P9-BAW-073

ESSENTIALS IN INTERVIEWING

HARPER'S SOCIAL SCIENCE SERIES

UNDER THE EDITORSHIP OF F. STUART CHAPIN

ESSENTIALS IN INTERVIEWING

FOR THE INTERVIEWER OFFERING PROFESSIONAL SERVICES
Revised Edition

ANNE F. FENLASON
LATE OF THE UNIVERSITY OF MINNESOTA

REVISED BY Grace Beals Ferguson, PROFESSOR
EMERITUS OF SOCIAL WORK, UNIVERSITY OF WASHINGTON

AND Arthur C. Abrahamson, ASSOCIATE PROFESSOR
OF SOCIAL WORK, UNIVERSITY OF WASHINGTON

HARPER & ROW, PUBLISHERS, NEW YORK, EVANSTON, AND LONDON

Contents

Component—Image of the Institution and Perception of Its Role—The Professional Role

PART TWO

ILLUSTRATIONS FOR CLASS DISCUSSION

Preface to the First Edition

The purpose of this book is to show how background knowledge afforded by the social sciences can be put to use in understanding and working effectively with people. Here we have attempted to abstract and highlight as concepts some of the thinking of social scientists on the make-up of the individual and the ways he reacts to his environment. Such concepts underlie the successful interview.

The interview is a tool common to many professions. Its skillful use has made it an art as well as a method. Some of its skills will be discussed. The emphasis here, however, will be on exposition of the common processes of the interview; the illustrative material will be drawn from a variety of settings.

One essential of good interviewing is that the interviewee be understood as a person. Another is that the interviewer understand himself as a person, dealing with an individual who differs from him in many significant ways.

The first part of this book will be devoted to a discussion of the meaning of backgrounds, in terms of general culture and individual environment, past and present, and of the part culture plays in the development of personality.

It is also concerned with the functioning of an individual in a culture and with certain concepts of behavior which are helpful in professional practice.

Selected processes will be discussed in detail for a more intimate study of the interview, and the effect of attitudes as a conditioning factor will be reviewed. Factors common to all interviews as well as some of the variations caused by different

professional uses and settings will be analyzed. Skillful and unskillful interviews will be contrasted. The discussion recognizes
a need for a philosophy of life and for a definite point of view on
the part of the person who intends to work in the field of human
adjustment.

The second part contains material for class analysis and assignment.

Much of the material in this volume has been tried out in suc-
cessive years at the University of Minnesota in an undergraduate
course open to all students who might later be using the interview
in their future professions. Many of the interviews are selected
from class assignments—not necessarily as examples of good interviews, but as dialogues, as accurate as recall would permit. Students were expected to use themselves and their environments as
a testing ground for the concepts presented. The reader of this
book may find it more profitable if he too tries out on himself
the applicability of the concepts.

The only processes which will be described and illustrated are
those of general application. Those who are looking for specific
answers as to what to do and how to do it in a given situation
with a given individual will see that the emphasis here is on
description of method rather than instruction in method.

The teacher's mission is to instill principles in the student's
mind, to give him knowledge of methods, to teach him how to
study reflectively and to distinguish between essentials and non-
essentials. The objective is to develop the student's capacity for
making use of what he has learned.

Although workers in fields of human adjustment approach their
work today with the increasing security which comes from knowing what they are doing and why they are doing it, they have not
yet formulated an acknowledged scientific methodology. But they
are approaching this goal.

This book, then, is intended as a basic background for a reader
group of nontechnically trained workers. Technical emphasis and
content, requisite for those who use the interview in treatment,

are afforded by advanced work in disciplines such as social case work, psychiatry, clinical psychology, and public health nursing. If this book gives the worker an incentive to know more about himself, the people with whom he works, and the interviewing method, it will have achieved its purpose.

Acknowledgments

Many people have cooperated or collaborated in the writing of this book. The original idea for it grew out of an attempt to provide course material which would be useful for students preparing for other disciplines who applied for admission to social case work courses not geared to their needs. The University of Minnesota provided the opportunity and the stimulus for experimenting with a generic course. Dr. T. R. McConnell, Dean of the College of Science, Literature and the Arts—now President of the University of Buffalo—Dr. Theodore Blegen, Dean of the Graduate School, Dr. F. Stuart Chapin and Professor Gertrude Vaile, then Director and Associate Director of the School of Social Work, made the opportunities and encouraged the experiments.

Such a course has been offered at the University since 1944. Dr. Alice Leahy Shea helped greatly in the formulation of the course in its early stages. Professors Edith Nagel and Anne Winslow, my successors in teaching the undergraduate course which evolved, have been generous in contributing their class material and suggestions. I am indebted, too, to the many students who participated through the class assignments which are used as illustrations in this book and the several hundred more from whom we learned some of the defects in content and manner of presentation.

My interest in the different uses of the interview and its common components has been stimulated by the opportunity of working closely with the Counseling Bureau and through the class lectures contributed by colleagues from the Departments of Anthropology, Child Welfare, Philosophy, Psychology, Public Health Nursing, Journalism, and Counseling. I, as well as the students, profited from the lectures given by Dr. Wilson Wallis, Mrs. Pearl Cummings, Dr. Starke Hathaway, Miss Ruth Freeman, Dr. Mitchell Charnley, Dean John Darley, and Dean Anne Dudley Blitz and I especially appreciated their generosity in giving me permission to make use of their lecture notes.

The preprofessional committee of the American Association of Schools of Social Work provided support for the idea that there was general descriptive content which could be suitably and profitably presented at an undergraduate level. Their continued interest in this has been a matter of great encouragement in trying to put the course material into the form of a textbook.

Dean Marcia Edwards of the College of Education, Miss Theda Hagenau of the Counseling Bureau, and Dr. Cornelia Williams of the General College; Professors Margaret Taylor, Director of Public Health Nursing, and Jeannette Vroon, psychiatric consultant of Public Health Nursing; Dr. Robert Hinckley, Director, and Professor Lydia Herman, psychiatric social worker, of the Mental Hygiene Clinic of the Student Health Service; and Mrs. Paul O'Connor have read portions of the manuscript and given valuable counsel.

Dr. F. Stuart Chapin, editor of the Harper series under which this book is published, Professor Grace Beals Ferguson, School of Social Work, University of Washington, and Miss Helen R. Fish have helped immeasurably throughout, in their criticisms and suggestions on the content and composition of the book.

The preparation of the manuscript has been the responsibility of many individuals owing to the fact that the book has been in progress for three years. Miss Dorothy Hill, Mrs. Ruth Nyquist, Miss Ida Erickson, Miss Louise Dorroh, and Mrs. Marjorie Owen deserve special gratitude.

Publishers and individuals have freely given permission to use material from books and articles. The graciousness of the responses to my requests was a delightful experience. My extensive use of the material of others makes me conscious of my great obligation to those who have permitted me to incorporate their thinking with my own. Montaigne says for me what I sincerely feel in writing a book on *Essentials in Interviewing*: "I have here only made a nosegay of culled flowers, and have brought nothing of my own but the thread that ties them together."

ANNE F. FENLASON

Preface to the Revised Edition

Anne Ferguson Fenlason was a social worker and a scholar with deep convictions about the infinite worth and value of every man, woman, and child. Her life as a professional practitioner, teacher, and writer was one of uncompromising commitment to this conviction. She insisted that those who prepared themselves to help others in need should apply themselves diligently toward this goal. In doing so, the professional student was charged with the responsibility for acquiring a wide range and depth of knowledge about the human organism, the peoples, and cultures of which man is a part, and the societal structure and social forces which influence the shaping of man's destiny. She was a skilled interviewer who knew how to apply knowledge in a practical, helpful way to others, and thereby she gave enduring life to her commitment. Mrs. Fenlason, even after her death in June, 1950, has remained the expert teacher.

In preparing this revision the collaborators have taken special care to preserve the content and style of the first edition. We consulted with instructors who have used this textbook throughout the past ten years to find out what in it they found especially useful as well as what portions of it they wished to see revised or changed.

Current and new case illustrations have been added. We chose those which had been tested in the classroom and had repeatedly stimulated provocative interest and discussion among students. A large number of the illustrations in the first edition were found, through consistent classroom use, to be timeless as well as stimulating and pertinent; these examples have been retained as Mrs. Fenlason originally presented them.

A major change is the new chapter on social and professional role which shows how the factors and components of the role concept have pertinence for the background and process of the interview. The late author had in several places implied some of the content on role in the first edition. We took these implied references and expanded them in conjunction with the current considerations in role theory. We did the same thing in respect to the time-bound continuum and its predisposing influences in interviewing.

The following people have earned our warm appreciation and thanks for their valuable assistance to us in preparing this revision: Professors Richard G. Lawrence, Robert W. Macdonald, Jack R. Parsons, and Grace Dewey Reiss; Miss Kay Laughrige and Mrs. Essey Wofrom. We are indebted to the many students whose scholarship and classroom participation evoked stimulating ideas and considerations throughout the years.

GRACE BEALS FERGUSON
ARTHUR C. ABRAHAMSON

Seattle, Washington
February, 1962

PART ONE

Chapter One

ESSENTIAL KNOWLEDGE OF BACKGROUNDS FOR THE INTERVIEWER

THE BACKGROUND OF CULTURE FOR THE PROFESSIONAL INTERVIEWER

What Do We Mean by a Professional Interview?

A good interview represents both a verbal and a nonverbal interaction between two or more people working toward a common goal. The interview is a purposeful conversation. When the conversation is aimed at furnishing insight and gaining information, or furthering understanding, or arriving at some form of help and counsel, its purpose is usually a professional one, and the interviewer is likely to be working in some field of human adjustment. The word *professional* implies that the interviewer has had special preparation for his work; that his training, based on transmissible knowledge and skills, has been acquired formally.

Professional service means more than a fortuitous meeting of an individual's needs. It presupposes an understanding on the interviewer's part of the forces in environment as well as of the attitudes and standards of the individual in relation to his particular need. It utilizes the skills which professional training affords and it emphasizes the principle that the trained individual, as the medium for meeting such needs, is also a person whose atti-

tudes and background affect in no small measure the reactions of
the individual seeking professional services.

The interview is a specialized pattern of verbal and nonverbal
communication which has been initiated for a specific purpose
and is focused upon some specific content area. The interviewer's knowledge of background factors and present situation,
and the reactions and attitudes of himself and the person being
interviewed, play a significant part in every interview. The most
essential background factors include culture, personality, and
role. Interviews involve two or more individuals whose heredity,
experience, role performance, and attitudes are different; and it is
essential that the interviewer be able to accept and understand
the other person on these terms. A key to such acceptance and
understanding is the concept of culture.

What Do We Mean by Culture?

We owe the concept of culture primarily to anthropology and
sociology, although psychology, economics, and political science
have all made distinctive contributions to a knowledge of man in
his social relationships. The capacity to understand an individual
in terms of his culture and the points and ways in which his culture and his response as an individual differ from one's own individual culture and one's unique way of responding is essential to
any professional worker who attempts to help another to better
adjustment in any area of personal and social relationships. Culture is an indispensable factual background in relation to which
the worker adapts his contribution to the situation before him.

The Meaning of the Concept of Culture to the Interviewer

Our common and our individual cultures play their parts in
shaping our personalities and destinies. Our cultural background
in the anthropological sense is our common heritage, whereas our
personal backgrounds form individual environments. Without an
understanding of our backgrounds both common and personal
we cannot understand the individual.

Custom plays a predominant role in experience and attitudes. No man is unaffected by custom. To quote the late Ruth Benedict, the anthropologist:

No man looks at the world with pristine eyes. He sees it edited by a definite set of customs, institutions and ways of thinking. Even in his philosophical probings he cannot go behind these stereotypes; his very concepts of the true and the false will still have reference to his particular traditional customs. . . . The life history of the individual is first and foremost an accommodation to the patterns and standards traditionally handed down in his community. By the time he can talk, he is the little creature of his culture, and by the time he is grown and able to take part in its activities, its habits are his habits, its beliefs his beliefs, its impossibilities his impossibilities. Every child that is born into his group will share them with him, and no child born into one on the opposite side of the globe can achieve the thousandth part of his culture.[1]

Lynd says that culture refers to all the things a group of people inhabiting a geographical area do, the way they do things, the ways they think and feel about things, their material tools, and their values and symbols. "Cultures the world over reveal the same identical institutional clusters, though almost infinitely varied in emphasis, detail, and functional linkages. Everywhere men are engaged in getting a living, in living with the other sex and rearing young, in making group decisions and maintaining sanctions and taboos, in performing some sort of religious practices and in carrying on patterned forms of leisure."[2]

This idea of identical institutional clusters, with their varieties of detail, emphases, and linkages, becomes clearer perhaps when we consider the eight common characteristics of all cultures according to Kardiner:

1. They all have some form of family organization which can be identified by a formal arrangement among parents and children, and

[1] Ruth Benedict, *Patterns of Culture*, Houghton Mifflin Company, 1934, p. 2.
[2] Robert Lynd, *Knowledge for What?* Princeton University Press, 1939, p. 19.

members of the extended family. The composition of the extended family varies. The extension takes place by marriage or the inclusion of others into the family group.

2. They all have an in-group formation of some kind. The nature and manner of its composition vary. (Father, mother, and children are the basic family unit, with such collaterals as they are tied to by blood relationship, sentiment, or economic obligations.)
3. They all have some larger group, clan or tribe, based on family organization, real or symbolic consanguinity, or common interests.
4. They all have definite techniques for deriving sustenance from the outside world, although methods of cooperation, organization of labor, and division of produce differ widely.
5. They all have basic disciplines, but what impulses, interests, or needs they control differ widely.
6. They all control mutual aggression according to a large variety of standards.
7. They are held together by certain recognizable psychological forces.
8. They all create definite, distinctive life-goals which vary widely and even change within the same culture.[3]

These eight characteristics may be applied to a better understanding of our own culture.

Characteristics in common do not mean that there are not great differences of behavior patterns in different cultures. Anthropologists through their comparative studies of disparate cultures have found a wide range of personality types in any given culture. Linton writes that in a large enough community one finds every existing type of individual personality.[4] What culture does is to set limits to the normal range of individual variation. This limitation is set (1) by the individual's experience of the effect that other people, acting in accordance with the pattern, have on him and (2) by what he learns from others by imitation and instruction.

[3] Reprinted from Abram Kardiner, M.D., *The Individual and His Society*, by permission of Columbia University Press, Copyright 1939, p. 6.
[4] Ralph Linton, "The Personality of Peoples," *Scientific American*, August, 1949, pp. 11-15.

THE CONDITIONING EFFECT OF BACKGROUND ON PERSONALITY

The part culture plays in the making of personality is well presented by Wilson D. Wallis, head of the Anthropology Department of the University of Minnesota:

Culture possessions are the blood and sinews of personality; the individual is a moving, walking, talking record of culture. Act, thought, and dress reflect the culture medium; and culture possessions fittingly become treasured heirlooms. We are not concerned about the past as such; we are concerned about the past of our culture, and only very remotely and indifferently concerned about a past that is in no wise part of our culture. We so thoroughly identify ourselves with our culture that it seems to belong to us and we to it. We are emotionally and intellectually attached to it, and we are dependent upon it in almost every respect. From birth to old age we are conditioned to a specific culture—to its language, its ethical, aesthetic, and intellectual standards, and the customs and procedures sanctioned by usage. The culture dimension includes the psychological and the consciously logical framework of the world in which one lives and functions. Culture is man's human and humanized environment, in which he lives and has his being. He makes it; but, once made, it furnishes the stimuli amid which he lives and to which he reacts. It is his spring-board to effort and achievement, and his only haven of rest.[5]

In his discussion of culture, Wallis has phrased his ideas so aptly and succinctly that we may take them as cultural concepts useful to the interviewer. We are employing the word *concept* in the sense of a generally accepted statement of a significant idea.

Although Wallis' concepts of behavior are those of an anthropologist viewing man in traditional groups, they are equally applicable to our everyday lives and our personal backgrounds. An understanding of backgrounds is necessary to the interviewer for the insight it furnishes into our thoughts and actions.

[5] Wilson D. Wallis, unpublished lectures given at the University of Minnesota before classes in case method, 1944-1946.

CONCEPTS OF CULTURE USEFUL IN BACK-
GROUNDING THE INTERVIEW

The following discussion of the background needed for interviewing is directed to those students who are looking toward
work in some field of human relationships; social workers, public
health nurses, ministers, school and vocational counselors are
among the workers in human adjustment who must have a knowledge of themselves in relation to their former backgrounds and
present environments before they can hope to understand the
background and environment of another. Wallis and others have
prepared the ground, but the seeds of understanding must be
cultivated by the workers themselves.

In the concepts to follow we suggest that the reader supplement
the examples contained in the text with those drawn from his
own experiences.

Concept 1. Every culture is of paramount importance to its
possessor. It is alien only to those of other cultures.

It is well for us to remember that *alien* is used by Americans
in different senses. Legally, it means a person who lives in this
country but is not a citizen of the United States. Colloquially,
it seems to mean anyone whose manners or customs are foreign
or unfamiliar to us. This is particularly important to keep in mind
because of the composite nature of our own culture.

Dr. Everett Clinchy, president of the National Conference of
Christians and Jews, has created from the cold facts of the 1940
census a vivid picture of the United States in terms of racial and
nationality components. He says:

This country is a family of many national, racial, and religious
groups. To read the list of the people who make up the United States
is to state a problem. We are one-third of a million Oriental, Filipino,
Mexican; sixty million Anglo-Saxon; ten million Irish; fifteen million
Teutonic; nine million Slavic; five million Italian; four million Scandi-

navian; two million French; thirteen million Negro; one million each of Finn, Lithuanian, Greek.

In addition, our national structure is complicated by religious differences. We Americans are two million Anglican-Episcopalian, forty million Protestant, one million Greek-Catholic, four and a half million Jew, two-thirds million Mormon, twenty-two million Roman Catholic, one-half million Christian Scientist. And these people of these varying cultures, with all their differences, are trying to live together.[6]

It is imperative that we try to understand all the implications of these diverse cultures—especially since our geographic boundaries are being eliminated and Western civilization, if it survives, will be on a world scale.

Removing boundaries will not suddenly make our American culture acceptable or palatable to everyone. Nor is that desirable. Adamic tells us that the quickest and most complete assimilation is by those whose own cultural adherences are slight. Understanding the new immigrant must be predicated not only on an understanding of his Old World background but on a comprehension of our own heritage.

During World War II, the late Gertrude Stein, expatriate American author, talked before a group of servicemen in Paris, chiding them for their lack of courtesy in their casual encounters with the French people. Such courtesy, she tried to explain, should be built upon an acceptance of a French culture different from and, in many ways, perhaps superior to that of the American G.I.

Miss Stein admonished, "Every day somebody should say something nice about somebody else. Every nation should say something nice about another nation—you must smile at least once a day at a Frenchman."[7]

Such seeds of wisdom are likely to fall on stony ground. The

[6] Everett R. Clinchy, *Unity in Diversity, The Family in a World at War*, edited by Sidonie Matsner Gruenberg, Harper & Brothers, 1942, p. 125.

[7] "Gertie and the G.I.'s," *Time*, April 16, 1945, p. 27. By courtesy of *Time*, Copyright Time, Inc.

politeness of the French is a conventional part of them; smiling at a Frenchman might lead to better rapport, but respect for and acceptance of the culture of a nation can be built only on a deeper understanding of it.

Individuals have a common tendency to place themselves and their activities in the center of the universe and to view other persons' acts and expressions in terms of similarities to and differences from their own. The greater the degree of similarity, the more likelihood of acceptance.

The tendency to cling to one's culture is amusingly exhibited by tourists to other lands. E. V. Lucas, in one of his delightful essays, wryly comments on the startling realization that one has become a foreigner from the moment he steps on alien ground.[8] He recalls Thomas Hood's surprise at hearing even the little children in France speak French.

The arrogance of certain travelers who try to browbeat natives of other cultures into conformity with their own, instead of adapting their habits to the others' customs, is often a discordant memory to the sensitive American traveler.

A young woman representing an agency interested in the welfare of American Indians acquired some appreciation of the importance of the Indian's culture from a difficult experience. Her assignment was to investigate illegal drinking among the Jicarilla Apaches of northern New Mexico and the extent to which it contributed to social and economic problems.

In order to get this information she interviewed agency officials and traders, as well as several members of the Apache Council. She found almost all of the younger Indians spoke English well, but many of the older people—from whom the Council members are largely drawn—spoke either haltingly or not at all. Therefore, she engaged as interpreter and guide an intelligent young man by the name of Bob B., a member of a respected Apache family and

----

[8] E. V. Lucas, *Giving and Receiving*, George H. Doran Company, 1927, pp. 126, 127.

student at the University of New Mexico, who conducted her to the home of a certain Mr. G., one of the most important members of the Council. Mr. G., Bob assured her, spoke English well. Bob, however, introduced her in Apache while the large, dignified councilman waited silently.

The worker's account of the interview is as follows:

I supposed from Bob's use of Apache that he might have over-estimated Mr. G.'s knowledge of English. So I accepted the introduction and began my questions: Did he think that there was a liquor problem of any gravity on the Reservation? If he felt there were any aspects of the matter that should be brought to the attention of the government, my association was able and willing to present his views. Mr. G. then answered in Apache at considerable length, but his answers when interpreted amounted only to a direct "no." Before I could go on, hoping to get a real expression of opinion, I suddenly found myself the target of a thorough-going tirade. Mr. G. shook his fist within inches of my nose, while Bob shrank visibly in his chair and reluctantly interpreted the vehemence of our host.

It seemed that Mr. G. had said that the association asked many questions but actually did nothing to help the Apaches; that if they wanted information they should call a meeting of the Council, because asking questions of individual members was underhanded; finally, that a woman had no business meddling in tribal affairs, and that Bob was likely to get into trouble by interpreting for me.

With the conventional Apache signal of a rising inflection and folded hands, Mr. G. indicated that the interview was closed, and we all rose. I stepped hastily to the door, commenting on the heat, when suddenly, in perfect English, the now smiling Mr. G. asked "Would you like a drink?" I thanked him, drank from a dipper and we began to chat amicably. I recognized that my interview had been a failure, but I began to understand also that the Councilman's fist had been aimed not at my nose, but at my questions.

I should have realized before beginning this interview that, after years of absolute rule by the government agency, the re-establishment of a self-governing Council among this proud tribe must be fraught with deep traditional significance. Naturally they could not speak of tribal matters except in the language of the tribe! And logically enough, the Council could not be strong unless it spoke as a body. Finally, to anyone who understood Apache tradition, it must be obvious that no woman, least of all a white woman, had a place in tribal affairs.

I learned from this experience to equip myself with an understanding of backgrounds before undertaking an interview.

The ability to work with others is determined in part by the facility with which we are able to understand others in terms of *their* backgrounds—not in terms of *our* faulty interpretations of their backgrounds.

Concept 2. To understand individuals in another culture it is necessary to have some appreciation of their culture.

A community can be *alien* in terms of culture. The South is often incomprehensible to a Northerner, and the Southerner often feels the North alien in sympathies and customs. Understanding the diversities among communities makes the professional interviewer more accurate in his interpretations.

The college personnel worker should know his college and its environs as a distinct community. The industrial counselor must know the economic, social, and political aspects of his area. Any district worker, public health nurse, social case worker, or attendance officer should know the characteristics of the district in which he works. Interviews with people within any area are varied to meet the local scene. The worker who notes political complexion, loyalty to the church, attitudes toward the local school, quality and kind of the key people in the community is more helpful than the worker who is not interested in the community as a living, evolving culture different from all others. When the worker knows the general pattern, he is on the way to knowing the community itself, as well as the persons in it; such knowledge is part of his job.

The Gersons, familiar with the pattern of life in rural Montana, assail the "happy assumptions" that there is no overcrowding in wide open spaces, that country people are healthier than city people, and that, although farmers may lack money, there is always enough to eat on the farm. Another set of false assumptions, which they reveal for the benefit of the urban-bred worker in a rural agency, is the belief that

. . . having a knowledge of rural life in one section of the country, a worker is thereby qualified to undertake social service in any rural area. With all their variation, cities are standardized in comparison with rural areas. The conditions facing the farmer of diversified crops in Ohio, the truck farmer of New Jersey, the corn farmer of Iowa, and the wheat farmer of the Dakotas are different in important ways. Doubtless the South, with its plantation system, presents another set of problems. Out of the High Plains we have the "dry farmer," the farmer using irrigated lands, the sheep rancher, and the cattle grower.[9]

Some of the procedures of interviewing which are involved in the attempt to understand another's background are outlined for us by Carl Carmer, a journalist, noted for his regional writings. *Stars Fell on Alabama* shows Carmer's method of acquiring an understanding of a culture not his own. One of his chapters, appropriately titled "The Twilight of the Races," is an account of the Cajans, a deprecated minority in the deep South.

Carmer, then a member of the faculty of the University of Alabama, made an appointment for an interview with a man known in the region as the most influential of the Cajans. In preparation for his interview he had gathered insight into Cajan culture from journeys by car into the Cajan country of Alabama. The people in the one-room shacks in scrub pine clearings impressed him as "tall, dark, and unfriendly." He presents a picture of these people, as he saw them in the drug store of the little town of Citronelle, Alabama.

A young man and a girl came in to buy ice cream cones. They were both dark and tall, the man about six feet. Save for their height, they looked like Sicilians. The man's hair was curly, his cheek bones high,

[9] Samuel and Jeanette Gerson, "The Social Worker in the Rural Community," *The Family*, January, 1936, pp. 263-264.

his features aquiline, his eyes large and gray. The girl was of olive complexion and her straight, well-formed nose and generous mouth under a wealth of dark brown hair that was braided and caught up at the base of her neck gave her exotic beauty. Her loveliness was marred only when she smiled, for then her teeth showed dark and neglected. Her companion wore blue overalls and a gray flannel shirt, and she a shapeless dark gray dress. Both were barefoot.[10]

The local townspeople gave him their varied versions of the Cajans, all of which indicated contempt and hostility. One said that they sprang up on the sand flats where "they couldn't even get Negroes to live." Another told Carmer they "really came from pirates that originally had headquarters at Mobile Bay," where they would divide their spoils of cargo, gold, and women. The women were said to be "Russian, Spanish, English, Negro—and so were the pirates."

You may be sure that Carl Carmer had more authentic sources of information. The encyclopedia, in which genealogy is unmixed with emotion, undoubtedly had supplied him with the information that Acadia was a former province of Canada, usually considered synonymous with Nova Scotia. The Acadians were farming people of French ancestry who were deported from their lands and homes by the British and settled in Louisiana during the French and Indian War. There and in Alabama we now find the Cajans—a contraction of Acadian—exiles who intermarried with the Creoles, native-born descendants of the French and Spanish conquerors. Indian or Negro blood is denied by the true Cajan.

Carmer's most objective and helpful informant on the Cajans of Alabama was the local doctor, who is described by the author as a "sun-browned healthy man on whom physical facts had impressed a breadth and tolerance not known to his immediate neighbors." It was he who took the visitor to a number of the Cajan hovels, all of which looked alike. The doctor explained: "They're all old houses built by their fathers and their grandfathers. They have a superstition that it's bad luck to move out of

[10] Reprinted from *Stars Fell on Alabama*, Carl Carmer, Farrar and Rinehart, 1934. By permission of the author. Pp. 257-270.

'em, so they stay no matter how rich they get or how many children they have; a sort of ancestor worship, I reckon."

The schoolhouse, a one-story frame structure which doubled as a church on Sundays, was taught by a white girl of about eighteen, pleasant and friendly. The school was in session only the three summer months in which their teacher, who had just finished her freshman year at the University, was available. The Cajans had refused to accept a mulatto teacher recently graduated from Tuskegee.

The children bore such names as Byrd, Weaver, Chestang, Rivers, Sullivan, Johnson, along with such French names as Bedreau and LeSolliat. They ranged from curly-haired, olive-complexioned types to yellow-haired, blue-eyed blonds. One of the children, when asked by the teacher to tell about the Cajan people, explained that they came from "French people that married Indians"; and then he added a little belligerently, "and not from Negroes at all."

It was, then, with some background of understanding that Carl Carmer went to keep his appointment with the man described as richest of the Cajans who lived down the road in "the bright blue house."

The interview is reproduced in full, interspersed with a running commentary on those parts which reflect culture traits.

"THE TWILIGHT OF THE RACES"

Carl Carmer gives us this setting for his interview with a Cajan:

The bright blue house was a rambling cottage built on the side of a hill. Green vines shaded its spacious veranda, affording a color contrast that was echoed by the sycamores and blue sky beyond. My host came to greet me, a sturdy man with sandy hair, reddish mustache and very blue eyes. We sat outdoors for a while looking down on the neat design of his fields.

Note an author's ability to observe and describe significant details. Against the contrast of the unpainted shacks of the other Cajans he describes a bright blue house; instead of one room it was a rambling cottage; instead of being in the scrub pines it was shaded by sycamore trees. He notes that the man had sandy hair, a reddish mustache, and very blue eyes. All this, which is contrary to the impression Carmer had previously been given of the Cajans as a people, is observed by him as part of the interview.

"Yours is a good name in South Carolina," I said. "Did you come from there?"

The journalist draws here upon his store of pertinent information. Names indicative of nationality, and with them all the cultural traits involved, are often used as introduction when one is feeling the way to a point of contact with another. More significant here is Carmer's alertness to variations in culture in geographic areas.

"It's just as good a name here," he said simply. "Yes, my folks live in South Carolina now. But I came here and married a Cajan woman and that makes me a Cajan and all our children, too."

From the standpoint of culture it is interesting that the Cajan admitted that marriage to his wife made him a Cajan. In many cultures, marriage is more likely to raise a woman to a man's status than to lower his to his wife's. In the description of his house and his title as the richest of the Cajans, we have some indication that this man was conceded to have superior socioeconomic status.

"That doesn't seem to have worked against you," I said. "You have a pleasant home—a fertile, profitable farm. They tell me you have plenty of money in the bank."

The comments were more provocative than direct questions would have been. It is probable that Carmer's sympathetic manner as well as his words evoked response.

He was silent for some time. Then, as if he had been making up his mind, he spoke determinedly:

"My farm and my money don't make other farmers friendly. And they can't buy my children a decent education. I don't so much care for myself or my wife—we get along. But I've tried hard to help my

children. They're as white as you or me—and I put 'em in a white
school. Soon as the teacher found out who they were, she sent 'em
back. So I went to law about it, spent a lot of money putting up a big
fight. They couldn't prove my wife wasn't white, but they decided
that technically my children were the same as Negroes. They could go
to the miserable Cajan schools or to Negro schools but they couldn't
go to school with other white children."

I had not expected such an outburst and I was a little embarrassed.
Probably, I thought, I am the first disinterested person this fellow has
had a chance to talk to about his life—and a man needs to let off steam
once in a while.

The ostracism of the Cajans by their "white" neighbors is
vividly portrayed by the farmer—himself not a Cajan.

Carmer's ability to say nothing and refrain from pointless conversation is shown here. His activity is mental and emotional but
not vocal, as he sits thinking over the meaning of their conversation and giving his partner in the interview a chance to do the
same.

While we sat there mulling it over silently, a bright-eyed woman
appeared in the doorway bearing two cups of steaming coffee. She
wore a checked blue and white apron over her blue dress figured in
yellow. Her straight black hair, parted in the middle and knotted at
the back, was flecked with gray, and her sun-browned face showed
interlaced delicate lines.

Again the observation of details and their cultural significance
should be noted. Her clothes are colorful; her black hair is
straight; her face is sun-browned.

"My wife."
"Howdy," she said. "Here's your before-dinner coffee. The rest'll be
on the table by the time you finish."
"But I mustn't," I said.
"We've been expectin' you," said my host. "We like to have some-
body from outside the state for our guest."

Before-dinner coffee would have registered in the mind of the
interviewer as a custom unique to a cultural area.

While we sipped our coffee, a bell rang at the back of the house. In a few moments two boys in blue overalls appeared on the veranda. "This one is Jack," said their father, pointing to the taller of the two— a tow-headed blue-eyed youngster of about fourteen; "and that's Tom," indicating a small edition of Jack, possibly two years younger.

We four went in to sit at a long plank table for dinner and while the menfolks ate, the wife and little ten-year-old Catherine, who looked like her mother, brought them salt pork, collards, turnips, and bread and molasses. I looked about the room that apparently served both dining and general living purposes. Aside from the table at which we sat, the furniture was store-bought, including a "mission" divan. There was a large framed photograph on the wall—probably of a South Carolina relative. On a small corner table was a portable phonograph.

Note again the observations which denote a recognition of significant living habits and cultural traits. The diet is that ordinarily found in a low economic level of the South, the furniture indicates existence at a comfort level; the wife's and Catherine's serving the men and boys may imply a recognition of their superiority or may be a custom of the region.

We sat outdoors again after dinner, and I tried to get the boys to talk to me, aided by their proud father. At first, they were very shy— but they got excited when I spoke of baseball and said I had seen Babe Ruth hit a home run. Their questions came quite as quickly as their active, squirming bodies. Finally their father said: "Better get your hoes on down to that lower forty if we're going to have a corn crop," and they left us.

When I rose to go a few moments later, the richest of the Cajans took my hand. "I'm proud to know you," he said, "and I wish if you're goin' to write a book, like you say, I wish you'd put somethin' in it about people like me that want their children educated but don't get a chance."

The Cajan's remarks indicate a colloquial manner of speech and limited education, as well as a re-emphasis of the social handicap of this minority group.

"I'll do the best I can," I said.

The author's leave-taking is honest, sympathetic, and without false promises. It left the two men each with an appreciation of the other as a man, even though their cultures were alien.

Appreciation of a knowledge of an individual's culture and a desire to know as many of its facets as possible is one of the earmarks of a skillful professional worker.

Concept 3. One who functions in a culture is part of it, and every phase of his life and thought reflects that culture.

We are only beginning to understand the full impact of early environment in an individual's life. For this developing understanding we are indebted to the contributions from the different approaches of biology, anthropology, sociology, and psychology.

The application of this concept may be seen readily in the life history of any individual.

Alexander Woollcott, for example, wit, *bon vivant*, sophisticate, and cynic, was on the one hand a product of the clubs, theaters, and smart literary society of New York. On the other he was a sentimentalist and humanitarian, a true scion of his grandparents, who had founded a cooperative Utopia in New York State.[11]

The democratic social theories of Franklin Delano Roosevelt were, as some of his biographers have revealed, a logical outcome of early background factors and environmental situations as a member of that mythical aristocracy which later called him "a traitor to his class."

Two student examples of the functioning of this culture concept may bring it nearer to some of our own experiences. Student A writes:

I was brought up in a home and a community where drinking of any alcoholic beverage was frowned upon. My parents believed wholeheartedly in prohibition and not only would not touch liquor themselves but went out of their way to give others the same point of view.

When I went away to school my first roommate in the dormitory

[11] Samuel Hopkins Adams, *Alexander Woollcott, His Life and His World,* Reynal and Hitchcock, 1945.

was a girl brought up in a type of home practically the opposite of mine. Her parents had died when she was fairly young. Her family and her friends were in the habit of drinking a good deal; in fact, they would go out on a drinking party nearly every Saturday night and come home intoxicated.

This difference in viewpoint between my roommate and myself was quite often the cause of misunderstanding between us. She could neither tolerate nor understand my viewpoint, nor could I in any way agree with her. Because of my background I could not see why all people could not see the situation as I did—that alcohol was injurious to health, was the underlying cause of many accidents, etc. We talked about it many times and the fact that she agreed with me on these points only made me less able to understand her point of view. And so far as she was concerned, the more I talked about it the more of a prude I became. When I stayed home nights she'd urge me to "come along and join the fun"; and the next morning, while she nursed a hangover, I'd say, "I told you so." That went on for three months—we never did come to an understanding.

The opposite side of the shield is pictured by Student B, who writes:

My parents have always been liberal in letting my brother and me indulge moderately in alcoholic beverages. Our parents always reminded us of the evils of excessive drinking, but never objected to moderate drinking.

With this environment, I have found that I am tolerant to "drinking." The other day I was present when a boarding mother was telling a staff nurse that the mother of her boarding child was married now and planned to take the child. She said that the husband was good-looking, well-mannered, and had a good job, but added that he drank moderately. The staff nurse raised her eyebrows and looked horrified; but to me moderate drinking was no especial blemish on a man's character.

The reflection of early culture is seen in the attitude of these two college girls, whose new environment makes each conscious of the effects of early conditioning.

Concept 4. Behavior may be a response to distant rather than proximate stimuli.

A remote rather than a current stimulus can make a considerable change in an individual's behavior. Where this occurs it means that memories unconsciously stored have been reactivated by some immediate situation. Whenever you find yourself saying, "To this day, I feel," or "I act," or "I react," so and so, you are illustrating this concept.

A certain self-reliant woman never goes out of her bachelor apartment without leaving the light burning, even in the afternoon, if it will be dark on her return. This in spite of knowing that her fear of darkness began at the age of four when both parents were killed in an accident and she confused death with darkness and emptiness. For years she has had the feeling that anyone close to her might disappear into space and darkness. She makes a pretense of laughing at her fears; still, at middle age she leaves her lights burning.

A public health nurse recounts the way in which the meaning of this concept became imprinted on her memory:

In the winter of 1944 I was working in the surgery of an Army hospital in France. Operating-room work was my first love; I had been doing it for four years and felt there was no phase of surgery which did not interest me keenly. Our work at the time included a considerable amount of eye surgery and plastic repair with which I often assisted.

Then a letter from home one day informed me that my mother was in the hospital with laceration of her eyelid. Complete assurance that she had received the best of care and perfect repair of the lid did little in allaying my fears. I seemed to experience an unusual amount of shock at the news, and my anxiety was increased by the fact that mails were slow and the accident had happened two weeks previously.

My friends tried to reassure me with little result. The day after receipt of the letter I fainted for the first time in my life while assisting in an eye operation. Then started a long and bitter battle to regain my lost self-assurance and the personal detachment which my work required.

Here the nurse, working in a familiar environment and on a familiar assignment, reacted to news of an event which was removed both in time and space. Her chagrin at fainting was replaced by a fear that she might faint again at ensuing operations. She tried to avoid a repetition by manipulating working hours and schedules to avoid having to assist in eye cases. Gradually her tension and the fatigue from it with long working hours and inadequate rest lessened and she was able to face her problem and eventually vanquish her fear.

Concept 5. A knowledge of the specific conditioning to which an individual has been subjected shows the functional relationship of things not logically related.

An item in a 1938 *New Yorker* on Thomas Mann shows the unbroken impact of Mann's German experiences even in the placid setting of an American college town.

With both Thomas Mann and Einstein settled in Princeton, that community can easily advertise itself as a centre of German intellectualism. Dr. Mann has rented a large red brick house at 65 Stockton Street, a short distance from the campus. . . . At the moment he is at work on a novel based on the life of Goethe. He says this will be a "tragicomic little thing." . . .

The Manns took out their first citizenship papers last May, about the time the author was completing a lecture tour. On this trip so many people wanted to hear him that frequently at his lectures the police had to be called in. In Cleveland the excitement was so great that Dr. Mann thought the police were present to shield him from enemies. He had scarcely regained his calm when two days later, in Toronto, he and Mrs. Mann awoke to find a note under their door reading, "We've got you now," or words to that effect. The Manns ran panic-stricken to their lecture agent, who had a room next door. It was later revealed that the note had been left for the agent by some ribald friends of his who made a mistake in doors. . . .[12]

The reaction of the Manns had been an automatic response to their former terrors. Only a knowledge of the specific conditioning to which the Manns had been subjected would account for Dr. Mann's fear of people and the panic engendered by a simple practical joke.

[12] Reprinted from *The New Yorker*, December 10, 1938, pp. 26, 27, by permission of *The New Yorker*.

Concept 6. One can be physically and geographically in a culture and yet not psychologically in it.

The student in the classroom who takes a course he dislikes because it is a prerequisite to a desired course is physically in the classroom but psychologically outside of it. He hears as little of the lectures and discussions as he can since his aim is to retain only enough of the content to pass the course.

A story of how well-meaning clubwomen tried to help Peter Pussick of "Hunkie town" toward a gracious way of living also illustrates Concept 6. The ladies would have felt less chagrined at the outcome of their experiment if they had understood that Mr. Pussick, although geographically a resident of a steel-mill town in the United States, was still living psychologically and to a great extent emotionally in his homeland.

Owen Francis[13] draws a graphic picture of "Hunkie town" in the steel-mill district, with its unkempt houses, unpaved streets, unsavory odors, and crowds of screeching children. He introduces us to Pete Pussick, who loved the town because there he was among his own people, and because he earned the solid wage of $4.40 a day with which to support his family, consisting of a comfortable Slavic wife and two little boys. Pete liked his rented house, where he could sit on the porch, his feet on the railing, drink his beer, and smell the spicy Hungarian food his wife would be cooking for dinner.

Now the Excelsior Club of the city, composed of women with good intentions and a reforming spirit but not too much knowledge of what makes people tick, decided upon this town as a field for their operations and selected the Peter Pussick family for their guinea pigs. They persuaded the mill superintendent to allow them to settle the Pussicks in a new model house, complete with fresh curtains, carpets, furniture, laundry tubs, and all the facili-

[13] Owen Francis, *The Ladies Call on Mr. Pussick,* Charles Scribner's Sons, reproduced in *Social Insight Through Short Stories, An Anthology,* by Josephine Strode, Harper & Brothers, 1946.

ties of a modern home. The Pussicks, scrubbed, bewildered, but flattered at this amazing display of interest in their affairs, were duly installed in these ideal surroundings where the Excelsior Club, exhausted and exulting, left them to lead sane and sanitary lives.

A week later, however, when the enthusiastic Excelsiors brought a dozen townswomen to see how a really modern home is operated, the home had undergone a change. They found curtains down and carpets up, the parlor rented to boarders, beer in the tubs, cabbage on the stove, and general messiness over everything, including the younger Pussicks.

So the family went back to their old house, with Pete's final comment, "By God, nobody's gonna play a joke on me again!"

Peter Pussick accepted only those cultural traits in his American environment which he found congenial; psychologically he remained a foreigner or an alien, according to your conception of the term.

Classic examples of people who experience psychological distance from cultures while being in them physically and geographically are seen in many Americans who tour or live temporarily in other countries. During periods of crisis and stress this isolation becomes accented. A nurse's interview with the wife of an army officer, at a dispensary on Saigon, Viet Nam, illustrates this. Prior to the interview cited below this forty-two-year-old woman, Mrs. Wall, had frequently called at the dispensary, complaining of many physical ills for which there was no organic basis; she had always patiently awaited her turn.

After entering the dispensary Mrs. Wall walked hastily down the corridor and directly into the nurse's office, announcing very loudly that she had tuberculosis and should be hospitalized immediately. The nurse felt considerable surprise because Mrs. Wall had completed chest X-rays ten days ago and these were negative. Mrs. Wall went on to complain that she had not slept well for many nights, that she was tired, had lost weight and "like every one else in this place, has tuberculosis." She complained that her servant's son was seeing a

Vietnamese doctor regularly and was certain that he, too, had tuberculosis. She repeated with almost a scream: "Everyone has it in *this* place!"

The nurse responded by commenting that one usually feels fatigue during periods of severe heat, and this becomes worse if one doesn't sleep well. The nurse went on to suggest that she might discuss this with the doctor.

The suggestion brought another storm of complaints, all of them directed at the French-speaking doctors and the Vietnamese physicians who spoke English well. She complained bitterly about her difficulty in understanding "their English," and in the next breath went on to talk about the barriers of living in a strange culture, her wish to dismiss the servants because she could not understand them and her suspiciousness about the medicines which had been given her previously. The nurse allowed Mrs. Wall to talk fully about her irritations with the culture and noticed that, after about fifty minutes of this, the patient's manner was considerably more like that which had been noted during earlier visits at the dispensary.

Finally Mrs. Wall remarked that she supposed that the doctors were "trying to be kind." The nurse pointed out that they did want very much to help Mrs. Wall and added that they had been very highly trained. Mrs. Wall reacted to this with a positive nod but made no other direct comment about it. She continued to talk more about her lack of familiarity with the customs. She did not mention tuberculosis and her own fear about it again in the interview. As the interview was closing the nurse suggested that an appointment be made with the doctor in view of her complaints. Mrs. Wall did not think this was necessary and left stating that she would, indeed, return if her weight were to drop sharply. When asked about the weight loss Mrs. Wall pointed out that she had lost about a pound.

The material brought out in the nurse's interview with Mrs. Wall also points out the necessity of considering behavioral factors in relation to and in conjunction with the particularized cultural aspects.

Concept 7. In order to understand present behavior we must view it as a cross section of the past. It is only in linking the present to the past that some behavior appears rational.

In cultures and in individual lives there is a continuity. The thread of the past is discernible even in the vivid pattern of the present. Our conventions of courtesy are derived from the past. For example, men accompanying women still take the outer edge of the sidewalk because of a former hazard; horses on the street might have run away and endangered pedestrians on the sidewalk, or even if that catastrophe didn't occur the mud splashed from horses' hoofs and carriage wheels might have damaged a lady's apparel.

A specific instance of the need to understand present behavior in its relation to the past is that of a young man who, as a spastic cripple, was considered unemployable before the last war but was given a roustabout job in a restaurant during the man-power shortage. Today, he is paying an income tax on his earnings. He has learned that he can work and do a good job; he has in fact performed so efficiently that he has been retained even though able-bodied men are now available. Whatever confidence and security he has acquired date from the time when the need for his services overcame the prejudice against employment of handicapped persons. His ever present fear today is that scarcity of employment may reduce him to his former status. The fear is well founded in that at any time the employer's prejudice against the handicapped may reappear.

Excerpts from a Swedish social worker's interview with a patient at a Stockholm hospital's cardiology department show how a thirty-five-year-old woman's reluctance to accept financial aid was related to a cross section of her past experience. The heart specialist had prescribed a necessary rest period which the woman could not initially accept, since, she said, she was without financial reserves. When the doctor explained the Social Aid Program for which all Swedish citizens were eligible, the woman said that she could not accept such help, in spite of the fact that the majority of people in this culture are able to do so. She did consent to talk with the social worker about this after the specialist told her that the rest period and the vocational restoration were equally crucial in treating her heart condition. The doctor had explained his patient's reluctance to the social worker, and she consequently began her interview on that basis.

The social worker gained considerable rapport with the patient by conveying to her that neither she nor the doctor would be angry at the woman's feelings of discomfort about accepting the commonly used state supported assistance. In the middle of the interview the patient was voluntarily reflecting about why she might feel such gross discomfort.

"Maybe my inability to take your kind help is due to some kind of pride. What do you think?"

The social worker said that she did not know if this was the patient's situation, but she did know that many people felt this way and that sometimes this was accounted for because of the values they acquired in their upbringing.

"Perhaps that is so, but I cannot accept it. Would you tell me about the re-training program that Dr. Bergstrom said you would help me with?"

The social worker outlined the program, and pointed out that if the patient was interested in retraining, various aspects of the plan would be worked out when the specialist found that she was able to undertake it. The woman agreed to return for another interview. When she came back for her appointment with the social worker, this was what she said:

"I thought about what we talked about a few days ago and remembered what you said about upbringing. I have done a lot of thinking about this and have come up with some ideas."

The patient explained her strict attentiveness to independence as a value that had been instilled in their children by her parents. Moreover, the patient's father died when the children were still in grammar school, whereupon her mother and the older children (including the patient) had taken over and managed the family business. She described many instances of long hours of hard work coupled with many anxieties. It was after she had talked about this that the patient progressed to the point of suggesting that she might accept some financial support for one month.

If the patient, doctor, and social worker had not had the opportunity to view a cross section of this woman's past experience, the behavior which interfered with her using the resources to bring about the physiological restoration of her damaged heart would not have been fully understood.

Concept 8. If we know past behavior, we can predict certain types of present and future behavior.

If we know earlier conditioning we can interpret behavior patterns and understand many motives for behavior which would otherwise be incomprehensible.

Professional workers know with a reasonable certainty that the spoiled, dependent little girl is likely to make a childish mother; that undemonstrative, intellectual parents demanding high achievement from their children often produce lonely child prodigies, unable to relate themselves to the people around them; that the child who has had to fight for recognition in his home generally develops into the aggressive adult still unconsciously fighting for love and attention; and that the man or woman who is well adjusted in later life is usually the one whose childhood has supplied him with love, security, and recognition.

A student's account shows the way her present behavior carries over and is predicated on the past.

When I was about eight years old my brother and I were taken to Coney Island. We were fascinated by the giant Ferris Wheel and had an overwhelming desire to ride it. We coaxed our mother almost continuously. Her response was that we could have our ride "later." Finally, in exasperation she warned us that unless we stopped our nagging we would have no ride. We did not stop; we did not ride. From this experience we learned that nagging did not pay. However, we learned afterward to cope with like situations. We found that if we accepted "No" with good grace, it often became "Yes." Arguments or pleas would not change mother's decision, but silence, which allowed her to talk herself into giving consent, was most effective. My brother and I have applied this knowledge with gratifying results over a great many years.

The technique of prognosis is now employed in such diverse fields as medicine, business, and social welfare. Our lives tomorrow will probably be foretold, not by soothsayers, but by social and biological scientists whose prognoses are predicated on studies of the past and present projected into the future.

Concept 9. All our worlds are self-complete and self-contained; clashes and discord are part of normal functions.

We live not in one world but in many, each characterized by cohesion of interests, geographical boundaries, factors of climate, and other material and psychological attributes. The greater the number of harmonious factors, the more self-complete and self-contained is the group.

Recently, in a large metropolitan area, a heated controversy arose concerning the expansion of airport facilities. Adjoining the present airport on one side were owners of homes in the middle- and upper-class economic brackets. On another side there was a veterans' hospital and other Veterans Administration facilities. On the other two boundaries were farm lands. The farmers to the west had swampy land and, therefore, welcomed the acquisition of their property by the Civil Aeronautics Authority. The air lines fought to retain the field. The residential homeowners formed an active protective association and sought to block the expansion of the field. The farmers to the south, not in the path of the flights, were divided in opinion, passive but not neutral. Here are self-complete and self-contained groups. Among them natural clashes and discords exist which are both discernible and understandable in terms of background factors.

In your own neighborhood you will find considerable community of interests and to a large extent the same socioeconomic status. These common factors do not insure harmony. You will occasionally find in these communities young children who are considered such troublemakers that other children are forbidden to play with them. You will also find within their family groups loyalties which withstand frictions. Indeed, as an observer once said, some families thrive on friction. It is therefore important that professional workers be alert both to elements of discord and to those which make for friendly relations.

There are other aspects of culture which, not broad enough to warrant being phrased as concepts, deserve passing consideration.

Lynd[14] calls attention to the modern inclination to attain the goal of happiness with a minimum of effort. A constant bombardment of advertising in daily press, magazines, and radio urges us to spend for luxuries instead of safeguarding our economic futures. The social worker who for personal reasons cannot understand why a client has bought an electric refrigerator with the first pay check her husband has received after a long period of unemployment may lose his chance to be of further service to the family in their other social problems.

Professional workers need also to keep in mind the present tendency to live in tomorrow and the fact that this tendency is not always a liability. Future goals are unique to the individual and may be sound for him, even if they seem unrealistic to the counselor.

In the city of X, professional workers covering a span of the last twenty years will never forget the Baer family—nor the lesson of their experience.

> The Baers first became known to the social agencies when the community nurse made a routine postpartum call on a woman with a new baby. The baby was a fine healthy boy, but Mrs. Baer, the mother, was a frail, timid little woman who reluctantly

14 Lynd, *op. cit.*, p. 87.

was made to tell that her black eye was caused by a beating her husband had administered the night before. She explained that he seldom drank and was abusive only when he did.

In addition to the baby, there were three other children, a girl of six and boys of eight and ten.

Against Mrs. Baer's protests the nurse reported the incident to Miss Bridges, a worker in an agency for the protection of mothers and children. The husband, trained in Germany as a maker of precision instruments, had told his wife that if she continued to take the advice of the agency, they could take over the family. Miss Bridges withdrew and for a year nothing more was heard from the Baer family. Then one morning a frightened voice came over the telephone asking Miss Bridges to come to the Baer home as soon as possible. When she found Mrs. Baer in the same deplorable state as before, she assuaged her own indignation by persuading Mrs. Baer to swear out an assault and battery charge against her husband. Before it could be served, irate Mr. Baer telephoned the agency that he was leaving his family to their supervision, which he did literally, by leaving town. The agency perforce took over.

Mrs. Baer is still recalled by the various agency workers who became responsible for the family as one of their most cooperative clients.

During those years the father wrote his wife and children an occasional taunting letter from Mexico. From this safe distance he reminded them he could not be brought back by extradition. However he conceded that he would be willing to have his family come to him in Mexico.

In the meantime, supported both from public and private funds, the children were the pride of their sponsors. Herman, the oldest boy, who finished grade school at the head of his class when he was thirteen years old, wanted to go on to high school and then to college. The welfare workers, in solemn conference, deliberated on the factors in the problem. The boy's tested finger dexterity slanted their decision that he should go to a trade school—which he did.

When Fritz, the second boy, not too apt in school, finished the eighth grade at the age of fourteen, the welfare workers decided that since he had average ability and no special talents he should go through high school.

When Louise, the daughter, eventually reached high school level she was advised to enter a vocational school, as her only talent was a flair for clothes.

During all this period, the flaw in the smooth functioning between the family and its professional helpers was that all efforts to move the family to better quarters provided by the agency had proved fruitless. The Baers gave no reason for remaining in a ramshackle building on a rear lot in a good residential neighborhood, but there they stayed.

By the time Louise entered Vocational High, the financial contribution of the brothers with the proceeds from the mother's home baking sales was sufficient income to make the family independent of any social agency.

In New York City one of the national agencies was making a spot study of successful case work around the country. The worker in charge wrote to a former colleague who had also known the Baer family, asking that a professional visit be made to the Baers in order to evaluate the help given by the agencies.

Mrs. Baer recognized the interviewer as a former worker and graciously invited her in. The Baer home, now across the street from their former abode, was modern and attractive. With quiet pride Mrs. Baer explained that the children had taken a great deal of satisfaction in buying the house. She revealed for the first time that they had remained in the hovel because it was the only cheap housing in the district, and because the children did not wish to leave their associates in church and school.

Mrs. Baer brought the family history up to date for the worker. She told how Herman had gone to the trade school; she had been afraid to tell the agency that he also attended night high school and from 4 to 7 P.M. had scrubbed floors in an office building and had finished college in extension courses while working at various odd jobs. With calm pride, his mother explained that he was now in a prominent law firm and had excellent prospects. His engagement to a girl in the neighborhood had just been announced.

"Fritz, the next boy? Oh, he's working now for the B. Instrument Company making precision tools." He ran away from home after the second year in high school, where his grades were mediocre, and got a job in a neighboring city. Being unmarried he was able to send home $250 per month of his $450 salary—one portion for his mother and the rest for his savings account.

Mrs. Baer's pride in Louise was also apparent. Louise, she explained, was always crazy about clothes. She left the Vocational School as soon as the family were no longer answerable to the agency and secured her own job as a stock girl in a well-known women's ready-to-wear shop, where she is now a buyer. Although happily married, she is definitely a "career girl."

Mr. Baer has kept in touch with his family. He occasionally sends gifts and writes that he is lonely. Fritz has visited him. Mrs. Baer explained for the first time that their basic quarrel had been over religion. She was a Lutheran; he was an agnostic. Whenever she refused to take birth control measures, they would quarrel and he would generally climax the quarrel with a drunken spree.

Her explanation of this success story, which had run at variance to the advice of her counselors, was quite simple. She said that the whole family had always known what they wanted but couldn't seem to make the people in the agencies understand!

And so it was a chastened social worker who sent the report of the triumph of the Baers to her former colleague in New York. Their design for living had indeed been patterned on tomorrow.

Another cultural phase of particular importance to professional workers is one to which Lynd has called attention.[15] It is the emphasis on the social value of youth in women which has been a destructive force tending to keep women emotionally immature. The woman who refuses to grow up to her responsibilities poses a problem not only to herself, her husband, and her children but to the family doctor, nurse, or social worker whom she frequently involves in her difficulties.

Naomi Brown is only one of a myriad of such women. She was married at seventeen to a boyhood sweetheart two years her senior. Her two small children have proved to be more than she can handle with the routine of the housework in their small apartment; so they spend most of their time "visiting" one or the other of their grandmothers.

Both her mother and her mother-in-law believe the evidence of illness visible in her dark-circled eyes, her chronic fatigue, her

[15] *Ibid.*, p. 93.

anemic appearance, and her extreme irritability, rather than the doctor's statement that she has no organic illness and that her physical state is a flight into illness. She accuses her husband of no longer caring for her whenever he tries to carry out the doctor's suggestions of encouraging and helping her to assume the care of the children. The children, still relegated to the status of visitors, hardly know where or to whom they belong and are becoming behavior problems. Naomi, because of her previous romantic ideals, lack of preparation for marriage, and dependence upon her family and husband, is emotionally a child failing at a woman's job.

Also cited by Lynd[16] is the culture trait of emphasis on the years of a man's maximum earning capacity, an attitude which reacts not on the man who is gainfully employed but on the one who is too old to work.

Grandpa Jones had been an honored, useful member of the family whose advice on farming was sought and often followed by his son. Now, his active days on the farm over, Grandpa Jones is left alone with his reflections while his son does a mechanized kind of farming foreign to his father. The housing shortage has made grandfather expendable. The family has no room for him in their home or in their busy lives. His only refuge is an old people's home or a room of his own maintained by old age assistance or possibly old age insurance.

The social worker or the nurse is often the only bright spot in such a lonely, aimless life.

The attitude of the interviewer is apt to be colored by his own experiences with the aged. Edna Ferber's "Old Man Minick"[17] reflects the author's sympathy for and understanding of the feelings of an old man who is unwelcome in his daughter-in-law's home. The picture of the self-centered daughter-in-law who found

[16] *Ibid.*, p. 93.
[17] Edna Ferber, *One Basket*, Thomas Y. Crowell Company, 1922, pp. 110-127.

her father-in-law an inconvenience and a handicap to her social
life is etched in acid with an artist's skill. After submitting silently
to refined torture at his daughter-in-law's hands, Old Man Minick
overhears her telling bridge-playing friends that her father-in-
law's presence in the home means that they cannot have a child.
At first his brain reels under the shock. "He stood there in the
dining room quiet, quiet. His body felt queerly remote and numb
but his mind was working frenziedly. Clearly, too, in spite of the
frenzy. Death. That was the first thought. Death. It would be easy.
But he didn't want to die. He liked life. The park, the trees, the
club, the talk, the whole show . . . Nettie was a good girl . . . The
old must make way for the young. They had the right to be born
. . . Maybe it was just another excuse. Almost four years married
. . . The right to live."

Mr. Minick steals away to return triumphantly as the bridge
club is leaving. He breaks through their polite greetings to an-
nounce that he is busy moving. He has just completed arrangements to move in to the Grant Home the following week. There,
in the refuge where he had gone daily to talk over the affairs of
the nation and the world with his contemporaries and his cronies,
he finds acceptance and has status. He can live as a man among
men.

Lynd[18] also makes the point that conflict between the sexes is
incited by their patterned roles. In America, woman is both a
pampered darling and the traditional homemaker, and man is the
breadwinner. Where either fails in the allotted role, there is
discord—often strife. Attempts to explain the conflict between
the sexes have been made by sociologists and others concerned
with marital discord and problems of family life; one of the most
provocative of these is a book on *Woman, The Lost Sex*.[19] Reviewed angrily by feminists and read avidly by housewives and

[18] Lynd, *op. cit.*, p. 95.
[19] M. F. Farnham and F. Lundberg, *Woman, The Lost Sex*, Harper &
Brothers, 1947.

career women, it is the collaborative effort of a psychiatrist and her sociologist husband to present the problem in a modern light. More recently Margaret Mead,[20] who has studied sexual behavior in many cultures, analyzes critically the behavior of man and woman and their roles in our cultures in terms of the genesis and significance of their different patterns to society.

The duel between the sexes is not a phrase or an abstraction. It gets down to cases with which the professional worker must deal. It is well for him to take a personal inventory of his own ideas on the respective roles of men and women as well as to understand the attitudes of his clients, advisees, or patients. These attitudes are of cultural as well as individual significance.

Present-day economics is changing the trend in regard to woman's working outside the home. More and more women are successfully combining the two jobs of marriage and career. Women work primarily for economic reasons, whether for security or for luxuries. Pin-money workers among women are now in the minority. The professionally trained married woman who is not compelled to earn money usually finds home and children more than compensate for the career she has given up.

A study made by McMurray[21] is relevant. Interviewing twenty-four women inspectors in a glass factory, twelve of whom were considered very good and twelve of whom were poor workers, he found that eleven of the twelve best workers were married and motivated for their work by heavy financial obligations: the support of dependents, doctors' bills, the education of children, higher standards of living. The one unmarried woman interviewed was a conscientious type, emotionally mature, accustomed from childhood to hard work and heavy responsibilities. The unsatisfactory workers, on the contrary, having had no early

[20] Margaret Mead, *Male and Female: A Study of Sexes in a Changed World*, William Morrow and Company, 1949.
[21] Robert N. McMurray, *Handling Personality Adjustment in Industry*, Harper & Brothers, 1944, pp. 141-142.

responsibilities and without family dependents, were irresponsible and easily upset.

The professional worker must remember that many of the people with whom he works come from alien cultures where the roles of the sexes also have been patterned, but with a different design. It is common in German-American communities settled originally by German peasants to see women doing heavy manual labor in farms and fields. Finnish women on American farms still do the milking. The Italian mother tries to hold the daughter to the same rigid restrictions in social relations to which she was subjected in her own youth.

THE APPLICATION OF CONCEPTS OF BACKGROUND TO AN INTERVIEW

For the application of the concepts on background, an interview which has become a classic has been selected. In 1923 Viola Paradise, then a field representative of the Children's Bureau of the Labor Department, was studying conditions of child labor. Her interview was published as an essay in the *Atlantic Monthly* titled "Only a Conversation."[22] Porter Lee, then head of the Charity Organization Society of New York and director of the New York School of Social Work, was perhaps the first to use it in his teaching of the interview. His example was followed by countless other teachers. Miss Garrett reproduced it, with pertinent comments, as one of the discriminating selections in her book on the interview.[23] We are reproducing it here, partly because of the skill it displays in interviewing, which will be referred to incidentally, but primarily because it illustrates most of our concepts of background. The concepts which are italicized will

[22] Viola Paradise, "Only a Conversation," *Atlantic Monthly*, January, 1923, pp. 81-93.
[23] Annette Garrett, *Interviewing, Its Principles and Methods,* Family Welfare Association of America, 1932.

not be rediscussed. Their application will be indicated, rather than analyzed.

Only a Conversation

Paragraph 1. Today, as always on days when the cannery was closed, Mrs. Kazalski wavered between relief at having free time for housework and distress at the loss of a day's earnings. Good, at least, that the weather was fine, she thought; and told Katie to take her cough out into the sunshine, and to see that the baby did not cut himself on the oystershells. Then she sent Dan to the pump, at one end of the "camp," for water, and turned to sort an accumulation of soiled clothes, which smelt unpleasantly of stale oyster-juice.

To understand individuals in another culture it is necessary to have some appreciation of their culture. The interviewer's purpose here was to study the conditions of an oyster and shrimp camp in Mississippi as they pertained to child labor. To do this she was seeking information not in the character of a census taker but as a person trying to understand why these people had come to the camps, and how they were affected by conditions.

Paragraph 2. Mrs. Kazalski accepted the distasteful odor with a dull fatalism, as she accepted the rest of her widow's lot; as she accepted everything in her life. A careless observer might have called her broad pleasant face stupid, might never have guessed that the thick crust of acceptance covered a shrinking sensitiveness, and had nothing to do with her thoughts. These, in so far as she thought at all, concerned themselves with obvious things: worry over Katie's cough, the debt at the company store, a mingled hope and dread of the early call of the factory siren on the morrow; for an early siren meant a big load of oysters, and consequently more nickels.

Paragraph 3. She had put the clothes in to soak, when she became aware of excitement in the camp, and the sharp voice of Mrs. Oshinsky's Annie in breathless recital. Mrs. Kazalski put her head out of the door, and saw a group of women and children—Katie among them—at the end of the building.

Paragraph 4. One of the women called her, and in the next sentence told Mrs. Oshinsky's Annie not to talk so loud. She arrived in the midst of the hushed importance of Annie's outpouring.

In paragraphs 1 to 4 such names as Annie Oshinsky and Mrs. Kazalski are indicative of Polish or Russian origins. The physical conditions of the camp have been noted by the interviewer; their effect is here emphasized by the literary license of allowing Mrs. Kazalski's soliloquy. The daily living of the camp is shown by homely but significant details. You can see and feel the squalor even before you hear about it from the speakers.

Paragraph 5. "Gov'ment ladies. It's men dressed like ladies. Two. One went to talk to the boss. Mike Salinsky says it's inspectors. The other went down to the lower camp, but she says she ain't a inspector. She'll be here after a while. If they catch on us kids is working, you got to pay fines. Twenty-five dollars, Mike says. He says the gov'ment pays them to be inspectors, and that's why things cost so much at the store. He's awful mad. He says if it wasn't for inspectors, everything would be better for us. He says maybe they'll take the work away from us. He says maybe they'll put us in jail. I think maybe they got revolvers!"

Paragraph 6. After some discussion, Mrs. Kazalski spoke: "It ain't nothing. They can't take money we ain't got. If we keep our mouths shut, they won't know the children work. The cannery ain't running today. Everybody's got to tell their children to shut up, and to shut up themselves, only be polite. No gov'ment lady or man neither won't get something out of me."

Paragraph 7. All morning as she worked, however, she worried about the gov'ment lady. Suppose that someone should let it out. Jail? No, surely not that. But if they should stop the children from working, how could they live? Suppose the company should refuse credit at the store. Once she had wished to cheat the Virgin Mary of a half-burned candle. Could this be punishment?

In paragraphs 5 to 7 you feel the insecurity and fear of the oyster camp workers and sense the ignorance on which such fear is based.

Annie Oshinsky, as well as Mrs. Kazalski, even in this little glimpse, is showing that *one who functions in a culture is part of it, and every phase of his life and thought reflects the culture.*

Paragraph 8. Suddenly, athwart her numb acceptance of life, came a passionate regret; if only she had never left Baltimore. Why, why, had she yielded to the persuasions of Mike Salinsky. She went over in her mind all the incidents that had influenced her to "come South to oysters." The day of Mike Salinsky's visit stood out as clearly in her mind as if it had been yesterday, instead of the day of her husband's funeral, three months ago.

Paragraphs 8 and 9 show us that Mrs. Kazalski's insecurity began, not with the threat of the children's losing their job, but with the death of her husband in an accident. We recognize that her *behavior is a response to a distant rather than a proximate stimulus. A change in a situation past rather than current may make a considerable change in an individual's behavior.*

In paragraphs 38 to 46, this is made quite clear when Mrs. Kazalski finds it a relief to tell Miss Egmont the facts which added up to the present situation—laying the bricks of hardship, one by one, into the structure of her life. Miss Egmont herself was a woman who recognized the meaning of background and believed in the worth of the individual. Her simple introduction of herself by name is the entrance into the protective façade Mrs. Kazalski has made for herself. Interviewers may forget that the interviewee's reaction to the interview is as important and direct as their own, and is much less impersonal.

Paragraph 9. The story continues with Mrs. Kazalski's introspection as she goes over in her mind all that had happened between the time of the funeral, three months ago, and today. She thinks of how she sat alone after the funeral, dazed, wishing only to be alone, but being pestered by her sister-in-law with, "What are you going to do now?" At last the sister-in-law left and then suddenly there appeared the smooth, oily, but persuasive Mike Salinsky with the offer, "How would you like to go South? How'd you like to go to the Gulf of Mexico, down in Mississippi where it's nice and warm, and where you and all the children could get nice easy work, and good pay, and free rent, and free fuel? How'd you like to go South and shuck oysters and pick shrimps for the winter? I'm row boss for the O. U. Oyster Company, and they sent me up here to get families to come down and work." It was particularly the lure of the warm South and his assurance that Katie's cough would get better there that finally persuaded her. She recalled all the awful disappointments upon her arrival. The miserable one-room accommodations in a long-sagging twelve-room row. The back-breaking work, the change in Mike to a brutal boss, prodding her and the tiniest child through the long working hours, the high prices at the company store, and the ever-increasing debt piling up there, and above all the worry over Katie's increased coughing. Now, added to this was the agonizing fear that the government ladies would find out about the children's working.

Paragraph 10. Mrs. Kazalski struggled hard against despair. If only she had never left Baltimore!

In paragraphs 9 and 10 we have a hint that although Mrs. Kazalski is in Mississippi, she wishes she were back in Baltimore. This and her reasoning lead us to the concepts that *one can be physically and geographically in a culture and not psychologically in it* and that *to understand present behavior we must view it as a cross section of the past.*

Paragraph 11. And now the government was sending inspectors, to find them, to starve them, to take the work away from their children! Twenty-five dollars! Suppose that they discovered that her children worked, that she had not the twenty-five dollars? Some of the neighbors might let it out. Well, the government lady would get nothing from her, not a thing. She would be civil, but not a word about the work!

Paragraph 12. The government lady was in the door. "It's not a man, dressed as a woman," was Mrs. Kazalski's first thought. "Annie Oshinsky is a fool!" She responded, unsmiling, to the "Good afternoon, Mrs. Kazalski. I'm Miss Egmont of the Children's Bureau. May I come in?"

Paragraph 13. "Sit down," she said, in a dull voice, but she thought, as she looked at the short, slight, brown-clad figure, the pointed piquant face under the close-fitting little round hat, "She looks—

almost—as if she could be happy!" It came as a revelation to her that any adult could look like this.

Paragraph 14. Afterward, thinking of her, Mrs. Kazalski wondered why she had seemed so remarkable. She was not pretty, nor yet clever; apparently she had not noticed Mrs. Kazalski's hostility, had acted as if she were welcome. She had said, easily, "May I take off my hat? It fits a little too tight"; and without waiting for permission, had removed it and hung it on a knob of the chair.

Paragraph 15. Afterward, as during the interview, Mrs. Kazalski felt about in her sparsely furnished mind for a word to explain this visitor, so unlike anyone she had ever met. The Polish word for "separate" kept coming to her mind; but, being unused to abstract thinking, she did not recognize it as exactly the word to express Miss Egmont's detachment—detachment for herself, apparent freedom from problems of her own—which was a quality that puzzled and attracted Mrs. Kazalski.

In paragraphs 13 to 15, Mrs. Kazalski's careful sizing up of the worker as one she could trust, appears the first turning point of the interview. Mrs. Kazalski's recognition of differences was as sharp but more unconscious and of even more importance than her visitor's. If she had not decided that she liked and respected the differences, the interview would not have progressed. "Backgrounding the news" is a technique made popular by radio. "Backgrounding your agency" should be a tool used by every worker at any new contact.

Paragraph 16. "Did you ever hear of the Children's Bureau?" began Miss Egmont. And when Mrs. Kazalski had said, "No'm," she continued, "Well it's part of the government that is trying to find out how children and mothers are getting along, and what they do, in order to learn what things are best for them.

Paragraph 17. "Now we are visiting all mothers with children in these little canning camps. How many children have you?"

In paragraphs 16 and 17 Miss Egmont attempts to explain the function of the agency she represents. But because her explanation fails to explain in terms that Mrs. Kazalski can understand and because it is followed by a direct question about her children,

Mrs. Kazalski withdraws immediately. A further cause for her withdrawal is the sight of Miss Egmont's schedule. Miss Egmont's personality was strong enough to counteract, to enable her to get over this temporary rough spot when the questions turned out to be the routine ones of names, ages, and school grades. These were questions Mrs. Kazalski had been asked before.

Paragraph 18. Mrs. Kazalski was immediately on her guard. Miss Egmont's pencil was poised over a large card, on which Mrs. Kazalski could see irregular patches of printing, combined with blank spaces, and red-and-blue lines. Miss Egmont was not looking at the card, but at her hostess, with half-smiling encouragement. And surely, thought Mrs. Kazalski, that was a harmless question. No harm, either, in giving their ages and telling at what grades they had stopped in school. In fact, Miss Egmont turned directly to Katie and Dan, who stood by, their wide eyes upon her, and asked them questions about school. Katie, who coughed most of the time, coughed harder now from nervousness; and Miss Egmont's face clouded, as she asked about the cough.

Paragraph 19. Despite her resolution to be circumspect in her dealings with this intruder, Mrs. Kazalski scarcely listened to what she was saying, so preoccupied was she in her personality. "If she had my life and my troubles," she thought, "would she be so—so different?"

Paragraphs 18 and 19 show the interaction of Mrs. Kazalski and Miss Egmont as two people with different backgrounds both interested in the same children.

Paragraph 20. "You 'Merican lady?" she asked.

Paragraph 21. "Yes," said Miss Egmont. "But my grandparents came from the old country. How long have you been in America?"

Paragraph 22. "Nine years. How old are you, lady?"

Paragraph 23. If Miss Egmont was surprised, she did not show it. "Thirty-two," she replied. "And you?"

Paragraph 24. Mrs. Kazalski's eyes opened wide. Thirty-two! Why she herself was only thirty. She would have guessed Miss Egmont fully ten years younger. Then surely this apparent happiness was not real. Why, she was not married; was an old maid.

Paragraph 25. Mrs. Kazalski softened, with something like pity. So busy was she speculating about her visitor, that she answered questions mechanically. But suddenly, one question brought her up short.

In paragraphs 20 to 25 the interview becomes truly one of interaction, with Mrs. Kazalski trying to find out why Miss Egmont was "so different." The differences in her cultural attitude toward marriage give Mrs. Kazalski a slight sense of superiority over Miss Egmont's single state. Miss Egmont accepted Mrs. Kazalski's questions with equanimity, and answered with poise, recognizing them as Mrs. Kazalski's attempt to understand her.

Paragraph 26. "Now tell me about the children's work. I suppose Katie can't help you very much at the factory because of her cough?"

Paragraph 27. Mrs. Kazalski's face hardened. She made no answer. Miss Egmont might ask until doomsday, she'd get nothing out of her. Yet it was strange that she would ask the question so directly —not at all as if she were trying to surprise an answer from her.

Paragraph 28. "I'd like to know," Miss Egmont went on, in her soft, even voice, "about the work you and the children do in the cannery—just what you do, and how much you earn, and what time you go to work, and some other things. But first, are you sure you understand just why I'm asking these questions? Sometimes people are suspicious, can't understand why the government, far off in Washington, should send someone away down here to ask questions. Maybe you'd like to ask me some questions before you answer mine?"

Paragraph 29. "Mrs. Oshinsky says you come to collect fines."

Paragraph 30. "Fines?"

Paragraph 31. "The twenty-five dollars for people, if their children work. You inspector?"

Paragraph 32. "No," said Miss Egmont simply, and it surprised Mrs. Kazalski that the accusation did not embarrass her. "There are inspectors," Miss Egmont continued, "and there are fines for employing children; but the bosses, not the workers, pay the fines. Only my work has nothing to do with fines. The government is making a study of what's good for children and what's bad for children. You see, children are the most valuable things in the world; but it is only lately that people have learned that in order to make them healthier and happier, we have to study them, and see how things affect them. The Children's Bureau is finding out how work affects them—how it affects their health and their chances of growing up strong and healthy, and happy. What do you think about it? How do you feel about the work your children do and the other children?"

In paragraph 26 Miss Egmont returns to the purpose of her interview but in the ensuing paragraphs, 27 to 32, is forced to amplify her earlier inadequate explanation of her agency, the Children's Bureau, in terms that Mrs. Kazalski can understand. She now could realize from her interviewee's misconception of the duties of inspectors the truth of the concept that *the specific conditioning to which an individual has been subjected shows the functional relationship of things not logically related.* We have another incident of this in paragraph 42, where Mrs. Kazalski's attitude toward receiving charity, obviously an outcome of her Slavic trait of independence, was vigorous enough to outweigh any outsider's attempt at bettering her family conditions.

The question, "How do you feel about the work your children and the other children do?" credits Mrs. Kazalski with ideas worthy of consideration. The way in which the interviewer frames his questions often reveals the extent to which he accredits the personality of another.

Paragraph 33. Mrs. Kazalski had never thought of it. But the question turned her scrutiny back from her visitor to herself. It half flashed through her mind that she had never before thought of anything aside from how to get money for the next day's living; how to keep her children and her house clean; what to cook; whether the oysters would be large or small; how to pick out the wettest car and to work quickly, so that as much water as possible would get in with the oyster-meat, before it was weighed.

Paragraph 34. But now, here was a new thing. Her opinion was being asked. She shrugged her shoulders. What had she to do with these things?

Paragraph 35. Yet something quite strange and new seemed to be pushing up in her mind. A low anger was part of it, but there was another element in it, too. She had an opinion, and she wanted, not to be silent and sullen with this government lady, but to talk, to argue with her. Presently she was answering: "I think too bad for children to work; but what you can do? It's better to work and live, than to starve and die. What would poor people without husband do, if children don't work? Without the children, I no could make half to live on. Even with the children, I got a debt, eighteen dollars, at the store. And you—the government—it don't give money, no? No, just questions it gives. How can help us— questions? The row boss say you get money for questions, that's why things cost too much—for tax. You say it's good for children— questions. Will it help my children?"

Paragraph 36. This was a long speech for Mrs. Kazalski. She was breathing hard and perspiring with the efforts of it.

Paragraph 37. Miss Egmont's face was thoughtful. "I'm not absolutely sure it will help your children." She spoke slowly, experienced in making simple people understand new things. "I'm not sure the results of a study like this will come soon enough, though they may come in time to help the younger ones. Do you know," she went on, "that some states give money to widows, so that their children can go to school? And that, in some countries, fathers and bosses and the government together pay for insurance, so that, if the father dies, the mother will have some money every month, and won't have to put the children to work? Well, how do you suppose those countries and those states came to do these things? They sent people like me to go and study what the people needed, how they lived and how they worked; and they then planned ways to help them. But it takes time, and to learn these things we must depend on what the workers tell us, and what the bosses tell us. You, when you tell me about your children's work and about your work, are helping the government to make things better for all children, even though the changes may not come tomorrow or for several years. I believe they will come in your children's lifetime. Don't you want to help make things better for children?"

Paragraphs 35 and 37 are again the interaction of two people trying to understand one another and working toward a common end. The effect of Mrs. Kazalski's recognition that she was considered by Miss Egmont as a person in her own right is dramatically told by the author. The interview moves from here to a swift conclusion as Mrs. Kazalski decides to return to Baltimore.

Paragraph 38. Mrs. Kazalski felt strangely moved. Only partly by the argument of her visitor, only partly by the visitor's personality. Mainly, it was the fact of this visit, the fact of this conversation, which swerved its familiar groove into the rough vastness of new thinking. To think, for the first time in one's life, of anything outside the range of one's experience and observation, is a profound experience. As Mrs. Kazalski's untutored but not stupid mind followed Miss Egmont's simple explanation, she forgot about her debt to the store, forgot Katie's cough (for Katie, listening intently, had not coughed for some minutes). A strange emotion welled up in her, a feeling of value, a feeling that her children were really important, not only to herself, but to the country.

Paragraph 39. She shook her head several times. "It should be good work," she said slowly. And when Miss Egmont took up her questioning again, with "How did you happen to leave Baltimore, to come down here?" Mrs. Kazalski found herself wanting to tell the whole story of her hardships. It would be a blessed relief to talk about her troubles, to put them into words, to a person quite detached from her life, someone she would never see again. Never had she done this; never had it occurred to her. She had always thought of her burdens as inevitable, inflicted by Providence, goading her to laborious effort which offered no reward. She was not a woman to pity herself, but now, as she poured forth her tale, it was as if she had been given the power to stand apart and see herself. A rush of self-pity, the first she had known, flooded her for the moment—a strange indulgence of pain that was hotter, but softer, than her hard, accepting silence of many months. Yet there was nothing in her voice, no moisture in her eyes. She sent the children out of doors, and in a low voice—that her neighbors might not hear—she had begun:

Paragraph 40. "Things were enough good with me, till the accident. After five months sick, my man dies; and was left in the house only five dollars thirty-eight cents. Katie coughed bad. That night the row boss—"

Paragraph 41. She told of Mike Salinsky's visit, of her trip down, of her disappointment; of the draughty coldness of the canning shed in bad weather; how the roof of her house "leaked like a basket" when it rained; how she lay awake at night, too tired to sleep, worrying, waiting for the siren, yet dreading it; waiting and dreading the watchman's pounding on the door, which never failed to fill her with anger; hating to force the children from their beds at four or five or six o'clock in the morning—according to the size of the catch; how fast the shucking gloves wore out—"one glove a day, and we cut our hands yet"; how much worse picking shrimps was than shucking oysters, because of the acid in the head of the shrimp; "after two days at shrimps, my hands look like butcher-shop, but that's the only one thing to make think there is in the world meat! and the stink! You smelt it once? So! !"

Paragraph 42. But worst of all, was the worry about Katie's cough. That kept recurring again and again in her outpouring. She talked with the simple vividness of a person unused to fluent speech. "I no would care about work, I no would care for nothing, if Katie could get well. When I go away from Baltimore, I say, charity the Kazalskis no take. But now I think foolish to be more proud than to care of your child's health. It ain't proud, having them work over mud and wet, in clothes soaked and torn like noodles. And I think maybe oysters no good for the cough."

Paragraph 43. "Did you ask the boss if he would send you back now instead of waiting till the end"'"

Paragraph 44. Mrs. Kazalski laughed bitterly. "He gave me a mouthful," she said.

Paragraph 45. "Excuse me, I tell you all this," she went on, "but you want to know why children got to work. That's why. But if Katie could get well, I'd give—I'd give—well, I ain't got nothing to give. Excuse me, miss, your face looks very sorry. But you ask—and now you know."

Paragraph 46. Miss Egmont was silent for a while. Then she said, "Did your husband's boss do nothing for you when he died?"

Paragraph 47. "Why should he do something? It was no his fault—the accident. My man, my man—" she paused, "—he good worker, nine year one boss; but he make himself the accident. Sixteen hours he work, and he was much tired. He was a good worker, but we no could ask something from the boss, when my husband make the accident."

Paragraph 48. "When you get back to Baltimore, what will you do?"

Paragraph 49. Mrs. Kazalski had asked herself this same question many times, and never had she found any answer. But now, miraculously, she discovered that she had a plan, a plan that sprang up of its own accord, that rushed forth, almost as a part of her outpouring.

Paragraph 50. "I go to a charity. I say, 'Let me take money for rooms; I take lodgers, so I can get a doctor for Katie; I take in washing; I pay back the money.' Maybe I pay neighbor to take care of baby; to go to factory maybe. But I send my children on the school; they should grow up, like you say, like people, not like pigs. What for I leave Baltimore, to come down to this pig life, I don't know. If only," she added wistfully, "if only Katie should live till we get back."

Paragraph 51. Miss Egmont looked away, out of the open doorway to the Gulf. The water was a deep blue. A white sail moved slowly, in the sunlight, along the horizon.

Paragraph 52. "Well," she said, bringing her eyes back to Mrs. Kazalski, "you have had a hard time. But there are only six weeks more, and you say, you have been here nearly fourteen already. Six weeks is not so terribly long. About the debt, I should not worry too much. Are you the only person here with a debt at the store?"

Paragraph 53. "Oh, no! All people got debt at the store!"

Paragraph 54. "Well, surely the company won't want to keep all of you here, for your debt. At the worst, they will take some of your bedding to pay for it. And there may be a heavy run of oysters. And thank you very much for giving me this information. Would you mind if I look over this card, to see that I haven't forgotten to ask anything? I'm supposed to have an answer for every question."

Paragraph 55. Mrs. Kazalski did not accuse her of indifference. Her mind was so occupied with her sudden new plans for the ordering of her life on her return to Baltimore that she was scarcely conscious of Miss Egmont.

Paragraph 56. Miss Egmont stayed a few minutes longer to get in detail the earnings of each member of the family, since their coming, and the hours of work. Presently she left, hoping things would go better, hoping Katie would improve, suggesting a Baltimore clinic.

Paragraph 57. Mrs. Kazalski went back to her washtub. She could hear Miss Egmont making the same explanation in the next compartment, could hear her neighbor's guarded, reluctant answers. She did not listen to the words, though she could easily have heard them—at first. But after a while her neighbor had some trouble as real as her own; perhaps—why surely every woman in the camp had some troubles. Most of them were widows, most of them had children to support. And perhaps other women, all over the country! Why, of course, it was right that the government should send someone down to see how things were!

Paragraph 58. That night she went to bed with a new feeling. It was as if, for the first time in her life, she was fully alive. Not happy, but awake. Sometimes in her youth—say fourteen years ago—at a wedding in Galicia, after a peasant dance, she had a feeling akin to this, yet different. Then the dancing made one forget the hard furrows and the heavy plow. Now there was no forgetting, rather a full remembering, a coming alive of her mind. A full remembering of herself, and therefore, of others.

Paragraph 59. Yet she told herself, nothing had happened, really. A woman had come, had asked questions, and had gone away. She had answered questions, had stated her situation. "Yet nothing has happened," she repeated to herself in Polish, "only a conversation. Talk, only." The debt was still unpaid, Katie was this minute coughing, and life in Baltimore, at the end of six weeks, would be a hard struggle, even though she now had a plan. . . . Why, then, this new courage, this strange, warm feeling, which reached out, even beyond this roomful of her own family—which included even more than the whole camp? Was this, she asked herself, what they meant by patriotism?

Paragraph 60. The wind blew, and the single palm tree outside her door cracked. The sound was like the rattle of hard rain. Other nights she had hated it, had thought it mournful, but now she liked it. She raised her head from the bed, and through the window she could see the tree. The moonlight seemed to drop off the sharp fingers of the leaves. Splotches of light and black shadows made a grotesquery; and for the first time she saw a beauty in it. She could close her ears to the heavy breathing of her neighbors, and to Katie's cough, and could listen to the orchestra of crickets and frogs, against the night's outer silence, with—was it possible?— almost happiness.

While Mrs. Kazalski was unable to solve her own problem without help, she could make up her mind to return to Baltimore

and accept help. Miss Egmont, out of her experience, and understanding, had shown her the way.

"Only a Conversation" reinforces the fundamental idea of this
book, that the basic need of the interviewer is to know something
of the meaning of background—both his own and that of the person whose life he has entered momentarily and professionally.

SUMMARY

An interview, as distinguished from an ordinary conversation,
has a purpose. The purpose for the interview in human adjustment ordinarily is to gain information, acquire insight, or give
help or counsel. The interviewer may be considered a professional
worker in this area if he has had special preparation for his work,
which encompasses knowledge of environmental forces, human
behavior, and interviewing processes and skills, all focused on
meeting the particular needs of an individual through the agency
designed to meet such needs.

The interviewer in human adjustment must be able to accept
and understand individual differences in heredity, background,
experiences, and attitudes as a basis for acceptance and understanding of the interviewee. The concept of culture contributes
to such acceptance and understanding.

Personality is affected both by our social heritage or the culture
of the past and by our more immediate background or environment.

Custom is a dominant force in the life of every individual.
Every individual's life represents accommodation to the patterns
and standards traditionally handed down in his community.

The eight characteristics of these patterns and standards, according to Kardiner, are: (1) some form of family organization;
(2) some extension of the family into the community as part of
an in-group; (3) a larger group fused by ties of real or symbolic
blood relationship or common interests; (4) means for self-

maintenance; (5) some controls of behavior enforced by discipline; (6) some control of aggressions; (7) a bond of recognizable psychological forces; and (8) distinctive life goals.

Culture sets limits for any individual through the impact of the behavior of other people upon him and by his learning from others through imitation and instruction.

Nine concepts of culture applicable to our daily lives are:

1. Every culture is of paramount importance to its possessor. It is alien only to those of other cultures.
2. To understand individuals in another culture it is necessary to have some appreciation of their culture.
3. One who functions in a culture is part of it, and every phase of his life and thought reflects that culture.
4. Behavior may be a response to distant rather than proximate stimuli.
5. A knowledge of the specific conditioning to which an individual has been subjected shows the functional relationship of things which are not logically related.
6. One can be physically and geographically in a culture and yet not psychologically in it.
7. In order to understand present behavior we must view it as a cross section of the past.
8. If we know past behavior, we can predict certain types of present and future behavior.
9. All our worlds are self-complete and self-contained; clashes and discord are part of normal functions.

Other characteristics of our American culture which have significance for the professional worker are our hedonistic goals and the emphasis given to the social value of youth in women and the economically productive years of men, with the resultant devaluation of age. The worker also must know the cultural implications of the trend toward the employment of women outside the home and the conflict created by this deviation from the patterned role of the sexes.

SUGGESTED ASSIGNMENTS

So far we have talked about concepts of culture which are operative in the interview, using lives and experiences of others as the basis for discussion. If you are planning to be a professional worker, or if you are already in your chosen field, you should know yourself. Unless you are willing to make an attempt to understand yourself, you might well question your right to interview others.

1. What about your own background? What have your ancestors given you as a material, physical, and psychological heritage? What factors in this background have aided you? What ones have hampered you? What are the salient psychological and material factors in your present environment today?
2. Describe the characteristics of any foreign neighborhood with which you are familiar. What features in its culture are foreign to your own? What cultural concepts are applicable?
3. Apply Kardiner's eight characteristics of culture to your own cultural background.
4. What novels have you read which have contributed to an understanding of the culture of a community? What specifically did you learn that you didn't know before which would help you to understand any individual in terms of his environment?
5. Do you know what steps your community is taking in behalf of displaced persons?
6. What is the Fulbright plan? How will it aid in an understanding of culture?

RECOMMENDED SUPPLEMENTARY READING

Adamic, Louis, *A Nation of Nations,* Harper & Brothers, 1945.

Alexander, Franz, *The Age of Unreason,* J. B. Lippincott Company, 1942.

Benedict, Ruth, *Patterns of Culture,* Houghton Mifflin Company, 1934.

Colcord, Joanna C., *Your Community,* The Russell Sage Foundation, 1939.

Dollard, John, *Caste and Class in a Southern Town,* Yale University Press. 1937.

Gorer, Geoffry, *The American People,* W. W. Norton and Company, 1948.

Kardiner, Abram, *The Individual and His Society,* Columbia University Press, 1939.

Lynd, Robert S., *Knowledge for What?* Princeton University Press, 1939.

Malinowski, Bronislaw, "Culture," *The Encyclopaedia of the Social Sciences,* The Macmillan Company, Vol. III, 1937.

Malinowski, Bronislaw, *A Scientific Theory of Culture and Other Essays,* University of North Carolina Press, 1944.

Mead, Margaret, *Male and Female,* William Morrow and Company, 1949.

The Family in a Democratic Society—A Symposium, Columbia University Press, 1949, with particular reference to the articles by Clyde Kluckhohn, "Variations in the Human Family," pp. 3-12, and Evaline M. Burns, "Economic Factors of Family Life," pp. 12-29.

Chapter Two

ESSENTIAL KNOWLEDGE OF PERSONALITY AND BEHAVIOR FOR THE INTERVIEWER

If I were given to prophecy, I should say the next significant emergence for man will be a realization by him that knowledge of himself is of at least equal importance to a knowledge of his environment.
—Dr. William Allen White

THE FUNCTIONING OF AN INDIVIDUAL IN A CULTURAL ENVIRONMENT

The Meaning of Behavior

In the foregoing section we have considered the importance of background and the need of the professional worker to understand individual backgrounds in both personal and cultural terms. In this section the emphasis is placed on the impact made by background on an individual. Behavior cannot be interpreted unless the interviewer is acquainted both with the client as an individual and with the forces which act upon him. The interviewer must also know himself and the significance of his own environmental influences, if the interaction between him and his client is to be helpful.

The following section will make no attempt to explain the development of personality or the mechanisms of behavior. It will omit any review of the extensive literature in this field and will refrain from any discussion of inherited physical and mental characteristics and tendencies, because this area of knowledge is too vast, too technical, and some of its facets are too controversial, to be profitably discussed except by an expert. For such material, readers who have not had formal courses dealing with the development of personality or the mechanisms of behavior are referred to an excellent book by Percival Symonds[1] or any standard text in psychology.

The Need to Understand Behavior and Personality

There is no doubt that professional workers in human problems are feeling the need to understand the springs of human behavior. Testimony on that point was given recently when 779 social case workers in Minnesota were asked what additional knowledge was most urgently needed for satisfactory performance on the job. The majority requested a more intensive study of personality. This subject, in their opinion, outranked all others as essential knowledge for practicing social case workers.[2]

Advancement in the understanding of behavior since World War I has been tremendous. Impelled by the experiences of the medical and allied professions in World War II, schools of medicine, nursing, and social work have added to their curriculums courses dealing with the *effect of illness on personality, mechanisms of behavior,* and *personality development.* A recent project of the Commonwealth Fund provides short courses for general practitioners to acquire a workable understanding of emotional problems and neurotic behavior.

The recognition by medical men of the importance of personality factors in illness has given rise to the psychosomatic approach in medicine, which recognizes and accepts the premise that many illnesses have a psychic component if not a psychic genesis.

[1] Percival M. Symonds, *The Dynamics of Human Adjustment,* Appleton-Century-Crofts, Inc., 1946.

[2] Anne Fenlason (with R. F. Sletto), "Problems in Education for Social Work," Studies in Higher Education, Biennial Report of the Committee on Educational Research, University of Minnesota, 1940-1942, pp. 94-104.

Counselors in industrial plants are realizing that job efficiency ties up closely with the well-being of the worker, emotionally as well as physically. Studies at the Hawthorne plant of the Western Electric Company which have been carried on since 1917 all support this statement.[3] The first investigations were concerned with the effect of physical environment on rates of production. Through these the discovery was made that it is not improvement in physical surroundings such as better lighting, a shorter working week, special lunches, and periodic health examinations which results in increased production; it is the way such changes are made. A group of girls segregated from the main body of workers and put to work in a special room responded to the change with greater productivity. Even when they were returned to the conditions under which the other employees worked, their high production rate was maintained. The investigators decided that the key to the improvement was a psychological factor. The girls were reacting to a social situation; they had acquired prestige in being selected for an important experiment. The records they had been asked to keep for the examiners of what they ate at home, what they did with their leisure time, how many hours they slept, etc., had given them a sense of their value as persons. As collaborators in a social and industrial experiment they took a different attitude toward their work not only for the duration of the test but after the experiment ended.

The Hawthorne plant now has a well-planned program of counseling based on the belief that cooperation of employees depends in a great part on how they feel about their job, their fellow workers, their supervisors, and the meaning of the whole work situation. Interviewing has now been substituted for experiments in manipulating working environment and has proved an excellent method of handling personal relations.

Workers in the field of juvenile delinquency have become in-

[3] Nathaniel Cantor, *Employee Counselling*, McGraw-Hill Book Company, 1945, pp. 20-22.

terested in the prevention of delinquent behavior through parent education, child guidance clinics, and, in some states, Youth Conservation Commissions. It is conceded by those concerned in the welfare of children that the child with behavior problems is an unhappy child who is generally unable to cope with his environment.

The teacher, as well as other workers, has an urgent need to understand personality development and the meaning of child behavior. A group studying parent-teacher responsibilities reports that a child's delinquent behavior is an unsuccessful attempt to attain some measure of success, security, or group approval. Delinquent or difficult behavior may be symptomatic of frustration, lack of judgment, inhibition, inherent individual deficiency, environmental lack, unfortunate personal relationships, or inadequate education and guidance. There is no single cure for a condition arising from so many complex factors, but the school, as one cooperating agency, by understanding behavior can help to direct it constructively. Prevention demands that every member of the school staff be alerted to telltale signs of potential or beginning delinquency. Teachers and other school personnel should be sensitive to the needs of children who come from broken homes, from homes ridden by poverty or from those where family relationships are inharmonious, from parents of limited intellectual capacity or conflicting cultures, and from those where family mobility is excessive. The symptoms of truancy, lying, destructiveness of property, membership in unwholesome gangs, sullenness, seclusiveness, and unhappiness should all be recognized not as personality characteristics but as symptoms and danger signals.[4]

A recent report by Lydia Herman[5] which checked the results of a course in mental hygiene given to a group of twenty-five

---

[4] *Report on School-Teacher Responsibilities,* National Conference on Prevention and Control of Juvenile Delinquency, Washington, D.C., 1946, pp. 2-5.

[5] Unpublished report of a study conducted by the Child Study Department of the Board of Education, Minneapolis, Minn., 1949.

teachers is further evidence of a recognized need of knowledge about human behavior on the part of those whose work is with human beings. Twenty-one of the twenty-five teachers answered a simple questionnaire. To the question, "If mental hygiene has helped you, please specify how you have profited," all of the teachers indicated that they had been helped markedly. More objective understanding of themselves with resultant personal security had contributed to a readier acceptance of their pupils, and modifications of their own attitudes, methods, and judgments.

Counselors in high schools and colleges see the behavior of the grade school child translated into adolescent and post-adolescent behavior. Poorly adjusted students are still exhibiting behavior symptomatic of failure to meet their needs. Their personalities are not the result of any one influence. They are the resolution of their encounters with each crisis of their lives—the record of their failures and successes.

Personality and Personal Adjustment

Further discussion of personality will be based on the acceptance of Plant's[6] concept that personality is the integration of the individual into his total environment.

Ways in which a process of integration is accomplished have been outlined by a committee of the American Council on Education in *Counseling for Mental Health*.[7] They define personality as a dynamic balance—or an emotional equilibrium amid the stresses and strains to which an individual is subjected and to which he must adjust.

The Council lists certain characteristics and their balances as follows:

[6] James S. Plant, *Personality and the Culture Pattern,* The Commonwealth Fund, 1937, p. 8.
[7] *Counseling for Mental Health,* Series VI, No. 8, American Council on Education, Washington, D.C., 1947.

On the one hand there are:

1. One's assets.
2. One's own assets.
3. The giving of affection, sympathy, and understanding.
4. Enjoyment of work.
5. Enjoyment of activity.
6. Enjoyment of working cooperatively.
7. Enjoyment of success.
8. Seeing failure as due sometimes to one's own limitations.

9. The ability to think.
10. The ability to be a leader.
11. The ability to use one's powers to the utmost.

12. The recognition of conscious factors as important in our motivation.
13. A respect for the mind.
14. The import of one's own sex.

15. One's worth as an individual.
16. The realization of the present.

These must be balanced against:

1. One's liabilities.
2. Assets of others.
3. The receiving of affection, sympathy, and understanding.
4. Enjoyment of play.
5. Enjoyment of rest and quiet.
6. Enjoyment of working alone.

7. Ability to accept failure.
8. Seeing failure as due sometimes to environmental difficulties.

9. The ability to feel.
10. The ability to be a follower.
11. The ability to recognize that there are powers beyond our control.

12. The recognition of unconscious factors in our motivation.
13. A respect for the body.
14. The import of the opposite sex.

15. The vastness of the universe.
16. The realization of the past and future.

When the balance of these factors has been achieved and assayed with a fair degree of accuracy, a personality profile emerges. A balance successfully maintained or re-established means a well-integrated personality—the integration of the individual into his total environment.

Symonds uses the word *adjustment* instead of integration when he defines adjustment as "a satisfactory relation of an organism to its environment."[8]

[8] Symonds, *op. cit.*, p. 1.

Chapin[9] sharpens this definition by differentiating the three ways in which an individual adjusts to his internal and external world in terms of: (1) how the person feels about his adjustment (the attitudinal component); (2) how he acts or behaves with others (the component of participation); (3) the way he fails to react or the way he rejects frustrations or obstacles.

Plant delineates three ways in which personality adapts to culture:[10] (1) the dominant personality which overrides all of the obstacles in the environment; (2) the relatively fixed personality which conforms to environmental pressures; and (3) the psychoosmotic personality which responds to and makes use of environmental forces. All of these types rest upon the hypothesis that environmental forces can and do change the personality. This change comes about either through action, force, and molding power which flows into and out of the individual or through mechanical forces to which the individual must adapt.

In the first type of relationship—*the self-sufficient personality who overcomes the forces of his environment*—we find a reflection of the individual's attitudes toward the events of his life. Many people who have achieved eminence come to mind under this category. Marie Curie, Sister Kenny, Michael Dowling might be cited as examples. All of them fought their handicaps and surmounted apparently unsurmountable obstacles.

Madame Curie, undaunted by ill health, bereavement, and the jealousy and antagonism of her peers, achieved her scientific goals. Sister Kenny, with indomitable spirit, fought for and won acceptance of her method of treatment for victims of poliomyelitis. Michael Dowling, while in his teens, lost both legs in an accident, also one arm and most of the fingers on the remaining hand. For an orphan supported by the county, this could well have meant a life of dependence. Through force of person-

---

[9] F. Stuart Chapin, class lecture in social organization, University of Minnesota, 1947.
[10] Plant, *op. cit.*, pp. 14-16.

ality, in spite of poverty and his tremendous physical handicaps, he achieved a college education. He became successively a teacher, a newspaperman, and a banker, and was able to live a happy, normal life with a wife and family. He became a leader in his own community of Renville County, Minnesota, a member of the legislature and later of Congress. A school for crippled children in the city of Minneapolis has been named for him.

All of these people counteracted the obstacles of unfavorable backgrounds or personal handicaps by achieving mastery over them. Individual differences in capacity or adaptability have to be taken into account.

The second type of personality is *resistant to environmental forces, because of a fixed and inflexible personality pattern* which is apparently congenital. This personality takes only those elements from the environment which fit the pattern. There is much evidence for the theory that personality patterns are set in infancy. Gesell's recent studies of the human fetus show distinct patterns of individual behavior in the womb. Even untrained observers can note that one infant is aggressive and fights to gratify his needs from the moment of his birth, whereas another, the so-called "good baby," more or less passively waits for his needs to be met. It is a safe prediction that the aggressive baby is better equipped to cope with his environment throughout life than the passive baby who has to learn how to compete for survival.

A relatively fixed pattern of the personality was found in a study of leadership qualities by Miles and Goodenough.[11] The study encompassed 500 high school children in Stillwater, Minnesota, a town with a population of 7173. Children were classified according to definite personality types. One group was composed of *successful leaders,* with leadership abilities acknowledged by

[11] Katherine A. Miles, "The Relationship Between Certain Factors in the Home Background and the Qualities of Leadership Shown by Children," unpublished Ph.D. dissertation, University of Minnesota, 1945, p. 49.

teachers and other students. Another group consisted of *attempted leaders*. A third group were *followers*. A good leader was found to be a good follower, although not all followers demonstrated qualities of leadership. A fourth group were the *voluntary non-participants*. A large number of students were typed as *over-looked*. They were those who had potentialities for group participation but were not given a chance to develop them. The last group, a small one, was that of the *outcast* or *social deviate*, set apart by teachers and students alike.

Miles' intensive study concerning home and personal factors of seventy children indicates that a child's social behavior is a product of a number of factors in the home background: (1) the location of the home, i.e., whether urban or rural; (2) the socio-economic status of parents; (3) the occupation of the father; and (4) the education of the parents.[12]

The findings are that successful leaders are likely to be urban children; to come from homes which are well above average, if not superior, in socioeconomic status; to have fathers whose occupations are in the upper three occupational classifications; and to have parents whose education is superior.

Within the family group, social children tend to come from smaller families. The social child tends to be the middle child with approximately the same number of brothers and sisters. Asocial children tend to be the older children of larger families, who have more brothers than sisters.

Parents of successful leaders are less inclined to be overprotective and restrictive. They permit more leeway in allowing children to make decisions, to use their own judgment, and to make experiments in new situations. The child's rights and opinions are respected in the family group. Parents of successful leaders appear to have unusually keen insight into the basic needs of the child.

The relatively fixed personality described in the Miles study is

[12] *Ibid.*, pp. 227-229.

one in which conformity to the environment affords the easiest path to adjustment.

These findings suggest a broad field for the counselor, teacher, and social worker in helping those who attempt leadership to attain it and in aiding the undiscovered to discover themselves.

Symonds also discusses the mode of adjustment in which *conformity to the environment is the chief feature*.[13] He states that the concept of conformity to the environment is the most widely accepted measure of adjustment today. Conformity requires an individual to restrain his appetites and to tolerate frustrations. It relates to cultural rather than physical environment. As implied in the discussion in the previous section, culture, the man-made product which enables us to live together and attain our satisfactions on a group basis, demands uniformity. The individual who fails to conform fails to do his part in the group enterprise and is therefore penalized by ostracism. The reward of conformity is security obtained through acceptance by the group in which one lives; the penalty for nonconformity is rejection by the group.

> Bob Jackson, a senior in college, is now beginning to overcome a deep sense of inferiority engendered by his high school days in a small town in Wyoming. His mother was formerly an actress; his father, before becoming a ranchman, had studied to be an engineer. Both parents had musical and literary ability as well as unusual intellectual capacity. The contrast between Bob's home influences and those of his playmates made him unable to relate himself successfully to his high school mates. His self-conscious and awkward attempts seemed patronizing to the students. It was not until his later years in college when he found others with compatible interests that he dared venture into friendships—with moderate success.

Although the personality pattern of each of us is relatively set, there are periods in our lives when we are separated from old influences and subjected to new ones which may change our pat-

[13] Symonds, *op. cit.*, pp. 8-10.

tern within certain limits. These separation periods may come at any time, but the earlier the period, the greater the probabilities for change.

An account by a student of the influence of a high school teacher exerted at a time when the girl was susceptible to change and when her motivation to conform was high seems to bear out Symonds' views on the relation of conformity to the development of personality. A young Ukrainian girl writes:

I am describing myself as I was four years ago, a senior in high school, just seventeen. Some of my attitudes and why I behaved as I did are related in this short essay.

My parents were Ukrainian having come from Rumania in 1921. Despite their 13 years of residence here, they had not abandoned some of the old country traditions. I was taught to decorate eggs at Easter, to make various foreign foods, and to study Ukrainian music and dance.

But there were things I resented and those were the old country theories my folks clung stubbornly to and would not exchange for American ideas. There were things such as *never* staying out later than ten P.M., never arguing with your elders, never picking out your own clothes, and above all, never making your own decisions, since the parent knows what is best! The fact that I was the only living child out of five caused my folks to shelter me from all possible harm. Riding bicycles or playing rough was forbidden, since I might become injured. There were plans made for me—I was to get a good education, and thus avoid being the "girl with the hoe," as my mother and her mother before her had been. I was encouraged to study much and, since I showed musical capabilities, I was given a fine musical education (violin and accordion), which proved an escape for my mixed-up emotions during my high school days and especially in my senior year.

And thus, as a senior I did not make a striking picture. My vocabulary, due to my speaking a foreign language at home, was limited. I was unable to express myself, had I had the courage to do so. I was shy, modest, extremely thin, wiry, and pale-faced. I was not allowed to use makeup except on special occasions. My dresses were always too long and one size too large, since my mother felt I would eventually grow into them, but I never did.

Especially do I recall the time as a senior when our girls' sextette was scheduled to sing for an assembly, and at the rehearsal discouraging looks were directed at my dress. My teacher very tactfully led me into the home economics department, and then and there my dress was shortened and the appearance of the sextette was saved. I was more than overjoyed at the procedure and from then on that dress got more than its share of wear.

My oversensitiveness was horrible. A reprimand from a teacher would bring tears to my eyes and I had to be excused from the class room.

I realized how different from the others I must have seemed, yet I could do nothing about it since I had no method of breaking away nor anyone to direct me.

My classmates treated me with respect however, since I had a goodly amount of musical talent. I attended class parties, played for them and sang for them, but having performed my part felt too awkward to join in the fun and went home. In spite of this, I belonged to twelve extracurricular activities—a greater share of them musical, such as orchestra, trios, double sextette, glee club, instrumental duets, and the like. These activities coupled with hard studying were physically wearing, but day after day I plugged on.

My social studies teacher was the first person to do anything toward correcting me. He told me that it was at the age of seventeen that habits were being molded and that if I did not do something to change my behavior, I would be a sorry sight. He very kindly told me how to go about making the change, and helped me constantly the entire year to make a satisfactory adjustment. By the end of the school year I knew that I would do what he had advised and that was to break away from home and go away to school. To this teacher I owe a world of indebtedness for his keen perception and willingness to take an interest in me, and for helping me to become a member of the student group.

Dr. Plant asks if it isn't easier to modify personality artificially, through creating a more favorable environment, than directly.[14] He believes that more effort is made to change a person's attitude toward a situation than to help him to change the situation; in

[14] Plant, *op. cit.*, pp. 24-43.

other words, that it is easier to alter circumstances surrounding people than to build up an inner strength which will enable them to face the circumstances. His contention seems supported by the story of Helen Keller's evolution from a handicapped child to one of the world's most beloved women.

Helen Keller is an outstanding example of a person whose capacities have been released through another's help. The first steps in this release were lessons in conformity to an environment which her teacher tailored to Helen's needs.

In 1886 the parents of little Helen Keller, a deaf-blind child living in Tuscumbia, Alabama, applied to the Perkins Institution for the Blind for a tutor for their daughter. Anne Sullivan, almost blind from birth, whose sight had been partially recovered, was just being graduated from the Institution.

The story of the lifelong association of Anne Sullivan Macy with Helen Keller is one of a devoted and great teacher and a brilliant, remarkable student.

Miss Richmond's account, which is quoted here, shows some of the procedures through which the freeing of a shut-in personality was accomplished and communication miraculously established with an ever-expanding world.

Helen Keller was six years and nine months old when Miss Sullivan came to Tuscumbia. . . . We have in Miss Sullivan's letters to a friend not only *what* happened but *how* it happened, and the teacher's own reactions as well as the pupil's.

On the educational side, some of Miss Sullivan's methods anticipate those of the most advanced school of present-day teachers. On the social side, also, they represent at many points our modern social case work procedure, though under conditions that social work can seldom command. . . .

Helen had been an "eager, self-asserting" infant. At nineteen months an illness, described as "acute congestion of the stomach and brain," had left her deaf and blind. She was learning to talk before the attack, but very shortly "ceased to speak because she could not hear." Soon she began to tyrannize over everybody, "her mother, her father, the servants, the little darkies who play with her, and nobody," wrote Miss Sullivan, "had ever seriously disputed her will, except occasionally her brother James, until I came." The parents gave the new teacher entire charge of the little girl.

"They have promised to let me have a free hand," Miss Sullivan writes, "and help me as much as possible. . . . Of course, it is hard for them. I realize that it hurts to see their afflicted little child punished and made to do things against her will. Only a few hours after my talk with Captain and Mrs. Keller (and they had agreed to everything) Helen took a notion that she wouldn't use her napkin at table. I think she wanted to see what would happen. I attempted several times to put the napkin round her neck; but each time she tore it off and threw it on the floor and finally began to kick the table. I took her plate away and started to take her out of the room. Her father objected and said that no child of his should be deprived of his food on any account."

Cut off from the normal approaches to a child's heart, Miss Sullivan had very early suggested that Helen be separated from her family for a few weeks. There were "two essential things to teach her, obedience and love," and neither could be taught without a chance to pursue a consistent, uninterrupted policy. Accordingly, teacher and pupil were established in a little garden house near the former Keller home. At that time Helen "was unresponsive and even impatient of caresses from any one except her mother." In the new surroundings she "was greatly excited at first, and kicked and screamed herself into a sort of stupor—"

. . . Helen Keller . . . was to become a citizen of the world. As every one knows, she was graduated from Radcliffe College, has written several books, is interested in education of the deaf-blind, and has had the deep satisfaction of winning for them many better opportunities. Her social endeavors have not stopped here, however, but have been extended to the much larger group of all the blind, and she has also been an active champion of woman's suffrage and of other social reforms. That Miss Keller was born with great natural endowment is obvious, but she herself has always been the first to proclaim that Miss Sullivan's ability to make her education a social one, Miss Sullivan's genius for ignoring routine and for using life itself as her best interpreter has meant the difference between a singularly happy life and one of utter wretchedness.

Miss Richmond summarizes her illustration by explaining the dynamics as follows:

This remarkable teacher had a true instinct for that greatest of all realities—the reality of personality. Beneath all the handicaps of her charge and the unfortunate effects of those handicaps she was able to divine the unusual character of the child. Building upon this discovery, she summoned one environmental resource after another, first to release, then to develop, that highly socialized personality of whom we speak today when we name Helen Keller.

Almost from the beginning it was possible to push beyond the negative side of the task. The preliminary lesson in childish obedience was necessary to orderly progress, and once learned, Helen's affection was soon won. To accomplish this, however, Miss Sullivan took upon herself the humblest duties, such as dispensing with a nurse for Helen and caring for her personally until she was able to care for herself. Here again the instructor was too wise to build upon influence gained through one channel, whether obedience or affection. Soon she was able to appeal to the mind of her pupil—doing this through everything in the child's world, even through the very persons and things that seemed at first to be obstacles in her path.

There is a sympathy, an affection, which makes us feel strong; there is another which makes us dependent and weak. Miss Sullivan's sympathy *released* her pupil from that dependence, and it did this by establishing her relation to a multitude of vital, growing things and ideas, first in space, later in time. One of the most pitifully isolated of human beings thus became one of the most completely identified with whatever is best in the world.

. . . In the first month of her teaching, Miss Sullivan used a change of environment so skillfully that it was possible to return Helen to her own natural world at the end of only two weeks.

Another mark of Miss Sullivan's intuitive social work sense was her willingness to turn to any one whose expert knowledge of whatever kind could supplement her own. She was wisely humble, for example, about Helen's ambition to learn to speak, and about the child's spiritual needs. . . .

Finally, she taught her charge to trust her absolutely by being worthy of that trust. In the service of personality—of a personality other than our own—there is a field of endeavor, whether we call it teaching or social case work or by some other title, that is of all fields the most exacting. We are "named and known" by such service: by and through it we take our "station and degree."[15]

Helen Keller's personality was fixed early in her life. As compensation for great physical handicaps, she had the heritage of

[15] Reprinted from: Mary E. Richmond, *What Is Social Case Work?* Russell Sage Foundation, 1922, pp. 10-25.

high intelligence, a family of means, and a gifted teacher who devoted her life to the mission of helping Helen to achieve all of her great potentialities. She was able to take advantage of the educational facilities then for the first time offered the blind. Her continued phenomenal growth should perhaps be credited both to material aids and to the wide scope for development inherent in her own character.

Helen Keller's story should serve as a reminder that the concept of limitations in personality development does not mean that limitations are insurmountable obstacles. It means that one develops within his capacities by use of the influences and opportunities within himself and his environment.

Plant[16] comments that certain implastic personalities search for an environment tailored to fit their needs, whereas others submit to the molding effects of environmental patterns upon plastic and malleable personalities. These two assumptions lead him to the formulation of a third: *Personality and environment are in constant interaction.*

Psychoosmosis is the term Plant has given the method by which personality relates itself to environment. The word, a hybrid of psychological and physiological processes, embraces a concept that the wall about the personality is highly permeable and that currents of environmental influence flow into the personality continuously, affecting the existing content. Growth in personality is the effort to adjust or overcome frustrations in either the internal or the external environment. The only completely satisfactory adjustment is reduction to a minimum of inner needs, strains, and conflicts. The well-adjusted person is one who has the least amount of inner strain and conflict, who meets his surroundings with a balance of mastery and conformity. Each individual has his own way of effecting this balance in terms of his personal equipment and his needs.[17]

[16] Plant, *op. cit.*, p. 27.
[17] *Ibid.*, pp. 15-17.

Thomas and Znaniecki have stated a cardinal principle of social psychology in their discussion of the interaction between a man and his social environment which would be well for the interviewer to remember.[18] They point out that the cause of a social or individual phenomenon is never another social or individual phenomenon but always a combination of the two; the cause of a value or attitude is always a combination of both an attitude and a value.

Here is an example of the way attitudes and values might operate on social phenomena with different results. Miss A and Miss B are both workers in a public relief department where clients can claim relief as a right if they qualify under the rules of eligibility. Miss A's father, although a diabetic, has never missed a day's work and has always supported his family in comparative comfort. Miss B's father, with a chronic heart condition, has been forced to have his family supported through Aid to Dependent Children. Consequently, Miss B tends to expect less from her clients with physical disabilities than does Miss A.

We have presented several views of personality adjustment to psychological and material environment as a foundation upon which to erect a framework of concepts about the functioning personality. These concepts, derived largely from psychology, were articulated and used as guides first by social case workers and public health nurses and later by clinical psychologists and other workers in personal adjustment. The concepts recognize the importance of inner as well as outer pressures, and the fact that adjustment problems may be caused by endogenous as well as environmental factors. Although simple and general, they are indispensable to the interviewer.

[18] William I. Thomas and Florian Znaniecki, *The Polish Peasant in Europe and America,* Alfred A. Knopf, 1927, p. 44.

CONCEPTS OF BEHAVIOR OPERATIVE IN INTERVIEWING[19]

Concept 1. The individual is a human being who functions in and is conditioned by his environment and his life's experiences.

This concept applies to the worker as to his client. In addition to a knowledge of another individual and his background, the worker must know himself and know how his own personality may help or possibly impede his work.

Any biography, the reader's own life story, or that of any member of his family or his friends will illustrate this concept.

Concept 2. Emotional needs take priority over reasoning.

To appreciate the importance of this concept we should realize the strength of emotions motivated by hidden needs or wants. *Need* is here used in the sense of Symonds' definition that needs represent both certain conditions of the tissues of the body and the irritation or discomfort which accompanies or follows them.[20] An emaciated body is in need of food. A dehyrated body is in need of water. In addition to tissue conditions there are life conditions, also called needs, which stand behind tissue deficits or tensions. A person exposed to hardship may need financial or medical assistance, clothing, or shelter. Any behavior trend in the service of some more basic trend may itself become a need. A need for achievement or dominance, a need for affection, a need for dependence as well as independence—these are all basic needs.

For an example, Mrs. James' needs were both material and psychological. Mrs. James was an old woman who was a source of irritation and confusion to the social workers trying to help her.

[19] The concepts to follow have been largely adapted from those articulated by the Committee on Training in Family Social Agencies, Family Welfare Association of America, New York, 1933. They are discussed in any basic book on psychology. The books recommended as particularly rewarding to the readers of this volume are noted at the end of the chapter.

[20] Symonds, *op. cit.*, p. 48.

Fortunately for her, she eventually came under the care of the worker whose interview is reproduced here. Not only Mrs. James' needs but some of the worker's attitudes concerning them are set forth:

Mrs. James, an Old Age Assistance recipient, was the widow of a prominent artist. After his death Mrs. James was left completely without resources. It had become necessary for her to apply for old age assistance even before his death. While he was alive he had received help from Family Welfare; the combined income made it possible for the Jameses to maintain themselves in fair comfort. After his death Mr. James' aid was of necessity discontinued, leaving Mrs. James with only $40.00 a month on which to live.

At the time of his death and for a few years previous, they had been living in a modest apartment for which they paid $42.50 a month. Even that was too expensive for Mrs. James to maintain now but she would not move. Casual gifts of money from friends supplemented her grant and enabled her to hang on precariously to the apartment.

I understood that she felt the apartment was the only tangible thread which held her to the past, to the happiness she had shared with her husband, and to all the associations of the place.

I understood how desperately she clung to the mental image of herself as the wife of a man who had been prominent in the city. This feeling of prestige had become an integral part of her personality.

I understood her feeling of isolation and loneliness, as if she were a boat drifting alone down some strange dark river. She was now more conscious than ever of her age—of growing old.

And now, I was to try to help her come of her own free will to a decision which would cut the last thread with all she had grown to love.

I understood how helpless she must feel in making a new venture when she had barely the physical strength to meet the problems of ordinary existence.

I think I understood her anxiety regarding her financial security. Even forty dollars meant security and protection. It helped waylay the nagging fear of what would happen to her without it. I understood, too, the justifiable attitude of my agency, not questioning her right to live in her apartment but needing to know how she was managing the rent if she had no other income than her OAA grant.

I understood that possibly I had identified my feelings too closely with those of my client and had lost an objective viewpoint. My problem was to be fair both to the client and the agency.

When we were both seated comfortably in her living room, I began: "Mrs. James, I have been having a little difficulty in figuring out your budget and I felt that if I talked it over with you, you might be able to clear up some points for me."

Mrs. James smiled, "Of course, my dear, I will be glad to help you in any way I can."

"I am glad you feel that way, Mrs. James, because I have been greatly concerned. When I was estimating your budget I noticed that your monthly expenditures average more than your grant."

I went on to tell her I could understand a sentimental attachment for the apartment which had been her home for several years; I realized how hard it would be to give it up.

She looked at me for a moment, as if a little startled. "How did you know how I felt? Mr. James loved this place; when he was in the hospital during his last illness he would beg me to bring him back here." She stopped talking and looked out the window. "This apartment is really more than I can afford, isn't it?"

I said, "Yes, it does seem that it is a financial burden and worry to you." I went on, "Have you thought about renting a room for yourself like the one I told you of near Lake Elmo? If you don't like that room we have a list of several places available for people with limited incomes."

"I have thought about it, Miss Mason, and I believe I would be as happy there as I am here. This place reminds me so much of him—so many memories."

I went on, "You might not like it at first, Mrs. James."

"Oh, I know, I don't like any place now—but I could get used to it and it might not be so bad. We all get used to anything in time."

The worker understood the basis of Mrs. James' need to remain in her apartment, and the recognition of this need enabled her to place the facts before Mrs. James so that she could accept them and come to her own decision. Her capitulation was not due to the worker's personal influence or to persuasive arguments, but rather to the fact that Mrs. James had been able to voice her need without fear of being misunderstood. The strength of her drives had up to this time overpowered her reasoning capacity.

Neglect of the truism that emotion transcends reason usually results in futile arguments with patients, clients, and students. A rise in blood pressure is often the sole outcome for both interviewer and interviewee.

Drive is defined by Symonds as the tendency to action aroused by a need.[21] He explains that it is both complementary to and an expression of need. It indicates the irritating qualities of a need and translates them into action. Thus need and drive operate together in the satisfaction of psychogenic, fundamental urges. Need is prerequisite for drive; the very existence of need implies irritation and the compulsion to seek a remedy.

A recognition of the strength of the resistance of old Mrs. James was probably the factor which enabled the worker to help her arrive at a solution of her problems. The interview shows the client feeling her way to understanding and adjustment.

Concept 3. Behavior is symptomatic, purposeful, and in response to our inner needs and strivings.

To realize this is to begin to understand behavior by looking for motivations instead of misinterpreting symptoms.

Symonds defines symptomatic behavior as an ineffectual effort to avoid anxieties and resolve conflicts by the use of adjustment mechanisms.[22] Natalie's behavior is clearly such an unsuccessful attempt. Her behavior is described by a relative:

> When I walked into Natalie's room the night after her little brother had been operated on for mastoid infection, I found her calmly admiring herself in the mirror. On closer inspection I discovered why—there wasn't an eyelash left on her lids! !
>
> Natalie was nine and had been left at home with a cold while

[21] *Ibid.*, p. 49.
[22] *Ibid.*, p. 3.

the rest of the family was spending their time at the hospital with a seriously ill brother. It was my turn to stay with Natalie. Left alone in her room for a short time she had carefully plucked out each eyelash! My first impulse was to scold but I realized that attention, even at the price of a scolding, had been her motive. At first I was puzzled as to why she chose this particularly painful method, but a backward glimpse into her life soon explained her behavior.

Natalie had been the center of attraction in both her maternal and paternal families for over five years. She was a beautiful child, intelligent and well mannered. It was a marvel that she was not more spoiled than she was. When Robert, her little brother, was born she was forced to give over, or at least to share, the attention of loving aunts, uncles, cousins, and grandparents. Robert, too, was a handsome child. No one ever saw him for the first time without mentioning his beautiful eyes and long curling eyelashes. Even Natalie pointed out this feature to relatives and friends. Often there would be comments such as "What a shame the boy in the family got those beautiful long lashes," or "Robert is even better looking than Natalie—his eyes are so lovely."

The parents had managed never to show any particular favoritism for either child. They carefully avoided mentioning Robert's eyes. They believed Natalie felt little sense of rejection, envy, or jealousy.

Now, however, her parents had bundled her little brother off to the hospital, leaving her completely alone with whoever could be found to stay with her. Robert had had a severe cold; Natalie had a cold, too. Robert had received presents when he was in bed; no one had showered her with gifts. And so, she had resorted to this painful but effective way of drawing attention to her eyes.

Concept 4. Behavior can be understood only in terms of our own emotional and intellectual acceptance.

This psychological principle, like the preceding one, is widely accepted by professional workers. It is particularly useful in helping students or new workers understand their relationship to their clients and the effect of the relationship on their work. Only such insight and self-awareness can make us accept ourselves and enable us to be tolerant of others.

The way in which attitudes conditioned the behavior of a student nurse toward her patients is described as follows:

> As a young nurse, I thoroughly disliked the overanxious relatives of a patient, especially if they attempted to pry too deeply into the progress of recovery, or the cause of various symptoms which arose as convalescence progressed. I was horrified if they attempted to read the notations on the chart. I felt that the patient was in our care and that, since we were doing all in our power to achieve recovery, outsiders should trust us implicitly and have no worries of their own. If they tried to suggest any form of relief for the patient, I was abrupt. In other words, I completely lacked any understanding of the fears and anxieties which beset those who are close to an ill person.
>
> Several years ago my mother developed a serious illness and had to be taken to the hospital. I wonder now how the hospital staff tolerated the family. We were continually pestering the nurses, the internes, and the attending physician for some scrap of reassurance. We committed all the unforgivable sins of hospital behavior; we made suggestions, we supervised treatments, and even snooped into the recordings on the chart.
>
> When she had finally recovered and I looked back on our behavior, I realized the pattern was no different from that of visitors to my patients; their families had been as precious to them as our mother to us.

Concept 5. Constructive, lasting results ordinarily come from satisfying, successful experiences.

It must be remembered that such experiences are often achieved through pain or discomfort. Symonds[23] cites Schopenhauer's trenchant remark that "a need is a push from the past, rather than a pull from the future." We achieve our satisfactions and acquire mastery over our environment by trial and error and we tend to repeat attempts which succeed. This means for the professional worker, as well as for parent and teacher, that deserved approval affords better motivation for better behavior than exhortation or censure.

[23] *Ibid.*, p. 17.

Mrs. James, who came to see the reality of her own situation and to face it, will eventually be better adjusted in her single room than she was in the apartment she could not afford. The adjustment won't be easy, but her ability to manage her own affairs better will bring real and lasting satisfaction.

The professional worker, with his ability to accept people as they are, and to assure them of his sincerity and his concern about their situation, may be the source from which satisfying experience is first secured.

Mrs. Owen is a woman who needed only a little approbation at the hands of an understanding worker in order to become self-sufficient.

Mrs. Owen was a 37-year-old widow with two sons, 8 and 12 years old, for whom she received an Aid to Dependent Children grant supplemented by the Family Welfare Agency. She had frequently expressed a wish to be financially independent. Her plan had been to earn a teacher's certificate. She had three years of college with a home economics major before her marriage. She had accepted the agency's plan to take a course in electrical assembly but as yet had not secured work.

Mrs. Owen had always looked untidy and uncared for. Her clothes had been shabby and inadequate. Her tension was apparent in continual weeping. In spite of herself the first worker in the Family Welfare Agency was relieved when she had occasion to transfer Mrs. Owen to Miss Lane, a new worker in the agency. The interview to follow was Mrs. Owen's first contact with the new worker.

When Mrs. Owen arrived, with apologies for being late, Miss Lane was pleasantly surprised to note that Mrs. Owen was an attractive woman. Her clothes although inexpensive were in good taste, clean, pressed and becoming. Her makeup was skillfully applied. Her new gloves and purse completed a harmonious ensemble.

She was still without a job, she told Miss Lane. Her eyes filled with tears as she explained, "I'm too old, I guess. They only want girls from 18 to 25. And besides, they don't want me when they know I have two children. I'm so discouraged I don't know what to do. The agency has been ever so good to me but I can't keep on taking help."

Miss Lane recognized the effort Mrs. Owen had made in her own behalf, acknowledging the present scarcity of work in the field for which she had taken training but assuring her the employment executive knew that there would be openings later. She was encouraged to feel that the intervening time was well spent in making a home for her boys. Mrs. Owen responded to this attitude of the new worker, obviously showing her relief from anxiety. Because she was not criticized for not working, she reacted positively to the worker's recognition of the effort she had made to develop the boys' interest in activities which would keep them busy when she finally got work. Miss Lane explained that funds were provided by the agency to help her raise her children with consideration for their future as well as present needs.

Mrs. Owen's last words were, "I feel so different about everything ahead than when I first came in today."

The contrast between Mrs. Owen's response to the first worker's critical attitude and Miss Lane's appreciation of her efforts needs no further comment. With Miss Lane's interest Mrs. Owen was able shortly to carry on without further assistance from the agency.

Concept 6. There is a tendency to be what others consider us to be.

This is not a new idea—it is merely a rephrasing of the old proverb: Give a dog a bad name and he'll bite you.

An underestimation of a student's abilities had far-reaching results. Mary O. was the attractive, 18-year-old daughter of a noted historian. She had had poor grades in high school and tended to be withdrawn socially. She herself asked to go away to school. Unfortunately, she selected the school where her adored sister had obtained her Ph.D. degree with brilliant success.

For two years Mary's work was so dismal a failure that she was convinced of the folly of continuing her course. A counselor found that her earlier college aptitude tests had rated her in the lowest percentile for her school; so she therefore suggested a series of retests which Mary undertook with conspicuous lack of enthusiasm. The results were amazing. Mary was astounded to find her college ability test was 99 percentile. Due to the earlier test, her self-confidence had been shattered and for two years she had been confused by doubts, because at that time, the high school principal had warned the family that she was not college material. The explanation of his unfortunate recommendation was the clerical error of 9 percentile for 99 percentile in grading her aptitude test—so Mary had been functioning at a 9 percentile rather than a 99 percentile level.

The faith of others is a powerful stimulent to confidence and success, as countless examples of achievement, great and small, attest.

From experience and observation everyone can give examples of response to the stimulus of confidence and approval, which often inspire one to perform at a higher level than he would have attained without such stimulus.

This concept should make the professional worker aware that there is danger either of overestimating or of underestimating a person's capacities.

Concept 7. Behavior may be symptomatic of a serious disorder in the body of society as well as an individual failure to adjust.

Medical science has demonstrated that heart cases are more severe in times of economic depression and emotional strains. Many able young people during the last depression found that their lives were distorted because their educational plans had to be deferred or laid aside. During times of full employment or man-power shortages, certain physical disabilities may be no bar to job opportunities. As a period of unemployment comes, even minor disabilities become job hazards.

One positive outcome of the last depression was the government's assumption of responsibility for a public welfare program to offset the personal hardships of unemployment. The Works Progress Administration was an outstanding accomplishment. The following account of a man now permanently employed as a result of his connection with WPA is personal testimony to the effect of unemployment on society and on the individual.

The following statement is positive and personal. I trust, therefore, that you will pardon the use of the pronoun "I," but it is necessary to use it consistently; for this is a personal experience.

Unemployment took away my employment status. It destroyed my daily routine as a wage earner. It took away resources that had accumulated and after they were gone, I was destitute. After I was destitute, I could not pay my rent, gas, light, fuel, dues, bills, or purchase food and clothing. My clothes became shabby, my hair long, my shoes leaky.

The mailman stopped more regularly at my door, and the letters usually ended, "or else." The landlord became emphatic and the public utility companies surmised that, inasmuch as I could not meet their demands, I undoubtedly no more needed their products.

Now this was all economic, and, although exceedingly embarrassing, it was not comparable to the accompanying mental suffering. This mental state took a heavier toll. I honestly believe that a man could die happy even from starvation if his mind were free and at rest, but if his mental faculties are upset and deeply stressed, there is agony. I became discouraged, hope was waning. I started to doubt our economic system and questioned the efficiency of our form of government to meet the economic demands of a large part of its populace. I shunned friends and acquaintances lest they should ask, "What are you doing now?" and then "How do you manage?" At church I sat in the balcony where no one could see how much I put in the collection box. I felt sorry that my family had so poor a provider. I became bitter toward God and man.

The economic system was adamant. If all else fails and you have no other recourse, then you must go on relief. Then bitter struggles and anguish, heart searching and renewed efforts all of no avail. All right—public relief, investigations, questionnaires and affidavits, waiting relief lines, sliding along groaning relief benches, hospital examinations, grocery orders, pride way down, sordid thoughts.

Then came WPA, not a panacea for all ills by any means, not a fat living, but an assignment for work. An assignment to the

University campus. Both trembling and elated, I contacted the Superintendent's office. The people there were kindly, cheerful, helpful. I was sent to Dr. Reynolds, Professor of Sociology. He was glad to see me. His smile was real. He showed no superiority in any way. He placed himself on my level and drew me up to his. He asked my qualifications. Yes, they were satisfactory, he needed someone like that for work already begun. I soon found the place which I hold to this day. Once more a man is a human being, courteously treated, having a right to live.

Shortly after work started again, there followed paydays. Paydays meant other choices of food, bills were paid with cash out of the pocket, with United States currency, honestly earned.

My morale was strengthened, cheerfulness and a keen sense of humor returned, so that now I can laugh heartily, even at a good WPA joke. Faith in God and mankind was rekindled and the future became brighter. There has come a deep understanding and sympathy for others in distress, never felt before. This is a brief outline of my experiences, incomplete in a large sense. There are thoughts and feelings humans cannot express, either because no words are adequate or their import is too deep and personal.

The professional worker's idea of fundamental needs embraces emotional and social needs as well as those of food, shelter, and clothing.

Concept 8. A person cannot achieve his potentialities unless his fundamental needs—physical and emotional—are cared for. This concept is obviously corollary to the preceding one.

Part of the training of professional workers is to learn of such needs in their clients, to fulfill them if it is within their province and to refer them to the proper agency if their own agency is not suitably equipped to do so. Society is working toward a minimum standard of health, shelter, and nutrition. Until that is provided it is impossible to achieve maximum personality growth.

The seeming apathy of those who have been subjected to great shock is often hard to understand. A Red Cross worker in a disaster relief area walked slowly toward Mr. Havala, wondering how to break the news of his wife's death. Mr. Havala was the sole survivor of his family; his four children had already died in the forest fire which had destroyed his farm.

"Mr. Havala, I'm very sorry to tell you that your wife—" the Red Cross worker began.

He interrupted in a voice without inflection, "My Mary—she die? You got some potatoes and flour?"

There was no lack of feeling; the emotions could not withstand a single additional assault, and physical needs must be met. Any attempt at consolation or rehabilitation would have to come later.

In the same way, poverty is a brutalizing affair. The public health nurse should not have been upset by the Murphys. When she called at the home after the birth of the Murphys' first child, she was distressed to find Mr. Murphy ill with arthritis and unable to return to the damp basement where he was doing rough machine assembly work. He hoped he would be able to work soon and repudiated with dignity the suggestion that the family apply for help if his unemployment security should become inadequate to their needs. Upon her next visit, a week later, it was apparent that Mr. Murphy's incapacity would be prolonged, if not permanent, and the family reluctantly permitted the nurse to refer them to the Public Relief Department. When she visited again, both Mr. and Mrs. Murphy complained about the amount and kind of help they were receiving, and in subsequent visits their complaints seemed to have become chronic. The Murphys' physical needs had been met by the agency; they themselves assuaged their battered self-esteem by their rebellion.

Concept 9. Ideas become active only when charged by the desires and inner needs of the individual.[24]

Before benefit of psychology people said, "You can lead a horse to water but you cannot make him drink." More than half a cen-

[24] This concept is amplified in any basic book on psychology. Joseph Folsom has an excellent discussion on it in his book, *The Family and Democratic Society*, John Wiley & Sons, 1943, chap. 9. Cf. also E. R. Guthrie and Allen Edwards, *Psychology*, Harper & Brothers, 1949, chap. 8, pp. 87-148, for a brief. clear exposition.

tury ago the discovery was made by psychologists that in men's lives conscious ideas are affected by a set of memories, thoughts, and feelings outside of consciousness, which reveal themselves by unmistakable signs. William James early called attention to the tremendous importance of this contribution to an understanding of human nature.[25]

The importance of the concept for professional workers is that it necessitates acceptance of a client as a human being capable of change and making his own decisions. The worker knows that decisions are stimulated by the individual's needs and desires. He also knows constructive behavior results only when the psychological needs and the concrete material needs of the individual can be brought to a satisfactory compromise.

The professional worker is skilled in enabling another to move in his own behalf. Gordon Hamilton, in explaining the processes of the social case worker, also is describing those of professional workers in other fields.[26] The skilled social case worker by understanding the nature of motivation can help the client to mobilize his feelings in the direction of change, growth, and adaptation to reality. The worker stimulates the client to participate actively in the study of his problem, to make plans for its solution, to put active efforts into the solution, and to use his own and whatever community resources are available and appropriate.

For the relatively self-directing person whose difficulties are tangible the goal is, through counseling, to enable the individual to change his own situation. For a less competent or more handicapped person, the worker must support the client's efforts and even under some circumstances actively intervene in the environment to lessen social or economic pressures.

A person can be stimulated to try to change his situation through an educational process that clarifies a course of action

[25] William James, *The Varieties of Religious Experience*, Longmans, Green and Company, 1902, p. 233.

[26] Gordon Hamilton, "Helping People—The Growth of a Profession," *Social Work as Human Relations*, Columbia University Press, 1949, pp. 8-10.

and shows him ways and means of achieving satisfaction. This may be done through counseling, which Hamilton distinguishes from advising. Through the counselor's discussion a person's capacity to make rational choices is released.

Also under this concept the worker helps the other person to tear down his destructive mechanisms of defense and substitute more satisfactory and effective ones for them.

Chuck was in need of such professional service when he sought a counselor for help in becoming popular with girls.

Charles Corner (he likes to be called Chuck) is now a young man of 18 and of more than average intelligence. For some years he had been the scourge and gang leader of the neighborhood in spite of the attempts of both parents to change his behavior. By the time he was 15 years old he had twice run away to distant cities from the comfortable home of his too anxious parents whose love he had begun to mistrust and whose nagging made him feel insecure. Well grown for his age, he applied for enlistment in the Navy and only when he received his birth certificate did he learn that he was adopted. The shock of finding that the parents he had failed to please didn't belong to him anyway was too violent.

In the Navy he copied models as far as possible from the ideals of his foster parents. He accented his rough speech and "dead-end kid" behavior. Whatever sense of security he had previously possessed had proved false. The Navy had given him the greatest security he had ever known. Today he is a swearing, swaggering show-off trying unsuccessfully to mask the effects of lack of love and understanding.

Love withheld cannot be summoned at will. Unless Chuck's parents can perform this miracle, or the counselor can give security and understanding and provide motivation for change in behavior, Chuck will continue his defensive behavior.

Concept 10. Modification of behavior results from facing the limitations imposed by the reality factors of any situation.[27]

[27] *Ibid.*, pp. 17-20.

Both the professional worker and the client must learn to face the realities of a situation calling for professional services. For the client, facing reality involves accepting the limitations which prevent his solving his own problems. For the worker, it involves knowing the limitations of his agency in its capacity to help. The limiting factors for the client may be health handicaps, economic pressures, personality defects, cultural factors, or any of the other elements which impede successful functioning in an environment. The limiting factors of the professional worker may be his own capacity and the function of his agency. For both worker and client the concept of limitations means taking stock of the potentials, external and psychological. Failure to recognize reality as a factor in behavior is to court failure and frustration.

In "Only a Conversation" Mrs. Kazalski accepted her situation with a full realization of its meaning. She still wanted to return to Baltimore. Miss Egmont, by calling up the resources within Mrs. Kazalski herself, enabled Mrs. Kazalski to make plans for her return which had previously seemed impossible.

The concepts of behavior we have been discussing are by no means the only ones seen in operation by the interviewer. They are, however, significant statements generally accepted and understood as partial explanations of why a person behaves as he does.

THE PERSONAL HISTORY AS A MEANS OF UNDERSTANDING PERSONALITY IN ACTION

So far we have been discussing some salient factors in the development of an individual. The professional interviewer is not interested in individuals in the aggregate but in a specific individual: an individual whose personality pattern is formed from factors in his culture, his immediate environment, the way he reacts to opportunities and frustrations, and his attitudes toward events, others, and himself. The composite of these elements is an impression of a unique personality. The arrangement of the elements into a form which has meaning for himself or others is his personal history.

Biography as a Form of Personal History

The most familiar nonprofessional form of personal history is found in a biography or an autobiography. Here the elements are arranged by a writer to highlight the significant forces in a human life. Biographies and autobiographies contain distortions, owing to the selection of what the writer conceives to be important influences.

The reliability of a biography bears a direct relationship to the reliability of the author's sources of information. A good biography needs extensive research to minimize distortion in perspective. It also needs sufficient lapse of time to insure objectivity.

The varied emphases in the many biographies of Franklin Delano Roosevelt remind one of the different pictures created by the five blind men describing an elephant. In time there will be a historian who can bring these different perspectives of personalities and events into a true one.

Autobiographies are more illuminating than biographies to a student of personality in that there is an attempt in an honest autobiography to explain reactions and causal relationships to events by the person who has experienced them. Even when the author lacks an appreciation of his own motivations, the reader of a well-presented autobiography is vicariously meeting an individual and getting to know him intimately.

More or less reliable personal histories are collected for various professional reasons. Dollard[28] offers a plan for organizing personal history material into a structural outline primarily for research. The material is selected according to seven criteria for a life history.

[28] John Dollard, *Criteria for a Life History*, Yale University Press, 1935.

Dollard's Criteria for a Life History

According to Dollard a life history is a deliberate attempt to define the growth of a person in a cultural milieu and to make theoretical sense of it. He observes that most case histories are an account of a life with events separately identified like beads on a string. A well-constructed life history is worked up and mastered from a given systematic point of view which then makes the material meaningful to the worker who uses it. For real use a life history should be written, not oral. Seen culturally, it is a long section view. The person is the focus. The culture is his environment. The history shows how the individual operates as an organism in his given environment.

In our brief review of Dollard's criteria we shall encounter some of the concepts previously discussed in a different setting and with a different focus.

Criterion 1. The subject must be viewed as a specimen in a cultural series.[29]

This involves the cultural concept previously discussed, that one who functions in a culture is part of it and every phase of his life and thought reflects that culture.[30]

Criterion 2. Organic motors of action must be socially relevant.[31]

By this, Dollard means that the organic activities of the body must come to meet the social influences it encounters. Organic activity must come within the possibility of perception directed inward. It must be an urge which the person consciously attempts to carry out. Our inner drives and emotional tensions must be expressed in socially acceptable patterns.

We have already expressed the operation of this criterion, first in the concept that the individual is a biological organism, functioning in and conditioned by his life's experience, and again in

[29] *Ibid.,* pp. 13-17.
[30] See Chapter One, Concepts 1 and 3.
[31] Dollard, *op. cit.,* pp. 17-20.

the concept that behavior is symptomatic, purposeful, and in response to our inner needs and strivings. Dollard stresses understanding the need of the individual to conform to his culture. In any culture one works for his food to satisfy his hunger but his food habits are peculiar to his immediate environment. He has conventions around his sexual satisfactions, but these conventions must be relevant to the society in which he lives. His instincts and drives are common to any culture, but his expression of them is peculiar to his own. We try to gear the satisfaction of bodily needs to our social environment; we want social approval insured by conformity. In this pursuit of social approval the individual may suffer. Psychiatrists know, for example, that too strict or too early toilet training of the small child may result in adverse personality traits later.

Criterion 3. The peculiar role of the family group in transmitting culture must be recognized.[32]

Recently a new word has come into our vocabulary. *Momism* is the term the novelist Philip Wylie has coined to express our recognition of the destructive role an overprotective mother plays in the development of personality. Gorer, an English anthropologist, considers the overprotective mother one of the salient causes of the restlessness and anxiety which he finds characteristic of America. A good mother neither overprotects nor unduly restrains.

Dollard recognizes the family as the institution for rearing and care of children which has never been supplanted in any society.[33] The earliest cultural influences are contained in the family group. The interaction of the child and parent, the child and siblings, is highly significant in the development of personality. The traits of dependence and independence are fostered in family relationships in various growth stages from infancy to adolescence.

[32] *The Family in a Democratic Society,* Columbia University Press, 1949, Part I, on "The Human Sciences and the Family."
[33] Dollard, *op. cit.,* pp. 20-22.

Emancipation from the family is one indication of maturity. Dollard states that a comprehensive life history will show the family as "the matrix of the individual's early life." This matrix will include the relationship of the parents to the subject, the interaction of the subject and his siblings, and the socioeconomic status of the family.

Criterion 4. The specific method of elaboration of organic materials into social behavior must be shown in the life history.[34]

A useful life history should be able to show adaptation of the individual to his social group. The transition from biological needs to socialized behavior can be traced in any life history. We saw how Helen Keller, in spite of her tragic physical handicaps, became an adult of unusual adaptability whose usefulness has been world-wide. In great contrast to Helen's history we have the story of *The Natural History of a Delinquent Career*. This story by Clifford Shaw[35] is the life history of a young boy, born in the Chicago slums, who responds to each degrading element in his crippling surroundings with appropriate but asocial and amoral behavior.

Criterion 5. The continuous related character of experience from childhood through adulthood must be stressed.[36]

Every act of life is a part of a life sequence. The life of an individual is a single connected whole. Crises are generally cumulative rather than cataclysmic. The ways in which an individual reacts to new stimuli are constant and predictable.[37] The life of any individual might be cited. Your own life would present the clearest example to you.

Criterion 6. The social situation must be carefully and continuously specified as a factor.[38]

[34] *Ibid.*, pp. 24-26.
[35] Clifford Shaw, *The Natural History of a Delinquent Career,* University of Chicago Press, 1931.
[36] Dollard, *op. cit.*, pp. 26-29.
[37] Review Chapter One, Concepts 7 and 8.
[38] Dollard, *op. cit.*, pp. 29-33.

There are two facets to this criterion: one, the situation as it exists to the observer; the other, the situation in its meaning to the individual. Where the general version coincides with the personal version we have normal conduct.

In the interview with Mrs. James[39] we saw the situation as it appeared to the agency, of a woman whose old age assistance, supposedly her sole income, was insufficient for the rent she was paying. We saw the situation as it appeared to Mrs. James. It was reasonable to her that her rent should exceed her income, because her need for security represented by the apartment obscured her reason and judgment. The worker, seeing both the agency's point of view and her client's, was able to redirect the current. If the whole of Mrs. James' life were to be written, this incident would make only one small turning in the stream.

Criterion 7. The life history must be focused on the use which is made of it.[40]

To be useful it must be organized and conceptualized. For example, Dr. Diethelm, a psychiatrist, has devised a method of securing data about an individual in which every event of the individual's life from birth to the period of study is related to his physical condition, emotional attitudes, reactions, and social status.[41] A sociological study[42] based on interviews with share-croppers and textile workers in the deep South, made around a comprehensive outline, highlights the social and economic factors in their lives. The two suggested outlines are for different uses and bear little resemblance to each other although both result in extensive and detailed personal histories.

[39] Review Mrs. James' interview, Chapter Two.
[40] Dollard, *op. cit.*, pp. 33-36.
[41] Oskar Diethelm, *Treatment in Psychiatry*, The Macmillan Company, 1936, pp. 111-133.
[42] *These Are Our Lives*, a Federal Projects Publication, University of North Carolina Press, 1939, pp. 417-421.

THE CASE RECORD AS A MEANS OF UNDERSTANDING PERSONALITY IN ACTION

Another source of understanding the individual and his behavior is the case history. In the *life* history there is a continuum from infancy on, with selection of the material determined by the use of the history. The *case* history is a focused account of an individual in his functional relations. The focus is upon that point in the person's life where his functional relationships have become impaired to the extent that professional help is required. The life history may be secured for a purpose unrelated to a need for counsel or assistance. The case record is the selective use by a worker of life history material for benefit of the person concerned.

The personal history is translated into a case record after the interviewer has assembled the cultural, familial, and personal data and forged them into an instrument for helping the interviewee.

Competent and responsible practice in any profession requires a record. The record is for the benefit and protection of the person receiving professional services. The case record is the objective means by which the worker organizes and develops his understanding of the individual. His activity is based on that insight.

The form and content of the case record are derived and determined by (1) the character and requirements of the profession and (2) the purposes of the professional activities of the worker. Gordon Hamilton has outlined the latter for the social case worker.[43] Her definition applies to objectives of case records generally. The objectives of the social case record, according to Hamilton, are to project the worker's observations and findings; to help the worker check his observations; to show his relation-

[43] Gordon Hamilton, *Principles of Social Case Recording,* Columbia University Press, 1946, p. 9.

ship to his client and his role in helping him; to aid him in formulating hypotheses and appraising movement, change, growth, or negative or unsuccessful results. The record is also useful in supervision, teaching, and social research.

The following case record[44] was selected from the field of vocational rehabilitation. It is the personal record of a man who applied to an employment research institute as a candidate for the retraining available to the handicapped.

THE CASE RECORD OF ROBERT BARNES

FAMILY BACKGROUND

Robert Barnes is a married man 39 years of age. He and his wife live with his parents. They have no children. Both have resided in St. Louis all their lives. Both are of Swedish parentage. Mr. Barnes' father is a retired contractor of considerable means.

EDUCATION

Mr. Barnes attended school until he was 19 years old, when he dropped out in his second year of high school. An eight months' course in shorthand at a business college completed his formal education.

WORK HISTORY

He began work at the age of 19 years as a shipping clerk in a boiler manufacturing company. He left this job to attend business school. For two years after finishing his shorthand course he worked as a bookkeeper in a wholesale hardware store. He left this to go on a trip west. Upon his return he secured a job with a traction company where he did clerical work for two years. He does not know why he left this job. He was earning only $95.00 a month at this time. For the next thirteen months he worked for an electric company. He claimed he left because of penalizing mistakes made by the checkers. The $125.00 per month he earned on this job represented his highest wages. For the next three years he sold real estate and automobiles on commission. Lack of success as a salesman, and a month's illness, forced him to accept a job

[44] Unpublished personal history from the Minnesota Institute for Stabilization and Research, Minneapolis, Minn., 1942. The story of Mr. Barnes is authentic, edited to conceal identity.

driving a truck for a hardware store. He stayed at this job four and one-half years, finally leaving because he couldn't make enough money at $.95 per hour to support himself and his wife during slack times. Since then he has had only an occasional odd job at truck driving.

He has been assiduous in making personal applications to firms. He estimates that he has made between 50 and 75 direct applications in the past year.

PERSONAL CHARACTERISTICS

Mr. B. is neat in appearance, his manner courteous, his mentality alert, and his social adaptability negligible.

CONFIDENTIAL EXCHANGE CLEARANCE

Not known to any social agencies.

MEDICAL RECORD

Mr. B. is fit for limited employment only, due to his lack of sight in one eye. He has dental caries, pyorrhea, a lowered vital capacity, and several minor physical defects such as flat feet, varicocele, and a deviated septum with obstruction.

INDIVIDUAL DIAGNOSIS RECORD

Mr. B.'s educational attainment of tenth grade at the age of 19 years is compatible with his score in the classification test which shows him able to do work of the IXth grade. He is below average in clerical aptitude (30-34 percentile) and in mechanical ability requiring manipulation of fine objects, finger dexterity (25 percentile), tool dexterity (20 percentile), and spatial relations (17 percentile). He rated 90 percentile in assembling mechanical devices, however.

His personality ratings are low in neurotic and introversion traits and in traits of submissiveness (23, 22, and 29 percentiles respectively). He rated high (70 percentile) for traits of dependence.

In the strength tests he was below average in strength for hands, back, and legs.

His vocational interests according to the Strong Vocational Interest Test show him to have the same interests as an engineer or a purchasing agent and many of the interests of a vacuum cleaner salesman and an office clerk. He would like to work in an experimental laboratory—to do "systematizing," "efficiency," manufacturing or salesmanship.

Supplementary Information Secured by the Social Worker

HOME VISIT

Mr. B. and his wife live in an apartment in his father's apartment house. The father, a retired contractor, resents his son's living there, as he could otherwise be getting an income from the apartment. He feels his son lacks aggressiveness for a selling job and that his impaired sight interferes with rougher work like truck driving.

INTERVIEW WITH MR. B.

In a subsequent office interview with Mr. B. he confided that his chief worry over his unemployment is the unhappiness his wife feels about being dependent upon his parents. The B.'s are receiving free rent and have a small amount of capital which was given them at the time of their marriage by both her parents and his. They are using this for food and clothing at present. The wife, a stenographer before her marriage, wants to return to work as there are no children. The husband is opposed to this idea, however. He is interested in phrenology, numerology, and character reading. He says that the results of a numerology test taken recently predict success as a salesman. He regrets that he lacked the capital to avail himself of the sales territory rights of a psychograph machine. He feels that by demonstrating it at fairs, etc., he could make money. He has recently heard of a vocational expert who gives vocational advice based on handwriting; he intends to consult him.

He talked expansively about himself and his lack of self-confidence based on his eye defect. He feels inferior, he says, in meeting anyone for the first time and therefore doubts his sales ability.

WORK RECORD

(The only employer consulted was the most recent one, partly because he represented the longest term of employment and partly because Mr. B.'s eye defect and low clerical aptitude make any clerical or office work impractical as a vocational selection.)

Mr. Roberts, for whom Mr. B. had worked for four and one-half years, is the owner of a retail hardware store. He employed Mr. B. because he was a friend of the family's. B. helped around the store and made deliveries by truck. He was a careful driver and knew the city well.

Mr. Roberts felt Mr. B. was "peculiar." He was not interested in anything except talking. He would stay in a house from 15 to 20 minutes when making a delivery. He talked about everything, but around election time was especially interested in politics.

His memory was poor; he forgot an order two minutes after it had been given. His father could have employed him as janitor of an apartment house he owns but didn't feel that his son was competent for the job. An uncle is of the same opinion. Because of Mr. Roberts' friendship for the family he kept Mr. B. much longer than he was warranted in doing. He discharged him repeatedly, but always took him back.

Mr. B.'s father had formerly owned a retail mercantile store in which it was intended his son would work. When the father found he couldn't make his son work, he sold the store.

Staff Recommendations[45]

INDIVIDUAL DIAGNOSIS CLASSIFICATION

Trade skill claimed in stenography. The dominant cause of unemployment is probably cyclical due to current unemployment conditions.

The chief contributing cause is probably personal, due to the physical handicap of the loss of one eye and a peculiar personality make-up.

Employment classification is limited fitness for work.

RECOMMENDATIONS

Referral to the State Department of Rehabilitation with the suggestion of possible placement as a repairman for small machines. Mr. B.'s personality difficulty is recognized but it is doubtful if he would be receptive to any treatment along this line.

THE INTERVIEWER'S USE OF THE PERSONAL HISTORY

It will be noted that any case record is essentially an account of an individual who has come for, or is receiving, professional

[45] All pertinent data were sifted by staff conference consisting of the psychologist, the doctor, the psychiatrist, and the social worker who comprised the clinical team.

help from an individual or an agency. The information obtained in each instance is selected to enable the worker and the individual needing help to work together in the latter's interest. Seldom is a complete, detailed case history obtained. The only information sought is that pertinent to the problems presented.

In the case of Mr. B. the data all related to his employability. The information given by him through the interview was supplemented, with his knowledge and consent, by others who could give a more complete and accurate picture of his employability than he himself could furnish.

The interest of the trained worker in the case history is not in eliciting a complete and detailed account but in discovering the pertinent and helpful facts in a given situation.

Further illustrations of different uses of case material by interviewers would make this point more clear. Students preparing for professions are already familiarizing themselves with case records in their fields.

The professional use of case material is different for the counselor, the public health nurse, and the social worker, depending upon their various functions and practices. These differences are reflected in comparative studies of the case records of different types of agencies. Excellent case studies have been published in various fields. In the belief that the study of actual, live interviews will be found more revealing to the student of interviewing than a study of case records as such, our illustrations are presented in the form of the raw materials from which records are made. The case record is the form in which the worker recasts and indicates the substance of his interview in accordance with his agency's use of personal history material.

SUMMARY

Any profession in which the human element of interaction is a factor calls for an understanding of personality and behavior.

This is essential in any calling in which one individual attempts to help another in the resolution of difficulties involved in the maelstrom of our complex civilization.

Personal liabilities must be counterbalanced with compensating assets. Personal assets need to be weighed with the assets of others. One must be able to receive as well as give affection, sympathy, and understanding. Play and rest must be in a dynamic balance with work and enjoyment of activity. The well-adjusted person must have the capacity to work alone as well as with others. He can accept failure as well as enjoy success, and recognize that such failure may be due to environmental forces as well as to his own limitations. He can feel as well as think. He can follow as well as lead. He can recognize that there are forces beyond his control and at the same time make the most of his own powers. He recognizes that behavior is motivated by both conscious and unconscious factors. He respects the functions of the body as well as the mind, and his adjustment to sex is on a heterosexual level. He values the worth of the individual but recognizes that he is but an atom in the cosmic pattern. He knows that the past and the future are tied in with his attitudes, desires, and behavior in the present. The equilibrium he is able to achieve and maintain is a measure of his integration into his total environment and a key to his personality.

Plant recognizes three personality types in relation to environment: (1) the dominant individual who overrides obstacles in the environment; (2) the relatively fixed personality who tries to resist the impact of his culture and to preserve his personality pattern; and (3) the plastic personality who reacts to and makes use of the forces of his environment.

Ten generally accepted ideas of behavior are phrased as concepts for the convenience of the individual who uses the interview in the practice of his calling.

1. The individual is a human being who functions in and is conditioned by his environment and his life's experiences.

2. Emotional needs take priority over reasoning.

3. Behavior is symptomatic, purposeful, and in response to our inner needs and strivings.

4. Behavior can be understood only in terms of our own emotional and intellectual acceptance.

5. Constructive, lasting results ordinarily come from satisfying, successful experiences.

6. There is a tendency to be what others consider us to be.

7. Behavior may be symptomatic of a serious disorder in the body of society as well as an individual failure to adjust.

8. A person cannot achieve his potentialities unless his fundamental needs—physical and emotional—are cared for.

9. Ideas become active only when charged by the desires and inner needs of the individual.

10. Modification of behavior results from facing the limitations imposed by the reality factors of any situation.

The personal history of any individual is a medium for understanding personality in action. It is a systematic presentation of the significant features of an individual, and his life's activities. The seven criteria suggested by Dollard for the study of an individual in his cultural environment are as follows: (1) The subject must be viewed as a specimen in a cultural series. (2) Organic motors of action must be socially relevant. This is another way of saying that our inner drives and tensions must be expressed in patterns acceptable to society. (3) The peculiar role of the family group in transmitting culture must be recognized. The family is the matrix of the individual's early life. His relationship to his parents, his siblings, and his family's status are among the chief determinants of his later attitudes and behavior. (4) The specific method of the individual's adaptation to his social group must be shown. (5) The continuous related character of experience from childhood through adolescence must be stressed. (6) The social situation must be carefully and continuously emphasized from the point of view of the observer and in its meaning to the person observed. (7) The life history must be focused on the use which is to be made of it.

The case record is another key to understanding personality in action. The case record is a focused account of an individual centered on that point where professional help is required. It is the selective use of personal history material for the benefit of the person concerned; it contains an account of the professional worker's intervention and interaction in the case. The case record is the form in which the worker recasts and indicates the substance of his interviews and activities with his client.

SUGGESTED ASSIGNMENTS

1. What factor, external or internal, has had a profound effect upon your life today? How old were you when it occurred? What was the situation or event, and its setting? What was your emotional reaction then? What has been its lasting effect?
2. Select any three concepts of behavior as discussed in this chapter. Illustrate them from literature, your own life, or the life of someone sufficiently well known to you to insure accuracy of facts.
3. Use Mrs. Roosevelt's *My Own Story* for an application of the concepts of personality discussed in this chapter.
4. Interview a person now a stranger to you for his personal history. Use the outline contained in *These Are Our Lives*, with such modifications as are desirable, as the structure for your interview. What were the successful elements in the interview itself? Why? What were the unsuccessful elements? Why?
5. Select a biography or a novel with good characterization. Apply Dollard's criteria.
6. Take a published case history from your own field. How is it used to further the interests of the patient or client?

RECOMMENDED SUPPLEMENTARY READING

PERSONALITY AND BEHAVIOR

Allport, Gordon, *Personality, A Psychological Interpretation*, Henry Holt and Company, 1937.

English, Oliver, and Pearson, Gerald, H. J., *Emotional Problems of Living*, W. W. Norton and Company, 1945.

Goodenough, Florence L., *Developmental Psychology*, Appleton-Century-Crofts, Inc., 2nd ed., 1945.

Guthrie, Edwin, and Edwards, Allen, *Psychology*, Harper & Brothers, 1949.

Healy, William, *Personality in Formation and Action*, W. W. Norton and Company, 1938.

Overstreet, H. A., *The Mature Mind*, W. W. Norton and Company, 1949.

Plant, James, *Personality and the Culture Pattern*, The Commonwealth Fund, 1949.

Richardson, Henry B., *Patients Have Families*, The Commonwealth Fund, 1945.

Shaffer, Lawrence Frederic, *The Psychology of Adjustment*, Houghton Mifflin Company, 1936.

Symonds, Percival, *The Dynamics of Human Behavior*, Appleton-Century-Crofts, Inc., 1946.

Towle, Charlotte, *Common Human Needs*, Public Assistance Report No. 8, U.S. Government Printing Office, 1945.

The Family in a Democratic Society, Anniversary Papers of the New York School of Social Work and the Community Service Society of New York, Columbia University Press, 1949, Part I.

THE PERSONAL HISTORY

Dollard, John, *Criteria for a Life History*, Yale University Press, 1935.

These Are Our Lives, a Federal Writers Publication, University of North Carolina Press, 1939.

The Use of Personal Documents in History, Anthropology and Sociology, Social Science Research Council, Bulletin 53, 1945.

CASE RECORDING

Hamilton, Gordon, *Principles of Social Case Recording*, Columbia University Press, 1946.

Sarbin, Theodore R., "The Case Record in Psychological Counseling," *Journal of Applied Psychology*, April, 1940, pp. 184-197.

Chapter Three

KNOWLEDGE OF ROLE

The foregoing chapters have considered cultural and personality factors as essential background information for the interview. Also essential is a knowledge of role factors and their interrelatedness to cultural and personality concepts. Researchers in the social sciences have given systematic consideration to role theory as a basis for understanding man's social functioning. Social research in this area has flourished during the past fifteen years, and is still being refined and expanded. Such research has brought fresh insights into the understanding of human behavior, by revealing how role perceptions, expectations, and actual functioning assist or play havoc with the personality's harmonious operation in the social order.

PRELIMINARY CONSIDERATIONS

Role theory considers cultural, personality, and social backgrounds together with the wide range of perceptions and expectations within each of them. Talcott Parsons,[1,2] Leonard

[1] Talcott Parsons, "Age and Sex in the Social Structure of the United States," *The American Sociological Review*, October, 1942, pp. 604–616. Reprinted by permission in Herman D. Stein and Richard A. Cloward (eds.), *Social Perspectives on Behavior*, The Free Press, 1958, pp. 191–201.

[2] Talcott Parsons, *Essays in Sociological Theory*, The Free Press, 1949; and *The Social System*, The Free Press, 1951.

Cottrell,[3] and Ralph Linton[4] are among the many contributors to role theory. Henry Maas[5] articulated and developed several useful propositions relating to cultural stress and social role which were presented at an advanced seminar on interdisciplinary roles and relationships at Howard University.

A basic premise which the interviewer must consider is that the role concept takes into account the personality in social interaction. Without this assumption the role concept becomes sterile and mechanistic, and consequently loses its value as a useful tool in giving help.

A second fundamental consideration is the necessity of distinguishing between *role* and *status*. *Status* refers to the position or place one occupies in a society by virtue of age, sex, birth, occupation, or achievement. Position in this context refers to an individual's location in a societal structure that is characterized by a given set of social norms. Norms are the commonly held or accepted behavior expectations; that is, the learned responses held in common by the members of a society or members of one of its subgroups. Status, then, refers to the relative ranking of a position within a society, and includes the value assigned to the rank and to the person fulfilling the role(s) constituting the position. Inherent in position are specific task-oriented roles, in the performance of which certain behavior is expected. For example, in many cultures a multitude of task-oriented roles are expected of the father; one who has father status is expected to play the roles of breadwinner, spouse, disciplinarian, supporter, and model

[3] Leonard S. Cottrell, Jr., "The Adjustment of the Individual to His Age and Sex Roles," *The American Sociological Review*, October, 1942, pp. 17–20; and Nelson N. Foote and Leonard S. Cottrell, Jr., *Identity and Interpersonal Competence*, The University of Chicago Press, 1955.

[4] Ralph Linton, *The Study of Man*, Appleton-Century-Crofts, 1936, chap. 8; and *The Cultural Background of Personality*, Appleton-Century-Crofts, 1945.

[5] Henry S. Maas, "Behavioral Science Bases for Professional Education: The Unifying Conceptual Tool of Cultural Role," in *Proceedings of the Inter-Disciplinary Conference*, Howard University Press, 1957, pp. 11–23.

for male identification, while fulfilling his role as leader in the primary family group.

Role is the part one is expected to play in each of the assigned or achieved statuses. It is *human interaction affected by structure and function* in relation to status and position, and when the helping professions view role in this context they find deeper insights into the meaning of human interrelationships in the social order. Both status and role are social products, and one could not exist without the other. Linton emphasizes this distinction, defining status as "the place in a particular system which a certain individual occupies at a different time" and defining role as "the sum total of the cultural pattern associated with a particular status."[6,7] The array of association roles which each status carries becomes a complicated network in the functioning of any human being. Just how complex the functioning of many roles together can be was glimpsed in the above example of the father. Students, too, are expected to play a number of roles relative to their status. This complexity of multiple roles is particularly illustrated by the field work or practicum student. His status is primarily that of a student, or learner. But in addition to the role he is expected to play in the student-instructor relationship, he is required to play roles in relationships with his fellow students, with personnel in the agency or institution to which he is assigned for practicum, with workers from other professional disciplines, and very importantly, with the clients or patients he interviews and to whom he gives specialized help.

A third basic consideration which the interviewer must remember is that the role concept encompasses not only specific tasks in relation to functioning, but also the individual's expected, perceived, and actual behavior in the performance of these tasks.

[6] Ralph Linton, *The Cultural Background of Personality*, Appleton-Century-Crofts, 1945, pp. 76–77.

[7] For a discussion of status, see Francis E. Merrill, *Society and Culture*, Prentice-Hall, 1957, pp. 190–199.

OPERATIONAL FRAME OF REFERENCE

The following is offered as a frame of reference to guide the interviewer in his consideration and use of the role concept: *The role concept relates the range of perceptions, expectations—individual, cultural, and societal—and performance of specific tasks and activities to membership, position, and participation in various groups and organized societal institutions.* This frame of reference encompasses the fusing of ego perceptions and strivings with societal expectations. It also takes into consideration the value symbols represented by organizations and institutions per se, including the professional role perceptions and expectations of both interviewer and interviewee.

As a practical abstraction, the role concept is a useful guide to understanding the background and stresses of the interviewee; it also permits practical consideration of the interviewer's role of interaction with the interviewee. In their discussion of social role, Stein and Cloward[8] make a particular point in emphasizing the personality in social interaction. Stress factors are considered in conjunction with separate role combinations of age, sex, family, occupation, friendship, and the like. Nurses, teachers, and social workers, for example, encounter various role strains deriving from age-range differences that carry certain prescribed societal expectations. Stress coming from role combinations is experienced by the child when he first goes to school and must suddenly assume the pupil role; by the adolescent when he begins to perceive the role expectations of adulthood; and by the adult when he steps into marital and parental roles. Complicating this stress syndrome are the numerous accompanying physiological and psychological stresses and changes that are normally present at certain critical age periods in the life span. Combinations in age, sex, family, occupational, and friendship roles are vividly illustrated

[8] Herman D. Stein and Richard A. Cloward (eds.), *Social Perspectives on Behavior*, The Free Press, 1958, pp. 171–174.

in the interview with the experienced public health nurse, given in the latter section of Part Two.

Role Performance and the Family Unit

As the basic unit of society, the family and the roles played within it constitute perhaps the most tightly knit pattern. The entire repertoire of family roles differs among societies. Moreover, within the system of family roles a high degree of flux brought about by social change can be observed. Traditional definitions of role performance patterns and the changes within them are noticeable, especially among married men and women. For instance, the married woman today is, by and large, no longer content to be only a wife, mother, and housekeeper. Our industrial development has provided labor opportunities that often attractively invite her services. Fifty years ago the opportunity to work outside the home was not as readily accorded to a young wife and mother as it is today. Nor did the attitudinal climate within society at large enable her, in earlier years, to express her dissatisfaction or confusion with regard to her position. Albeit, there are still residual attitudes regarding both status and role expectations, which linger from the past and, together with individualized and internalized strivings, intermingle and produce areas of conflict in a number of married couples. Some conflicts which arise are also partly, and in some instances largely, accountable for varying degrees of stress factors which exist within marital relationships themselves and in parent-child interrelationships as well. In dealing with the latter, the interviewer is faced with a wide range of complex ramifications and variables which will not be dealt with here since they involve the intricate and complicated processes of the particular disciplines that handle such problems.[9]

A lucid narrative showing the prescription of definitive tasks within family roles is presented by John Steinbeck in his novel

[9] This text is conceived to be one that attempts to get at essentials for the beginning interviewer.

The Grapes of Wrath. Included among his many colorful descriptions of a subculture in social upheaval is the following:

And as the cars moved westward, each member of the family grew into his proper place, grew into his duties; so that each member, old and young, had his place in the car; so that in the weary, hot evenings, when the cars pulled into the camping places, each member had his duty and went to it without instruction: children to gather wood, to carry water; men to pitch the tents and bring down the beds; women to cook the supper and to watch while the family fed. And this was done without command. The families, which had been units of which the boundaries were a house at night, a farm by day, changed their boundaries. In the long hot light, they were silent in the cars moving slowly westward; but at night they integrated with any group they found.[10]

In our attention to the family unit as a group, we must consider the interacting relationships of all members to it and the presence or absence of leadership roles. In our present-day cultural patterns we think in terms of allocating the normal leadership responsibilities to the husband and wife—father and mother. There is usually a division of leadership responsibility, with certain behaviors and expectations within this division related to sex differences that are determined by the culture. Age is a factor of difference too. Sometimes the dominant leadership role is extended beyond the immediate family unit and is executed by such key related family members as grandparents, aunts, uncles, and the like. For instance, in some cultures where girls normally become mothers at a very early age, their mothers assume many maternal roles in caring for the infant, and while doing so apprentice their daughters until they are socially and psychologically ready to fulfill more independently the cultural expectations of the mother role. The interviewer who is forced to deal in one way or another with the many health, educational, social, and psychological problems of children will do well to know about

[10] John Steinbeck, *The Grapes of Wrath,* The Viking Press, 1939, p. 267.

and be sensitive to these factors. Failure to consider them could seriously disrupt or disorganize the best intended plan of help.

Lyle Saunders[11] and others have pointed out that with the birth of each child into a family unit, some modification in each member's role status and function takes place. Undoubtedly, more noticeable and stress producing modifications are necessitated by the prolonged absence of one parent and the accompanying changes in leadership tasks. This type of change may occur during periods of illness, separation, divorce, incarceration, or vocational assignments that take the adult away from the family unit for an extended period. Examples of such incidents are only too well known to teachers, nurses, doctors, psychologists, and social workers.

The records of school counselors and juvenile court officers show time and again the results of stresses placed on older children when the adult leadership in the family unit has been excessively weak. In these circumstances, parents have in many instances assigned leadership tasks to the oldest child, these tasks often being clearly excessive in terms of the age and social and psychological development of that child.

Family roles among siblings are frequently based on age and sex differences. Special privileges may be given to the eldest and youngest members of a sibling group. In certain cultures the oldest male child is accorded particular privileges as well as responsibilities. These factors also bring with them a range of expectations among all members in terms of behavior.

When parents are absent from the home for short periods there may often be an extension of role functions, with particular responsibilities delegated to the older children during these periods. In some cultures certain leadership tasks may be assigned to the

[11] Notes taken from a sociological lecture given by Professor Lyle Saunders at the Institute "Preventive Action Through Social Work in Health, Medical Care and Rehabilitation Programs," Pacific Northwest Regional Institute of the Medical Section, National Association of Social Workers, Lake Wilderness Lodge, Maple Valley, Washington, September 11–16, 1960.

oldest son, even when daughters older than he are present. This type of sex differentiation will depend on a particular culture's value with reference to sex difference. Frequently such a realignment of role and status, even when it is very temporary, brings discord within the existing family group.

A child welfare worker was made aware of these factors when he was asked to intervene in a disrupting squabble resulting from such a role rearrangement in a Mexican family which was being helped by the State Department's Child Welfare Division. The family unit consisted of a forty-four-year-old father and ten children ranging from five to seventeen years of age. The two oldest children were girls, age sixteen and seventeen; the oldest son was fourteen years old. Their mother had deserted them four years previously. Whenever their father had to be away from home during hours when the children were not in school, he delegated the disciplining of the children to the oldest son, who was sternly commanded to keep the children at home and warned that if he did not keep order he would be beaten upon the father's return. Once, while the father was away, a crisis developed because the two oldest daughters had arranged a double date and planned to leave before the father's return. When they announced their intention to the oldest son, an angry dispute emerged, and all ten children became excitedly involved in it. In the midst of what looked like unmanageable chaos, the eldest daughter telephoned the child welfare worker. The following excerpted account shows what developed and how the social worker gave practical considerations to the role concept and its implications:

When the worker arrived at the house, several of the children were sitting outside on the doorstep. Joe, the oldest son, was autocratically giving orders to several of the children, yelling quite loudly and threatening to beat them if they did not do what he commanded. The worker gathered the children into the house to discuss the problem which had arisen.

The older children sat around a large table and the smaller ones stood nearby. The two oldest girls explained the situation which they felt was not only unfair to them but unreasonable to the smaller children who were threatened with physical punishment. The worker gave each child a chance to express his or her feelings and opinions about the whole situation and to discuss their reasons for rebelling against Joe. Joe was also given an opportunity to explain his role. As he did so, he expressed his fear that the two older girls would "run around on dates and not stay at home." He also openly expressed his fear of the punishment he expected to receive from the father were he to come home and find the girls out.

Acting upon knowledge that there were four adolescents in this group, the worker suggested that limits be set for all in that no one should be going out of the house until the father returned and, also, until the worker had had a chance to discuss the situation with him. In the discussion which followed there was emphasis on the importance of sticking together rather than fighting among themselves. The children concluded that the authority should be delegated and distributed among the four adolescents, including Joe. They all agreed to work together and help each other. The chores of the household and each's task in completing them were decided upon and divided among them as a joint responsibility.

Later the social worker had an interview with the father who was able to modify some of the role functions previously delegated to one child, doing so after the worker had explained in as simple terms as possible some of the natural implications which had arisen from the former arrangement.

In assessing the immediate problem, the child welfare worker realized that he could not take the authority away from the oldest son without jeopardizing or breaking up the forces which were also being used to help the family remain together. Therefore, this social worker saw his function as one of helping the sibling group to function as a family and keeping it united until the father returned. The oldest son's role, as well as the culturally determined reason for it, had to be considered and then modified in such a way as not to be destructive to him or to the group. Care also had to be taken not to complicate the role of the father. It was also necessary to take adolescent behavior into account when dealing with the age, sex, and family roles as observed in this family. Cultural and personality factors were dealt with in direct relationship with the facets of role considerations.

Embodied in the illustration of Joe's behavior is the implication that he had informally learned, however badly, some of the behavioral aspects of the role he was to perform in connection with his status. It is apparent that he had observed his father's behavior in setting down limits and discipline. The point to be made is that human beings learn, often very informally, in preparation for the roles they will perform in connection with future statuses they will have. They perceive kinds of behavior which they assume to be expected of persons with particular status carrying particular roles. When this perception is distorted, as it was to some extent with Joe, the behavior may have to be modified. With this modification additional learning is called for.

The interviewer will also recognize that role functions and their interrelating aspects with other persons are extended and expanded as each child and adult moves outside the family unit. Some members carry over many of the qualities and characteristics of the role they assumed earlier in the family unit; but only rarely, if ever, are they carried over in exactly the same way. Indeed, there are others whose tasks and the ways in which they carry them out in other groups are radically different from those performed in the family unit. Teachers, child care workers in institutions, social group workers, and nurses have observed that most groups consist of leaders, followers, or isolates. Within the same group these characteristics may differ somewhat in the subgroups existing within them. For instance, the child who is a follower or an isolate when role-functioning on a school playground may reappear in the classroom as the leader of that assembly, and vice versa. A case like this is not common, however. It has also been reported that some children who have been forced to take on excessive leadership tasks in their homes often willingly abdicate them when away from home; many of these children may even be the isolates in the neighborhood, school, and church groups of which they are members.

Age and Sex as Role Factors

Knowledge of role must take into account the fact that status may derive from age and sex. The status values of age and sex are influenced by forces expressed through the social, economic, and political conditions of a society during a given historical period. Linton[12] points out that from earliest infancy, man is given a progressive set of roles appropriate to his age and sex, and he is expected to play them with reasonable persistence and accuracy. Certain types of behavior are prescribed and, also, certain kinds of behavior in certain age and sex roles are expressly forbidden. Parsons[13] has also pointed this out, and he goes on to state that this definition is not deliberate, but arises in spontaneous social interaction and is handed down in the same way.

Age and sex roles differ between societies and subcultures. Pubescent boys are thought of as children in one society, whereas in some cultures they are considered ready for the adult role. A similar difference is noted with reference to girls in their early adolescence—we consider them to be children but in other cultures they are married or at least marriageable. Currently, dating, in many sections of the United States, usually begins at an earlier age than is common in most European countries. The roles and status of older people also vary from culture to culture. In considering the age and sex elements of role along with its other components, the factor of constant social change, and the disruption which accompanies it, must also be taken into account.

Value-emphasis between adults and children and the ways of its expression are modified by changes in social structure. Some rather bold shifts in the status accorded to and the roles expected of persons among the younger and older age groups have evolved

[12] Linton, *op. cit.*
[13] Talcott Parsons, *The Social System,* The Free Press, 1951.

from structural changes in society. During the Victorian Age, and for a short period thereafter, children were "seen but not heard." Since the second quarter of this century "the age of the child" has become a well-known adage in North America. More recent popular and professional articles have protested against applying this standard excessively, explaining that it may derive from an exaggerated reaction to inhibitions imposed on children in the past.

Another aspect of change is illustrated by the present-day emphasis on social gerontology, its objective being to restore the status value of older people in society. There are those in Western cultures who call attention to the values ascribed to older people in the Oriental cultures. In this context it is important to point out that social welfare personnel and public health officials in China and Japan report some modifications now taking place in the Orient in the status accorded to age, resulting from increased industrialization and changes in political ideologies. In the Orient the frequency of family crises that have been brought about by this change and which have reflected a modification of attitudes and values in relation to people in the older age groups is increasing. An understanding of the cross section of the past, together with that of the present, is as important in assessing groups and societies as it is as background knowledge for understanding the person in them.

Occupation as a Role Component

School guidance counselors, personnel workers, vocational counselors, and workers in the fields of health and rehabilitation are most apt to encounter the many facets of occupational role functioning when they attempt to help students, clients, and patients whose stresses tend to focus on this area of role performance. Intellectual, physical, and native endowment, together with the cluster of one's interest and emotional equipment, are crucial considerations. Also to be taken into account with the interviewee's vocational and social aspirations are the value judgments that society places upon certain statuses and roles with respect to occupation.

In a discussion of value judgments and occupations, Merrill's reference to American society in this connection is a case in point. He explains that "our own society values the roles of business executive, industrialist, salesman, and entertainer. These roles are rewarded accordingly. Our society does not place a high valuation upon the roles of minister, teacher, scholar, artist, and (ordinarily) soldier. In other societies these roles are highly valued and remunerated accordingly."[14]

The interviewer must also, he says, consider the fact that within and among families, and within individuals themselves, there may be a different ordering of value judgments with respect to occupational status and the various roles within these.[15]

Particularly critical are the stress periods brought on by enforced modification or radical shift of occupational role. Occupational change necessitated by illness is a clear example of such an instance. In the cycle from the onset of illness to vocational rehabilitation, the patient moves through a continuum from an active and productive worker to a sedentary patient, then to convalescence, and finally (and hopefully) to full-fledged productivity. During each phase he faces and moves through role adaptations. The outcome and adjustment become more stressful when the return to work involves a realignment of former tasks, necessitated by permanent, though partial, disability.

Modification of occupational role may also be brought about by technological advances or by periods of economic recession and depression. War, or threat of war, may influence and even necessitate one's change of occupational role; value judgments about occupations may also shift during these periods. With re-

[14] Francis E. Merrill, *Society and Culture*, Prentice-Hall, Inc., 1957, p. 191.

[15] It is essential to mention that value judgments are also factors for consideration among the other components of social role.

gard to the latter, the present-day value on nuclear physics is a case in point.

Executives and administrators are often made acutely aware of the stresses which accompany shifts in occupational role when the shift is upward rather than downward. For instance, workers promoted from so-called line positions to supervisory or administrative positions usually undergo a short period of considerable stress during such a transition period. Guidance counselors are often forced to deal with this aspect of transition among graduating students who are about to enter the labor market. Indeed some organizations, in recognition of this factor, have attempted to make assignments that would accommodate a gradual, rather than sudden shift. In most instances much of the anxiety mentioned during the role transition phase is due to the individual's perception of the presumed and actual expectations inherent in such role performance.

IMAGE OF THE INSTITUTION AND PERCEPTION OF ITS ROLE

Although it is the personnel employed within institutions of society who carry out the helping roles, it is difficult to escape individual perception of the institution *per se* as a factor which influences expectations about its services and the way in which they are administered. An individual's perceived image of an institutional role may be relatively realistic or it may be a distorted misconception that is an overly positive or unduly negative expectation.

Every day probation officers hear their probationers voice the assumption that they are expected to be excessively authoritative because they work in social institutions (courts, detention facilities, and probation departments) that society perceives to be legal authority with binding implications. Workers in this field need to be especially sensitive to the distinction between having an authoritative manner and being a symbol of authority; they must be exceedingly secure and skillful in the way they acknowledge and carry out the authority role without unnecessarily acting in an officious manner that is perceived by the probationer to be more punitive than helpful or corrective. Stressful to workers in correctional institutions and juvenile courts is the ill-perceived expectation on the part of society that this social institution can and should be able to correct all antisocial pathology.

A counselor in a YWCA was made aware of the importance of preconceived institutional role perceptions and expectations when she interviewed a mentally ill transient who appeared there looking for lodging. The sick woman had suddenly abandoned her husband and five children under a siege of emotional panic and had hastened to a large urban center fifty miles from her home. Her exaggerated tension was instantly obvious and this prompted the counselor to talk with her. In the course of the short interview the counselor asked the newly arrived transient how she had happened to select the YWCA for lodging. The transient's instant response to the gentle inquiry was this: "I saw the sign YWCA and seeing something called 'Christian' I thought I would be safe and you would be kind to me."

The influence of the church or synagogue as a social institution (as well as a parochial one) cannot be underestimated in considering role as perceived through the institutional image. Ministers, priests, and rabbis are quickly exposed to the impact of role perception and expectations as they become involved in helping people who come to them for assistance. A Jesuit priest explained how his attentiveness to the role concept helped him understand why a Protestant sought him out as a counselor during a marital crisis. In this instance, the interviewee was seriously considering a petition for divorce. She made an appointment with an attorney; however, before it was due she decided to see a priest and selected one at random from the telephone directory. She began her interview by emphatically pointing out that she was a Protestant. After she had repeated this affiliation with equal vigor, the priest asked her why she had chosen to talk with him. The woman exclaimed: "I expected *you* would stop me from getting a divorce because the Catholic Church does not believe in divorce."

Cultural factors may also influence one's perception of an institution and its helping function. By way of example, this is borne out in an excerpt from the manual of social agencies published by the London County Council. Several organizations in England are established to take care of a particular social class. Included among these are three agencies whose purpose it is to aid those of "gentle" birth or education. In one instance, the following is the stated objective of an agency: "to assist those in need who, owing to birth or education, hesitate to apply for help to sources open to other classes."[16]

THE PROFESSIONAL ROLE

The multiplicity of prescribed tasks which any professional person is expected to carry out in assuming his role responsibility is discussed by Gordon Hearn. Discussing the application of the role concept to social work, Hearn points out:

Every relationship in professional social work involves work with individuals, in groups, in organizations, and in communities. The worker is concerned with this total complex at all times although his immediate concern may be with a particular part of the total complex. Usually the total activity of any social worker will involve some direct experience with all four categories of human organization. At any given moment, whether he be working with an individual, a group, an organization, or a community, he is doing so in one or more of several status-roles. At all times he has the status and performs the general role of social worker. But beyond this he may occupy alternately the position and perform the roles of agent, consultant, teacher, leader, or member. As an *agent* he acts as the extension of the agency

[16] *The London Relieving Officer,* Policy Manual of the London County Council, Public Assistance Department, The County Hall, S. E. 1, 1931.

118   ESSENTIALS IN INTERVIEWING

and gives the kind of direct service to clients which, in terms of its function, it is the responsibility of the agency to provide. As *consultant* he is one whose opinions and reactions other workers seek in order to increase their own understanding and skill. As *teacher* he facilitates the processes by which workers accumulate, integrate, and internalize knowledge, develop attitudes which are consistent with a well-articulated personal philosophy of social work and develop and refine their skill. As *leader* he carries administrative responsibility for executing some phase of the agency's programme. And as a *member* he is related in some degree to other persons for purposes of social welfare but is not, at that moment, performing the roles of agent, consultant, teacher, or leader.

If we were to examine more closely the relationship implied by each of these status-roles, we would probably find that the worker interacts with or in the system in a somewhat different way and for a somewhat different purpose. Leader and member imply a position within the system whereas agent, consultant, and teacher suggest a position external to it.[17]

The interviewer giving professional services must make a distinction between the social role ascribed to friendship and the friendly behavior which is a characteristic of the interviewer's conduct. Although this is to be considered as an essential factor in *skill*, it is a part of background knowledge as well. Many parents of adolescents report that they have had such a role distortion painfully pointed out to them by their teen-age children who normally have wanted a friendly parent rather than one who has tried to carry out in detail the role prescriptions of a friend. So it is in professional behavior too. The social role attributed to friendship takes into account, consciously or unconsciously, the fact that a friend is ordinarily so identified with the other friend that he or she has incorporated many of the same subjective appraisals and "blind spots" which distort the person's objectivity of a given situation. One normally expects and wants this attribute in a close friendship. Whether one desires it to be other-

[17] Gordon Hearn, *Theory Building in Social Work,* University of Toronto Press, 1958, pp. 69–70.

wise or not, the character of role changes the nature of both the social relationship and of the professional relationship when one deliberately or unwittingly tries to carry out both roles simultaneously. Frequently the constructive features in both roles have been annihilated in such circumstances.

At some point in their careers, professional people inevitably get involved in having to make this distinction or face the implications arising from failure to deal with it fully. A young social worker told about how she was able to handle this distinction comfortably with a close friend who came to her pleading for professional help with a complicated marital problem. The social worker explained to her that because she was a close friend she would be unable to view the problem much differently from the way in which her friend did, and that if she were to try to do otherwise it would undoubtedly change the quality of their friendship. The social worker also pointed out that she highly valued this friendship and did not want to undertake anything which might possibly jeopardize it. The explanation offered apparently prompted the friend to reply that she, too, treasured their friendship and, therefore, it would be wiser for her to go to a family agency for objective appraisal and help with her problem. In many instances, solutions do not come about as quickly and easily as this one did, particularly in the small communities where social intermingling between professional persons and their clientele is inevitable. When this mixture of role performance cannot be avoided it should be dealt with directly in the interview and early in the helping process.

Role factors especially complicate the background and stage of the interview when persons in the same or allied professions are forced to take specialized help from a peer or from one in a profession closely related to their own. Doctors and nurses report the extreme difficulties which arise when other doctors and nurses become patients, particularly when they require hospitalization. Social workers have experienced similar problems when other social workers are clients of social agencies, and they are forced to deal with role differences. The impact of such a change in role is as powerful for the giver of the professional service as it is for the recipient.

Perception and Expectation of the Professional Role

Research in medicine, the social sciences, psychology, nursing, and social work has dealt with the recipient's perception and expectations of help offered and given by professional workers in these fields. The nature of a given professional role as perceived by other professions and workers in the same institution has also been investigated.

A study reported by Alfred Kadushin and C. F. Wieringa[18] highlights some relevant data on the expectations of the Dutch and Americans regarding the social caseworker's behavior in carrying out the professional role. Groups of sociology students in Holland and in the United States were studied as an initial part of this research project. The results showed that the Dutch conception of the potentially helpful person is similar to the American conception of it. The two investigators found that the Dutch picture of the "good" counselor is that of a person who accepts the client's problems as important, who is anxious to encourage communication, and who shows a willingness to maintain it. The Dutch expectation of the able caseworker (counselor) is that of a person who permits broadening the range of communication, who seeks to make the client comfortable, and acts to minimize client tension when it arises.[19] The American picture was found to be strikingly similar with one notable difference in the degree of emphasis—the American respondents expected the caseworker to be more permissive and less disapproving than the

[18] Alfred Kadushin and C. F. Wieringa, "A Comparison: Dutch and American Expectations Regarding Behavior of the Caseworker," *Social Casework*, 41 (10), 1960, pp. 503–512.
[19] *Ibid.*, p. 506.

Dutch respondents did. In Holland occupational class differences were noted in that a group of Dutch factory girls perceived "less favorable" conceptions than the Dutch college students did.[20]

Marsha Worby's[21] earlier study of adolescents' expectations of the behavior of a helpful person in the professional role concluded with a number of findings that are similar to those of Kadushin and Wieringa. Other factors related to the recipient's expectation of professional role were brought out in the Worby study:

1. The adolescent expected the helping person to be willing to expend considerable effort to do things for him in relation to his problem; but expected the caseworker to remain unbiased, in regard to requests made of him, by structuring the situation through asking further exploratory questions and by offering suggestions and alternative conclusions.
2. The adolescents studied expected the caseworker to show his understanding of the adolescent by being aware and sensitive to situations which cause embarrassment during the interview. They saw, further, that the helping person would not be critical either by questioning the adolescent's maturity and intelligence or by laughing or becoming angry.
3. The helping person was perceived as one expected to respect the confusion that the "child-adult" role causes for the adolescent. Moreover, the caseworker, if regarded as helpful, would not force the adolescent to accept his opinion nor impress the adolescent with his superior status. It was expected that the helpful caseworker would respect both the adolescent's viewpoint as well as that of the parent's.
4. When the helping person could not assume the task of carrying out requests made by the adolescent, he was expected to offer an honest explanation for his decision. The adolescents studied expected to be encouraged to share in accepting responsibility for the task.
5. The adolescents studied expected that the helpful social worker

20 Ibid., p. 508.
21 Marsha Worby, "The Adolescent's Expectations of How the Potentially Helpful Person Will Act," Smith College Studies in Social Work, 26 (1), 1955, pp. 19–59.

would set some limits. For instance: when a falsehood was told, the worker would correct this in a polite but effective manner. During the interview, these adolescents expected that they would be permitted to digress from the problem but that the helpful interviewer would make some effort to gradually refocus the interview.[22]

It is not uncommon that consumers of professional services frequently hold, even with the best efforts to help them to do otherwise, limited perceptions of the professional role and tasks inherent in it. This factor is especially observed among many clients who receive casework services in public assistance agencies. A number of these clients have severe interrelationship and other social adjustment problems in addition to financial hardship. Yet many of them perceive the casework role solely in terms of dispensing monies. Moreover the behavior of these clients reflects their strong attitude that the social worker has the power to give or to withhold money. A large portion of this client group requires patient and skilled help over a long time before they can modify this limited role perception sufficiently to accept the caseworker's help with other than monetary difficulties. Some clients are never able to ovecome this barrier. Others may not be sufficiently motivated to move beyond attention to the needed economic assistance even though they know that social workers in public assistance do give help with other adjustment problems.

Personnel on hospital and clinic staffs will encounter a wide range of perceptions and expectations of professional role which exist among patients and among other staff personnel as well. The patient may either perceive an extremely limited task-oriented role or may expect functions of an unrealistically wide range. Past experience, behavioral stresses affecting expectations, and other factors may and often do account for this. The following, which is an excerpt from the social service record of a hospitalized

[22] *Ibid.,* pp. 56–57.

patient in a state mental hospital, shows such a limited perception and movement beyond it.

Patient was introduced to the social worker on the ward and her quick response was: "You help people find jobs." After explaining in simple terms a few of the areas that social workers helped patients with, the patient nodded and closed the introduction by saying that she wasn't looking for employment at the moment but when she needed to do so she would talk to the social worker about it.

The worker continued to see her, at first for brief periods on the ward, and the patient did talk about her family; however, in the first four interviews that patient continued to emphasize her perception of the social worker as one who found jobs for people and indicated that this was about all she saw. After two or three more interviews the patient's perception showed noticeable change when she verbalized directly her wish that the worker would talk with her husband and children.

The fact that this patient's perception of the social work role was a limited one was verified by her during the last phase of her hospitalization when the interviews were focussed on plans for discharge and return to her home and community. It was at this time that the social worker asked if she was interested in or had considered employment, mentioning the reference to the job finding expectation which had been brought out earlier. The patient replied that she had no intention nor wish to take employment (nor was this indicated as a need) and then voluntarily brought out her previous limited notion about the social worker's function and role in a hospital. When she was assessing the areas in which the social worker had helped her she also voluntarily referred to the fact that her perception of social work functions had radically changed, pointing out, in passing, how her own recent experience had brought about this change of professional role expectation.

The interviewer must recognize that the client's or patient's perception of the behavior and tasks inherent in the professional role may be different from the way the interviewer himself perceives it. This difference in perception may also be apparent among other disciplines which function within the same institution.

Varying ranges of professional role perception among other staff members in an institution are noted in a study done and reported on by Essey Wolfrom[23] who is Supervisor, Psychiatric Social Services, in the Mental Health Research Institute of the Washington State Department of Institutions. The study attempted to learn: (1) how employees of the Division of Mental Health rated seven selected social work tasks in their importance to the patient, and (2) whom they perceived as carrying out these jobs. Completed questionnaires were returned by 91.6 percent of the 724 employees who received them. Social workers rated the social work items higher in importance to the patient than did the total employee group. Because it does show a marked difference in role perception from what was preconceived to be the case by the social work staff, it is noteworthy to mention in the context of this discussion that one of the seven items ("helping patient adapt to hospital admission") was not seen as a social work function at all. In addition, only two of the selected social work jobs ("consulting with community agencies on behalf of patient" and "preparing patient's social history") were seen by employees as clearly and primarily the function of social work. In contrast to this, social workers themselves perceived that six of the social work items were now done by social workers.

Research studies in nursing also point up a wide range of perceptions of the nursing role by the doctors, and show that doctors often perceive certain aspects of the nurse's role differently than the nurse herself or her professional group perceives it. It is also

[23] Presented at the Research Meeting, Mental Health Research Institute, Ft. Steilacoom, Washington, on October 14, 1960. Reported in "Abstracts: Completed Work," *Mental Health Research Institute Bulletin,* 2 (6), December, 1960, pp. 130–131.

noted that there are differences in nursing role perception among individual doctors themselves.

One of the implications of these studies which involves the interviewer directly is that he or she must be prepared to clarify the nature and extent of the professional role and must also anticipate that the modification of professional role expectation will take time. Furthermore, the amount of time needed to make this modification will depend upon the constellation of individualized circumstances in the client or patient population and within the staff population of a given institution or in the immediate society itself.

SUMMARY

Roles are highly dynamic motivating forces in behavior rather than mere abstract categories of it. As dynamic forces in social functioning they are influenced by societal and institutional factors and conditions, and by physiological and psychological forces within the individual. These forces converge and both interact and interrelate with each other to produce a range of perceptions and expectations—individual, cultural, and societal—and a range of the performance of specific activities and tasks in conjunction with one's membership and position in groups or participation in various organized societal institutions.

Social roles are learned in the course of socialization during the entire course of one's life span. Such learning demands constant modification and a reordering which may be relatively simple, moderate, or intensely complicated. Moreover, to learn one must undergo varying degrees of stress ranging, again, from a mild force to a severe impact which may even threaten the disorganization or breakdown of the human organism.

Social roles and the patterns within them are reciprocal. Each role is related to other roles which an individual carries out in his social functioning. Reciprocity in role performance not only comprises the expected behavior of the individual in a situation, but also the behavior of others toward him.

Application of the role concept must take into account the self-evaluation of the individual as to his comparative success or failure in his role as well as the evaluation of peers, of seniors to him in role position, of those subordinate in status and position, and the evaluation of society at large. Evaluation of role is also influenced by individual and collective value judgments, particularly in relation to occupation and to age and sex factors.

The interviewer offering a professional service has not only to consider the role concept with reference to a special set of factors within the individual organism and the societal forces which impinge on and interact with these, but must also consider the perception and expectation of the organized institution under whose auspices help is provided. Also a factor of major consideration is the professional role itself and the person who carries it out as these are perceived and expected by the interviewee and by other staff members in the same institution.

SUGGESTED ASSIGNMENTS

1. What types of roles do you perform within a given week? How do you perceive them? What do you think your teachers, parents, peers, and group leaders expect of you in these various roles? To what extent does your student status affect others' perception of your role and the expectations accorded your various roles?

2. Select a time in your life when you remember being under considerable stress. How did this influence your role performances and the way you felt about the expectations perceived of them? What noticeable changes were apparent when the stress was removed or modified?

3. Select an incident when someone asked you for help. How did the person appear to perceive your performance in this role and what did he or she appear to expect?

4. Describe an instance in your experience when you expected something from the role performance of someone you perceived as potentially helpful to you and found what actually happened to be quite different.

RECOMMENDED SUPPLEMENTARY READING

Bott, Elizabeth, *Family and Social Network—Roles, Norms and External Relationships in Ordinary Urban Families,* Tavistock Publications Ltd., 1957.

Chance, Erika, "Mutual Expectations of Patients and Therapists in Individual Treatment," *Human Relations,* 1 (26), 1957, pp. 167–177.

Kadushin, Alfred and Wieringa, C. F., "A Comparison: Dutch and American Expectations Regarding Behavior of the Caseworker," *Social Casework,* 41 (10), 1960, pp. 503–512.

Linton, Ralph, *The Cultural Background of Personality,* Appleton-Century-Crofts, 1945.

Maas, Henry S., "Socio-Cultural Factors in Psychiatric Clinic Services for Children: A Collaborative Study in the New York and San Francisco Metropolitan Areas," *Smith College Studies in Social Work,* 25 (2), 1955, pp. 1–90.

Merrill, Francis E., *Society and Culture,* Prentice-Hall, 1957, pp. 181–220.

Motz, Annabelle B., "The Role Conception Inventory: A Tool for Research in Social Psychology," *American Sociological Review,* 17, 1952, pp. 465–471.

Parsons, Talcott, *The Social System,* The Free Press, 1951.

Stein, Herman D. and Cloward, Richard A. (eds.), *Social Perspectives on Behavior,* The Free Press, 1958, section II, "Social Roles," pp. 171–263.

Thomas, Edwin, Polansky, Norman, and Kounin, Jacob, "The Expected Behavior of a Potentially Helfpul Person," *Human Relations,* 8 (2), 1955, pp. 165–174.

Worby, Marsha, "The Adolescent's Expectations of How the Potentially Helpful Person Will Act," *Smith College Studies in Social Work,* 26 (1), 1955, pp. 19–59.

Chapter Four

ESSENTIALS OF THE INTERVIEWING
METHOD

The knowledge which a man can use is the only real knowledge which has life and growth in it, and converts itself into practical power. The rest hangs like dust before the brain, or dries like raindrops off the stones. —FROUDE

THE INTERVIEW AS A PROFESSIONAL METHOD

Froude's words are the bridge on which we shall cross from the concepts of culture and personality to their use by the professional worker. Concepts have been presented to workers in the fields of human adjustment as basic knowledge for an essential understanding of the individual and his environment. Such knowledge would be academic unless it could be brought into professional use. The medium through which it becomes useful is the professional interview. Its employment professionally— with the competence that the word *professional* implies—is through *the interviewing method.*

A *method* of accomplishment in any field implies that there is system and order in its performance. A scientific method always involves identifiable and logical ways of progressing or advancing from one step or point to the next. Knowledge of a method is transmissible. Interviewing is a method in a popular sense of the term. It does not progress in a series of definitive steps to a standardized, finished product. It is a general manner of working toward the accomplishment of an end. The ends or purposes of the interview are varied.

The interview as a purposeful conversation is found in the literature of past centuries in the writings of theologians, philosophers, educators, and novelists. Its application by professional workers is less easy to trace. It has been used as an instrument in many callings without much thought or study of its processes. As the various callings formulated their own distinctive methods and became increasingly analytical in their methodology, interviewing came in for its share of study. Until very recently such study of the interview has been almost inseparably tied to its specific professional use. Today there is a recognition that the interview has the same attributes wherever it is used. Some of the common background of understanding necessary to all interviewing has been indicated in preceding chapters. Here we are interested in components of the interview common to all skillful professional interviewing. These are *purpose, structure,* the dynamic *processes* inherent in the interaction of individuals, *technical procedures, attitudes,* and *predisposing elements.*[1]

INTERVIEWING COMPONENTS

Purpose in the Interview

Purpose distinguishes an interview from a casual conversation. Interviewing objectives are many and varied. The purpose of the

[1] Definitions from *Webster's New International Dictionary,* Second Edition:

"*Purpose, n.* an object to be attained; end or aim to be kept in view; intention: *v.t.* to resolve to bring about: *v.i.* to intend" (p. 2018).

"*Structure, n.* form; arrangement of parts" (p. 2501).

"*Process, n.* a series of actions, motions or operations definitely conducing to an end" (p. 1972).

"*Procedure, n.* manner or method of proceeding; order or system of conducting" (p. 1972).

"*Technique, n.* expert method of execution" (p. 2590).

"*Technical, adj.* appropriate to any art, science" (p. 2590).

interview may be: to explore another's mind or sentiments; to obtain information in regard to specific situations or attitudes; to establish eligibility; to impart health information; to ascertain health habits; to evaluate resources; to motivate to action; to give advice; to seek advice; and so on indefinitely.

There may be a general purpose for the entire interview with more specific minor objectives which may be modified during the course of the interview.

The purpose of the interview should be intellectually formulated. Some workers insist that the interviewer who cannot formulate the objective or objectives of his interview before he undertakes it has neither reason nor right to conduct it.

Purpose is an intellectual action—achieved through conscious use of processes and techniques within the structural limitations of the interview.

INTERVIEW STRUCTURE AND THE TIME-BOUND CONTINUUM WITHIN IT

Structure[2] is the element of the interview which gives it form and, in some instances, content. The concept of structure has its greatest value in the analysis of completed interviews. Analysis of one's own material may be more illuminating than the study of someone else's more skillful interview. Planned structuring of the interview, which serves to determine its form and content, is exemplified by the various outlines for conducting different types of interviews for specific use, such as the determination of eligibility, the developmental history of a child, or the schedule of a research study. These outlines bear directly on purpose and objectives.

---

[2] We regard *structure* as synonymous with organizational pattern rather than in its usual systematic meaning of a static pattern. Chapin explains the difference between these two conceptions of structure in *Contemporary American Institutions*, Harper & Brothers, 1935, pp. 60–61.

Aristotle supplied the basic elements of structure in his simple statement that everything has a beginning, a middle, and an ending. The late Porter Lee, one of the leaders in the'field of social work and one of the first teachers of the art of interviewing, amplified this by listing the four structural elements of the interview as (1) the start, (2) crises in the trend of discussion, (3) psychological moments, and (4) conclusion.[3]

Although Lee's discussion is in terms of social case work, his structure holds true for all professional interviewing in which the interviewee is a full and free participant. Carl Rogers,[4] among others, considers these factors in theoretical presentations and research on psychological and psychotherapeutic interviewing methods.

The continuum of time (beginning, middle and ending) is affected by the *critical incidents* in each phase. The term "critical incident" refers to what Lee earlier categorized as "crises" and "psychological moments." Critical incidents are characterized by crises and turning points which lead to a forward or backward movement toward or from the objectives of the interview. The critical moments which arise in interviews may come about in the following ways: (1) through a stimulus response of feeling and attitude *in the interviewee* himself as he reacts to the purpose of the interview and the circumstances which brought him to it, the setting of the interview, the memories and associations which the discussion evokes in the interview, and his feelings and attitudes toward the interviewer's personality and the interviewer's responses; (2) through responses of feeling and attitude *in the interviewer;* (3) through responses evoked by circumstances for

---

[3] Porter Lee, "Interviewing," in Mary Antoinette Cannon and Philip Klein (eds.), *Social Case Work*, Columbia University Press, 1933, p. 561.

[4] Carl R. Rogers, *Client-Centered Therapy*, Houghton Mifflin Company, 1951.

which the interviewer and the interviewee have little or no control. Studies of both single interviews and a long series of them show that both singly and collectively there can be determined certain characteristics of interviewee behavior and response and of interviewer activity that are peculiar to each of the three time-phases mentioned. While much is dependent on the skill and discipline of the interviewer, *time* itself has a structural influence on the interview. While learning the disciplined art and method of interviewing, remember always that the elements of structure can never be divorced from the dynamic processes that are spontaneous and inherent in it.

The *start* involves an obligation on the part of the interviewer to make the purpose of the interview clear to the interviewee at the earliest possible moment and where necessary, if it is a first contact, to explain the function of the agency he represents briefly and in terms that can be readily understood. Even as simple and direct as this point appears to be at first glance, there are critical incidents that can and often do arise which affect both the interviewee and the interviewer. There are numerous occasions when no matter how clearly the interviewer has stated the purpose and it is intellectually understood by the interviewee, there are critical situations which make for a difficult beginning. Records show a number of instances where the interviewee is unable to begin spontaneously, and in a groping fashion he will, after the explanation of the purpose, turn to the interviewer and ask, "Where shall I *begin?*" This initial feeling of awkwardness, uncertainty, or other discomfort is a critical event for the one being interviewed; if the interviewer is a novice it may be an equally critical moment for him as well. The commonly accepted principle which should act as a guide in beginning an interview is this: *Begin where the client or patient is.* In many instances, this beginning involves the interviewer and the interviewee talking for a few moments about the mere difficulty of *getting started.* On some occasions the interviewee may mention this but will not need to talk about it and can proceed directly to the underlying purpose of the interview.

The *middle phase* of an interview is in motion when the interviewee's and the interviewer's discussion progressively centers on the purpose for which the interview is being conducted. The adjustment period of "getting started and into the swing" of the underlying purpose is sufficiently over the initial hurdle to enable the interviewee to move on. However, critical moments arise in the middle phase. Most often noted are the psychological blocks within either the interviewee or the interviewer which interrupt the smooth flow of discussion. A personnel officer in a large industrial firm experienced such an incident when he was interviewing an employee to ascertain the reasons for absenteeism from work. It soon became apparent that the absenteeism was due to marital and in-law friction in the home. When the employee was discussing the stresses in his marriage he came to a sudden halt and exclaimed: "This is too painful to talk about." It was at this point that the interview focus shifted to a discussion of referral resources for help with family stress and with it the personnel officer pointed out that one of the purposes in this was to help make it easier for the employee to come regularly to work. Had the primary purpose of this interview been to work out the stresses involved in the family interaction pattern, it is likely that the discussion might have centered on amplification of the discomfort itself or some other focus related to primary purpose.

The *ending* of an interview may be established by the expiration of a predetermined period of time, or it may come about when either the interviewee or the interviewer decides that the purpose of the interview has been achieved and, hence, there is no reason for the conversation to continue. (The ending may abruptly come about because of the acting-out resistance, a point which will not be discussed in detail here; but certainly when such is the case it becomes a crisis. Understanding and management of such crises are topics for consideration in the specialized methodologies of specific professional processes and their practices.) When time is prescribed it is usually done by the interviewer who, at the beginning, states the exact amount of clock time which can be offered and used; it may also be prescribed by the client who announces the amount of time he can devote to the appointment. When time has been predetermined, the approach of this fixed ending is usually apparent to both the interviewer and the interviewee. Moreover, it is observed that both the interviewer and the interviewee behave in a characteristically different manner at this time in the interview than in the beginning and during the middle time periods; the stimulus for such behavior arises from the time factor itself. The following excerpt illustrates an occurrence characteristic of this factor. It is from a counseling interview with a young woman whose school adjustment was complicated by tension. In this instance, the counselor has stated that each interview could last for a fifty minute period.

The client looked at her watch and commented that in five minutes her time would be over. She reached for her gloves while remarking that she had talked about so many things that she now felt "at loose ends."

The counselor summarized the highlights of the discussion and connected these with the client's reason for coming to the Center for help. She was asked if she wanted an interview at the same time next week. This was arranged.

This brief illustration points out the influence of a predetermined time period and the interviewee's active response to it. Discussion of the interviewer's response to the same phenomenon will be considered in the section on skills which appears later in this chapter. Inherent is the critical incident element which brought about a turning point in discussion and also responses which were different in both character and outcome than the movement of discussion in the beginning and middle portions of the interview.

Critical incidents may also arise in interviews because of external interferences over which the interviewer and the interviewee have little or no control. These may occur during any one of the three interview periods and when they do the flow of discussion is interrupted. It is for this reason that many clinicians will not receive or take telephone calls during an interview. Outside noises and the way in which they interfere with the flow of conversation are only too well known. Workers who interview on the wards of hospitals or conduct interviews during a home visit have constantly to deal with such incidents and the range of crises situations which they produce. Another common event in this connection is the arising of physical discomforts.

Another exposition of the structure of an interview is found in Bogardus' theory of the circular or spiral response.[5] This is a useful concept for those who tend to be authoritative in their interviews and feel a need to dominate the situation. The theory is that each party in turn furnishes the stimulus on which the next response is based. Each response brings the interview to a new step or level and provides the stimulus for the next step or level. Each response becomes a new stimulus until the spiral ends by the accomplishment (or failure) of the purpose of the interview.

Dr. Bogardus comments that most of the work of the interview comes after the interview starts, since the interviewer does not have the predetermined role of questioner but adapts himself to the role of an associate or a joint student in each interviewing situation.

Rogers[6] has given the term *nondirective interview* to his interviewing method. Like Bogardus, he regards the structure of the

---

[5] E. S. Bogardus, "Interviewing as a Social Process," in Pauline Young's *Interviewing in Social Work*, McGraw-Hill Book Company, 1935, pp. 2-4.

[6] Carl R. Rogers, *Counseling and Psychotherapy*, Houghton Mifflin Company, 1942. Carl R. Rogers and John L. Wallen, *Counseling with Returned Service Men*, McGraw-Hill Book Company, 1946.

interview as a process of interaction between the interviewer and his client. The responses of the interviewer, according to Rogers' method, however, represent an attempt to understand the client in his own frame of reference and particularly to understand his feelings about his own situation. The theory behind this structure of interviewing is that, after the client has stated his problem in his own words, the body of the interview is formed by selective responses designed to force the client to a better understanding of his own feelings.

Dr. Porter, in an ingenious method of testing counselor attitudes, has shown how the interview is structured by the counselor's making and testing hypotheses with respect to his client and by the interaction between the two parties.[7]

Although Dr. Porter's discussion is based on counseling, he suggests its applicability to all types of interviews. He implies that the interviewer's attitudes condition his responses and result in five recognizable structures. These are the responses designed to: (1) bring to the attention of the interviewee some idea that the counselor has thought would be helpful; (2) identify the counselor with the client's values, to reassure him, to support him; (3) see the client from the client's point of view and understand how he feels about the situation, consciously withholding the counselor's own opinions and feelings; (4) teach, point out, interpret to the client his own behavior and its significance; (5) seek further information for the purpose of arriving at a diagnosis of the client's problems. The interviews resulting from predominant patterns of responses could well constitute the structure of (1) the evaluative or value-setting interview, (2) the interpretative or educational interview, (3) the interview for understanding, (4) the supportive interview, or (5) the diag-

[7] E. H. Porter, Jr., "A Simple Measure of Counselor Attitudes," in *Trends in Student Personnel Work*, edited by E. G. Williamson, University of Minnesota Press, 1949, pp. 119-135.

nostic interview. While these categories show patterns or structure, it would be an unusual interviewer whose methodology would be so rigidly adhered to as not to overlap from one category to another in some of the responses.

Darley describes some of the attributes of a skillful interview by drawing a parallel between a well-built movie or play and a well-contrived interview: (1) it cannot be dull or dreary; (2) it cannot be too talky; (3) it cannot be aimless or vague; (4) it should have one or two dramatic high points; (5) there must be a summary to tie the loose ends; (6) there must be a natural and reasonable ending.[8] The last four points are structural.

Processes and Techniques[9]

Structure, while important, is not a dynamic of the interview. The elements which make it move to the accomplishment of its purpose are *processes* and *techniques*. A process is a change or transformation of activity in any object or organism as contrasted with the constitution of the structure of that organism. It also is defined as a manner in which a change is effected. A technique is a characteristic way of achieving a given end by special procedures. A process in interviewing is the encompassing, descriptive word for movement in the interview. The technique is the propelling device. A process is discernible as the large pattern in the fabric of the interview. Techniques are the small designs which are skillfully blended to form the pattern. Interviewing processes are the same in any interview, but techniques are the variables which make each interview unique.

Observation is a process employed by all interviewers. An interviewer may consciously create a psychological or material

[8] John Darley, *The Interview in Counseling*, Retraining and Reemployment Administration, U.S. Dept. of Labor, 1946, p. 11.

[9] Chapin comments that our conception of process and technique is descriptive of verbal operations performed to implement the realization of a desired purpose.

setting for his interview. He may also create an atmosphere conducive to a favorable interview. He may encounter and effectively reduce resistance. He may be in a position of authority which he uses with skill. Use of observation, use of setting, the establishment of rapport, meeting resistance, conscious use of authority are all processes descriptive of movement in the interview. The movement itself is effected by such procedures as asking questions, a selective use of responses, remaining silent, and many other devices. A number of years ago a group of Twin City social workers isolated and named seventeen different processes and sixty-four techniques.[10] Their effort was valuable in that it was a serious attempt to know what was involved in interviewing. It was sterile because it lacked fundamental knowledge of the interviewee as an individual. In the light of the knowledge of personality and behavior available today, these processes and techniques could be reviewed with profit to the student of interviewing.

Today we recognize that the skillful interviewing processes of the news reporter resemble those of the public health nurse, the speech pathologist, or the social worker, whereas the way of using techniques varies in each case.

The interviewing techniques of the trial lawyer with his carefully phrased questions in examination and cross-examination differ from the procedures of the psychiatrist or analyst, where the stimulus to response is furnished by the setting and by the patient's need to free himself from his chaotic thoughts and impulses. The structured interviewing procedures of the "nondirective" interview of Carl Rogers are distinguishable from those of the psychiatrist or analyst. The interviewing procedures of E. G. Williamson, who stands for a school of clinical psychologists in contrast to that of Rogers and his followers, emphasize the use

[10] J. C. Colcord, "Study of Techniques of the Social Case Work Interview, with Discussions," *Journal of Social Forces*, July, 1929.

of tested aptitudes, interests, capacities, and skills as a necessary foundation for the interview.[11]

We are taking for granted that the beginning interviewer will feel awkward in consciously using processes and technical procedures. It is only when the interviewer's consciousness of their purposeful use has disappeared that he will have attained some degree of skill.

Understanding Motivations of Behavior as a Prerequisite to the Skillful Use of Processes and Techniques

The use of processes and technical procedures is dependent on understanding what is involved in the interaction of two such diverse individuals as the interviewer and the interviewee. Such an understanding brings with it a sensitivity to the reaction of the other person, an interpretation of the response, and the ability on the part of the interviewer to adapt his own response to the purpose of the dialogue. Although many individuals have an intuitive appreciation of factors in personality, the consistent application of such appreciation comes from formal training and discipline.

Benjamin Franklin in his autobiography tells of his metamorphosis from a curmudgeon to an affable gentleman by a conscious use of techniques.

I made it a rule to forebear all direct contradiction to the sentiments of others, and all positive assertions of my own. I even forbid myself the use of every word and expression in the language that imported a fixed opinion, such as certainly, undoubtedly, etc., and I adopted instead of them, I conceive, I apprehend, I imagine a thing to be so and so, or so it appears to me at present. When another asserted something that I thought an error, I denied myself the pleasure of contradicting him abruptly, and of showing immediately some absurdity in his propo-

[11] E. G. Williamson, *How to Counsel Students,* McGraw-Hill Book Company, 1939. Also "Counseling and the Minnesota Point of View," *Educational and Psychological Measurement,* Spring, 1947, pp. 141-155.

sition; and in answering I began by observing that, in certain cases or circumstances, his opinion would be right, but in the present case there appeared or seemed to me some difference, etc. I soon found the advantage of this change in my manners; the conversations I engaged in went on more pleasantly. The modest way in which I proposed my opinions procured them a readier reception and less contradiction; I had less mortification when I was found to be in the wrong; and I more easily prevailed with others to give up their mistakes and join with me when I happened to be right.

What Benjamin Franklin had discovered was that every individual was a human being like himself who would react not only to what was said but to the way in which it was said. So Franklin developed certain ways or techniques of getting the response he wanted. His use of such procedures, however, would have been unwarranted and probably unsuccessful if they had not been applied with sincerity and employed in appropriate situations.

Miss Garrett sounds a warning on the inexperienced interviewer's tendency to rely upon certain procedures which have been used skillfully by someone else in another situation but which would be entirely inappropriate to the present case.[12] The appropriateness of any technique is contingent upon the total interviewing situation.

An example of what can happen when a technique is used out of context and inappropriately is furnished by a student who had been impressed by a skilled worker's use of silence as an effective technique.

As the student nervously waited for her client to come into the office, she had made up her mind not to inject herself into the situation, but to be determinedly silent. The interview would be a trying one for both participants, she feared, because Mr. B., the interviewee, was under pressure to bring his wife home from the State Hospital to which she had been committed two months previously. The hospital authorities had advised against this course

[12] Annette Garrett, *Interviewing, Its Principles and Methods,* Family Welfare Association of America, 1942, p. 30.

but Mrs. B. was eager for the move and her husband was coming to enlist the worker's help in securing his wife's release.

When Mr. B. arrived it was obvious that he was upset. His chin quivered and tears were in his eyes as he fought for composure. As he spoke of his love for his wife and the conflict he was in, the interviewer "looked directly into Mr. B.'s eyes but made no comment." He said, "I'm distracted. Someone who knows more about this than I do has got to help me." In conflict herself at this point the worker remembered her technique and "gazed fixedly out the window." Mr. B. went on, "If no one's going to help me I might as well give up." At this, the interviewer records that she got up, went to the window and looked out. This was too much for Mr. B. He pounded on the desk—no longer tearful but very angry as he said, "I came here for some advice and I'm going to get it, or know the reason why." The young interviewer threw her silence technique out of the window, came back to her desk and the interview began again as an interview of participation.

Such ineptness, while discomfiting to both the client and the worker, is insufficient argument against trying to know more about the processes and techniques of the interview and to use them deliberately. In time the worker should lose self-consciousness and become aware of his part in the interview. Self-confidence, however, must rest on a real comprehension of why each individual behaves as he does.

Garrett discounts the fear that a self-conscious study of interviewing processes and procedures may detract from warm friendliness and real interest in others by reminding us that an informed person is not necessarily an unfriendly person.[13] Where interviewing is a stereotyped affair, the stereotype is in thinking of the interview as a matter of merely asking questions and recording answers, leaving out the human element. Even a partial understanding of the motivations of the interviewee's behavior and the processes of interaction between him and the worker makes the interview alive and personalized.

A reporter may play on the vanity of the people he interviews

[13] *Ibid.*, p. 8.

to obtain his feature story because he knows that most people, in spite of their protests, like to see their names in print. Radio interviewers have abundant evidence that liking to hear the sound of one's own voice is a well-nigh universal trait. The modern doctor interested in the psychological factors of illness is skilled in looking below the surface for the motivation of behavior. He knows, for example, that certain skin diseases may be caused by suppressed hostilities. He knows that the surplus pounds of his overweight patients are more than probably caused by eating excessive food for personal gratification or for solace. With this knowledge, his interview may seek for the psychological cause before he prescribes for the physical effect.

Although the interviewer tries to bring his knowledge of human motivation and resultant behavior to bear directly on the interviewee, he must not assume that the interviewee may not have similar perceptions. The *Ediphone News* once carried a lesson for their salesmen in the following account:

> The new salesman of cream separators had been coached on the interview in modern salesmanship, he had studied the correct approach, how to make contacts, how to interest the prospect before starting on his direct sales talk. He took instructions on these procedures literally and carried them out in accordance with the rules.
>
> On one of his calls he arrived at noon time when the farmer was sitting in the shade of the front yard while his wife sat in the window, darning socks. The farmer greeted the salesman cordially and invited him to come into the shade.
>
> "Don't mind mother," he said, "she's deaf."
>
> The salesman glanced without interest at the woman in the window and began his routine. His aim was to attract the attention and hold the interest of the farmer in preparation for the sales talk. So he talked of cows, breeds, comparative productiveness of different breeds, and various kinds of feed. Busy following directions and establishing himself as an expert, he noted with satisfaction that the farmer was attentive until he was abruptly jolted out of his complacency by the woman's voice, "What does the young

man want?" "Wants to sell me something," the farmer shouted back. "What is it?" she insisted. "Don't know yet—he's just laying his bait," was the farmer's answer.

It was then that the salesman abandoned his techniques and got down to selling a cream separator.

SKILL IN THE USE OF PROCESSES AND TECHNIQUES

Processes and techniques divorced from expertness in their use can have little meaning for the professional worker. When the interviewer has a basic understanding of motivations of behavior, skill in the use of processes and techniques can be enhanced by instruction and practice. To this end we have selected some of the more common technical factors for descriptive review.

Listening is singled out first, as a universal and basic process.

The Skilled Artistry in Listening

The most fundamental prerequisite for any interview is the ability to listen. Effective listening demands not only that the interviewer hear and understand what is being said but that he also hear and understand what is communicated through silence. The human value in the art of listening and the benefits accrued from its expression were understood by the wise leaders at least five thousand years ago. An Egyptian proverb proclaimed about 2750 B.C. emphasized this human value and pointed out:

If thou art a leader, be kind in hearing the speech of the suppliant. . . . The compliant setteth greater store by the easing of his mind than by the accomplishment for which he came. . . . To listen kindly comforteth the heart.[14]

Stated in contemporary phraseology is a significantly appropriate quotation from a modern writer:

There is an art of listening. To be able really to listen, one should abandon or put aside all prejudices, pre-formulations and daily activities. When you are in a receptive state of mind, things can be easily

[14] *Proverbs of Ptah-Lotep.*

understood; you are listening when your real attention is given to something. But unfortunately most of us listen through a screen of resistance. We are screened with prejudices, whether religious or spiritual, psychological or scientific; or with our daily worries, desires and fears. And with these for a screen, we listen. Therefore, we listen really to our own noise, to our own sound, not to what is being said. It is extremely difficult to put aside our training, our prejudices, our inclination, our resistance, and, reaching beyond verbal expression, to listen so that we understand instantaneously. This is going to be one of our difficulties.[15]

Krishnamurti's brilliant counsel strikes pointedly at the influence of attitudes which will be discussed in the next chapter. It is included here because without this preliminary caution the listening component would be valueless.

Skilled practice of an art demands discipline. In a commendable volume on the art of listening. Dominick Barbara has stressed four salient components of the discipline required of an artful listener: (1) *concentration* that allows for patience with ourselves and our removal of distractions in the paths of our listening; (2) *active participation* which involves keeping our minds in a state of relaxed alertness, open and flexible to all relevant changes in a given situation; (3) *comprehension*—understanding and grasp of the true idea or meaning of what is heard; (4) *objectivity* or hearing the other person out without imposing our preconceived notions or opinions.[16] The author also emphasizes that in order to listen well, one must have the capacity and the desire to examine critically, to evaluate and reshape values, attitudes, and relationships to oneself and to others.[17]

Children and adults are quick to perceive lax discipline in the interviewer's listening. Under stress they are often even more sensitive to it. Children tend to verbalize or express in other ways their perception of this fault more openly than many adults will. However, adults will usually discuss this observation with others if not with the interviewer at some later point in the professional contact. A common comment heard about such a reaction is often

[15] J. Krishnamurti, *The First and Last Personal Freedom*, Harper & Brothers, 1954. Quoted in the frontispiece of Dominick A. Barbara, *The Art of Listening*, Charles C. Thomas, 1958.
[16] Dominick A. Barbara, *op. cit.*, pp. 1–6.   [17] *Ibid.*, p. 81.

this: "I felt that he (or she) wasn't listening to what I was saying," or the following often-heard complaint, "If he had only listened to what I was saying he would have known the cause of the trouble sooner." Researchers who have investigated clients' and patients' responses to services given report that when these consumers felt the person listened to what they were saying and understood what they were experiencing, they reported this spontaneously to the researchers doing the follow-up study and did so with an easily recognizable nuance of genuine sincerity.

The skilled listener will hear both harmony and discords among the thoughts and feelings expressed by the interviewee. Often it is not the spoken words themselves that convey the most relevant meaning but the feeling and tone expressed in the speaker's voice and the gestures he uses to communicate. Frequent, too, is the impact behind what was *not said* that suggests clues about the source of a difficulty.

The guiding principle for the interviewer is that he *listen to all that the interviewee says and expresses, and that he be acute enough, also, to sense and note the significant omissions that are relevant to the purpose of the interview.*

Skill in Observation

Observation is a process operative in an interview from its inception to its close. The interviewer does not *observe* in the scientific sense of observing and noting phenomena in controlled experiments. Because he works with a human being in a fluid situation, his observation consists of noticing what he sees, hears, and apprehends in the interview. The interviewer with all his senses depends primarily on his eyes and ears for his information —although his olfactory organ is often a source of pertinent data. A nonsighted home teacher of the blind tells us she can "observe" such details as the height and weight of the interviewee, the size of the room, taste in interior decoration, and many other features by substituting her tactile and auditory senses for those of sight. Skill in observation is the ability to illuminate by imagination and accurate inference the facts apprehended by the senses.

The role of the skilled observer is suggested in the following chart:[18]

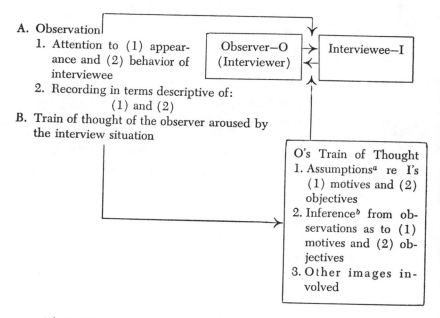

A. Observation
  1. Attention to (1) appearance and (2) behavior of interviewee

  Observer—O (Interviewer)

  Interviewee—I

  2. Recording in terms descriptive of:
        (1) and (2)
B. Train of thought of the observer aroused by the interview situation

O's Train of Thought
1. Assumptions[a] re I's (1) motives and (2) objectives
2. Inference[b] from observations as to (1) motives and (2) objectives
3. Other images involved

[a] Assumption: a proposition taken for granted; a presumption.
[b] Inference: passing from data to conclusions.

Sir Arthur Conan Doyle, who drew many of his fictional characters from his own contacts, made a conspicuous and unique use of observation. His biographer reveals that Sherlock Holmes was drawn largely from the character of Dr. Charles Bell, under whom Doyle studied medicine at Edinburgh University. As one of Bell's assistants, he would usher patients in to the diagnostic clinic.

"This man," Dr. Bell would declare in rich Scots, "is a left-handed cobbler." Then he would wait, with carefully concealed glee, for the puzzled looks of the students.

"You'll obsairve, gentlemen, the worn places on the corduroy breeks where a cobbler rests his lapstone? The right hand side, you'll note.

[18] We are indebted to F. Stuart Chapin for this graphic analysis of observation.

is far-r more worn than the left. He uses his left hand for handling the leather."

Or again, with finger tips together: "This man is a French-polisher." Then opening his eyes and rolling it out: "Come now. Can't you smel-l-l him?" . . . "The trained eye," he would say. "A simple matter."[19]

The trained eye is not a simple matter—but the eye and the other senses may be trained to observe. The trained observer senses many details and sifts out those irrelevant to the interviewing situation. The skilled worker has capacity for accuracy in observing details; the ability to know the significance of the fact he observes in relation to its genesis; its effect in the individual's present situation; and whether it represents a characteristic, static or modifiable.

Lawyers and doctors must be acute and accurate observers of the slightest reactions of their clients and patients. Successful writers are dependent upon observation to bring a sense of reality into their creations. The late Virginia Woolf has described for us the importance of observation as part of the writer's equipment. In this essay, called *Mr. Bennett and Mrs. Brown*, it is interesting to note the observations Mrs. Woolf makes as a writer and compare them with those which might be made by workers in other professions.

Mr. Bennett and Mrs. Brown[20]

. . . I have said that people have to acquire a good deal of skill in character-reading if they are to live a single year of life without disaster. But it is the art of the young. In middle age and in old age the art is practiced mostly for its uses, and friendships and other adventures and experiments in the art of reading character are seldom made.

But novelists differ from the rest of the world because they do not cease to be interested in character when they have learnt enough about it for practical purposes. They go a step further; they feel that there is something permanently interesting in character itself. When all the

19 John Dickson Carr, *The Life of Sir Arthur Conan Doyle,* Harper & Brothers, 1949, p. 23.

20 Virginia Woolf, *Mr. Bennett and Mrs. Brown,* Hogarth Press, London, 1924. A paper read to the Heretics, Cambridge, England, May 18, 1924. The excerpt of the conversation between Mr. Smith and Mrs. Brown precedes an imaginary conversation between Mrs. Woolf and Mr. Arnold Bennett, the novelist.

practical business of life has been discharged, there is something about people which continues to seem to them of overwhelming importance, in spite of the fact that it has no bearing whatever upon their happiness, comfort, or income. The study of character becomes to them an absorbing pursuit; to impart character an obsession. And this I find it very difficult to explain: what novelists mean when they talk about character, what the impulse is that urges them so powerfully every now and then to embody their view in writing.

So, if you will allow me, instead of analyzing and abstracting, I will tell you a simple story which, however pointless, has the merit of being true, of a journey from Richmond to Waterloo, in the hope that I may show you what I mean by character in itself; that you may realize the different aspects it can wear; and the hideous perils that beset you directly you try to describe it in words.

One night, some weeks ago, then, I was late for the train and jumped into the first carriage I came to. As I sat down I had the strange and uncomfortable feeling that I was interrupting a conversation between two people who were already sitting there. Not that they were young and happy. Far from it. They were both elderly, the woman over sixty, the man well over forty. They were sitting opposite each other, and the man, who had been leaning over and talking emphatically to judge by his attitude and the flush on his face, sat back and became silent. I had disturbed him, and he was annoyed. The elderly lady, however, whom I will call Mrs. Brown, seemed rather relieved. She was one of those clean, threadbare old ladies whose extreme tidiness—everything buttoned, fastened, tied together, mended and brushed up—suggests more poverty than rags and dirt. There was something pinched about her— a look of suffering, of apprehension, and, in addition, she was extremely small. Her feet, in their clean little boots, scarcely touched the floor. I felt that she had nobody to support her; that she had to make up her mind herself; that, having been deserted, or left a widow years ago, she had led an anxious, harried life, bringing up an only son, perhaps, who, as likely as not, was by this time beginning to go to the bad. All this shot through my mind as I sat down, being uncomfortable, like most people, at traveling with fellow passengers unless I have somehow or other accounted for them. Then I looked at the man. He was no relation of Mrs. Brown's, I felt sure; he was of a bigger, burlier, less refined type. He was a man of business, I imagined—dressed in good, blue serge with a pocket knife and a silk handkerchief, and a stout leather bag. Obviously, however, he had an unpleasant business to settle with Mrs. Brown; a secret, perhaps, sinister business, which they did not intend to discuss in my presence.

"Yes, the Crofts have had very bad luck with their servants," Mr. Smith (as I will call him) said in a considering way, going back to some earlier topic, with a view of keeping up appearances.

"Ah, poor people," said Mrs. Brown, a trifle condescendingly. "My grandmother had a maid who came when she was fifteen, and stayed till she was eighty." (This was said with a kind of hurt and aggressive pride to impress us both perhaps.)

"One doesn't come across that sort of thing nowadays," said Mr. Smith in conciliatory tones.

Then they were silent.

"It's odd they don't start a golf club there—I should have thought one of the young fellows would," said Mr. Smith, for the silence obviously made him uneasy.

Mrs. Brown hardly took the trouble to answer. . . .

It was plain, from Mrs. Brown's silence, from the uneasy affability with which Mr. Smith spoke, that he had some power over her which he was exerting disagreeably. It might have been her son's downfall, or some painful episode in her past life, or her daughter's. Perhaps she was going to London to sign some document to make over some property. Obviously against her will she was in Mr. Smith's hands. I was beginning to feel a great deal of pity for her, when she said, suddenly and inconsequently,

"Can you tell me if an oak-tree dies when the leaves have been eaten for two years in succession by caterpillars?"

She spoke quite brightly, and rather precisely, in a cultivated inquisitive voice.

Mr. Smith was startled, but relieved to have a safe topic of conversation given him. He told her a great deal very quickly about plagues of insects. He told her that he had a brother who kept a fruit farm in Kent. He told her what fruit farmers do every year in Kent, and so on. While he talked, a very odd thing happened. Mrs. Brown took out her little white handkerchief and began to dab her eyes. She was crying. But she went on listening quite composedly to what he was saying, and he went on talking, a little louder, a little angrily, as if he had seen her cry often before; as if it were a painful habit. At last it got on his nerves. He stopped abruptly, looked out of the window, then leant toward her as he had been doing when I got in, and said in a bullying, menacing way, as if he would not stand any more nonsense,

"So, about that matter we were discussing. It'll be all right? George will be there on Tuesday?"

"We shan't be late," said Mrs. Brown, gathering herself together with superb dignity.

Mr. Smith said nothing. He got up, buttoned his coat, reached his bag down, and jumped out of the train before it had stopped at Clapham Junction. He had got what he wanted, but was ashamed of himself; he was glad to get out of the old lady's sight.

Mrs. Brown and I were left alone together. She sat in her corner opposite, very clean, very small, rather queer, and suffering intensely. The impression she made was overwhelming. It came spouting out like a draught, like a smell of burning. What was it composed of—that over-whelming and peculiar impression? . . . I had no time to explain why I felt it somewhat tragic, heroic, yet with a dash of the flighty, and fantastic, before the train stopped, and I watched her disappear—.

The story ends without any point to it. . . . What I want you to see in it is this. Here is a character imposing itself on another person,—but you will reflect that the very widest interpretation can be put upon these words. For example, old Mrs. Brown's character will strike you very differently according to the age and country in which you happen to be born. . . .

Virginia Woolf's story shows the processes of observation from a writer's standpoint. Observation for the writer is not limited to the immediate facts apprehended by the senses; these facts are illuminated and extended by imagination and experience. For the professional worker, the form the observation takes, the pictures evoked, are extended by the interviewer's experience but with imagination carefully controlled. A conditioning factor for both writer and worker is the use to be made of the observation. Two examples, taken from Virginia Woolf's story to contrast her assumptions as a writer with those of a professional worker, will make this point clear.

A professional worker, for instance, would not be free to assume that "They were both elderly, the woman over sixty, the man well over forty." To a young person, a man well over forty may seem elderly, but forty years is considered middle age physiologically. The appearance of aging in either case might have been apparent but not real.

In the following instance, too, the writer has transferred her impressions to her readers without the necessity of being concerned about the accuracy of her assumptions. The professional worker would be more guarded in interpretation. The author is not limited in her inferences. She assumes that the man had been "talking emphatically" from his "attitude and the flush on his face." When he sat back and became silent she assumes "I had disturbed him and he was annoyed."

Every interview has its nonverbal accompaniment of emotional factors shown by variations in facial expression, movements of the body, muscular tensions, changes in volume and quality of voice, volubility, or silence. The professional worker, knowing this, would be alert to the symptom but slow to do anything but note it and would wait for further knowledge of the person before he could interpret. He would be still slower to attribute the display of emotion to any specific cause. The novelist can give free rein to his imagination in order to enhance the meaning of the observation; the professional worker must check his imagination until he has further confirmatory knowledge.

Virginia Woolf as a writer could describe the feelings of Mrs. Brown; and, as a writer, she had no obligation to know whether these really were Mrs. Brown's feelings. A professional worker may react just as definitely to the personality of the one to whom he is talking, but he is under the obligation of knowing the genesis and accuracy of his assumptions. Wrong interpretations have unfortunate consequences.

At each stage in every interview the interviewer is constantly making assumptions. These are subject to change as the interviewer develops new insight and understanding of his client and himself in their interrelationship.

Many workers make assumptions on insufficient evidence or in a superficial or merely routine manner. The unskillful public health nurse, for example, may make false assumptions by concentrating too carefully on physical ills, thereby shutting off the basis of understanding the emotional and environmental complications of her patient's condition. A nurse has been warned, for instance, against placing too much weight on a sick woman's reactions to her husband's unkindness. What might seem to her intolerable brutality may be only the exaggeration of illness where small grievances assume unwarranted magnitude; on the other hand, complaints may have an actual basis. The correct interpretation of what is observed is as important as the observed data.

A young public health nurse learned this truism in the first two visits she made as a new community health nurse. Her first visit was at a doctor's request to a woman in comfortable circumstances who seemed overwrought at her husband's neglect. The nurse observed the woman's tense manner, high-pitched voice and rapid speech as she listened attentively to a long account of "humiliations" suffered at the hands of her husband. The nurse, trying to sift the chaff from the wheat, at length decided that her report to the doctor would have to be that the patient needed psychiatric help. As she ended the interview and was going to the door, the nurse sensed that her patient was anxiously trying to detain her. When she paused, the woman blurted out, "Are you married?" The nurse's answer, "No, I'm not," was given somewhat reluctantly, fearing that as an unmarried worker she would be considered inadequate to understand marital difficulties. Immediately the woman's look of depression changed to one of envy as she exclaimed, "My goodness, aren't you lucky!"

The nurse's next visit, made at the request of a family agency, was to a woman whose husband had beaten her in a drunken rage. The woman was in bed. One of her eyes was blackened, her mouth was cut and her arms and legs showed ugly, purple discolorations. The nurse, inwardly quivering with indignation, forced herself to be calm while she administered aid. After she was through, her patient placed her hand timidly on the nurse's arm and with a sweet smile, somewhat marred by swollen lips, asked with an appeal for understanding in her voice, "Are you married, Miss Murphy?" The nurse answered with meaningful emphasis, *"No, I'm not."* Patting the nurse's arm gently, the woman, smiling still, this time with pride in her tone said, "Oh, well, you'll have your chance. You're young yet."

Later, the nurse found her assumption that the first woman was neurotic and exaggerating her grievances was not borne out by facts. The woman's husband was alcoholic and subtly cruel; her illness in great part was caused by her inability to cope with a tangible problem. In the second case, the woman herself drank and went on drinking bouts with her husband; only occasionally did the two reach a quarrelsome stage. All they asked of society was to be allowed to go on their debauched way together.

In making assumptions and interpretations based on observations, one can never be sure that alternative assumptions or explanations might not apply. The range of possibilities is so wide that there is a tendency to select those conveniently applicable and to avoid looking for all available circumstances or those which might contradict the assumptions the worker has already made.

The supervisor in an attendance department of the public schools in Zenith relates an incident. A woman came into the office. Her general appearance was of one accustomed to hard, heavy work. She had gnarled red hands, a bent back, a shuffling walk, and even more noticeably a "shut in" expression on her face. She approached the counter without responding to the worker's automatically cheery, "Good morning." Her demeanor seemed to challenge, "What's good about it?" as she thrust across the counter a notice which demanded that John F. return to school at once or be subject to court action as a truant.

The attendance officer recognized immediately the behavior of a deaf mute; so she started the conversation by writing in longhand on a slip of paper, "What can I do for you?" The woman wrote her answer slowly in the big, ill-formed letters of an illiterate person that she didn't see why her son had to be in school; he had a chance to get a job; they needed his help; he was nearly sixteen and large for his age. The worker in her written reply, contended that the compulsory education law provided for no exceptions.

Arguments continued in this vein until the heat generated was visible to an interested office force by the increased vigor with which each was writing, by head shakings and frowns on the part of the mother, and by the tense posture of the worker emphasized by a forced, set smile. The climax was reached when the deaf mute threw down the pad, saying loudly, clearly, audibly, "Well, I certainly think that is a senseless law and I'll take it to court!"

The tension of the office listeners was broken; both the worker and the woman joined in laughter. Then after a brief interval of embarrassed explanation by the worker, they proceeded with an orthodox interview.

The explanation was that the worker had been going over the absentee cards and had been annoyed to find that one of her most troublesome cases, a John M., whose parents were deaf mutes, was listed among the absentees. The woman entering at that point had worn an expression which seemed to the worker similar to that of John M.'s deaf and dumb mother, and instead of beginning the interview by speaking, she had handed the attendance officer a written notice. The false assumption, which in this case proved merely a cause of embarrassment, is easily understood when the circumstances are known.

There are many instances in which the interviewer, if he had followed through, would have seen that his interpretation was founded not on the actual situation but on factors he himself had contributed to the situation. It is true that we never assume or interpret without drawing upon our own backgrounds and experiences. It is also true that a remote happening can be a powerful present stimulus.

Theodore Reik[21] calls the psychoanalyst's faculty of sensing the meaning of what he observes "listening with the third ear." He explains that this process begins on the conscious levels of

[21] Theodore Reik, *Listening with the Third Ear,* Farrar, Straus and Company, 1949.

intelligence, is integrated with previous knowledge and emotions in the unconscious, and is brought back into consciousness after it has been transmuted into a meaningful and useful interpretation of what the patient himself has revealed by his appearance, his story, or his dreams.

Reik's description of this process, within the limitations of each worker's equipment, is perhaps as near an explanation as need be made, until investigation under controlled conditions can be undertaken, of the interviewer's skillful and selective use of observation.

Skill in the Use of Setting

An interviewer's skill is often evidenced in the way he uses the setting of the interview. Although not always thought of as such, the conscious employment of setting to further the purpose of the interview is a process.

Dr. Oliver's description of the material setting he created for the students at Johns Hopkins University who came to him for counsel is an illustration of a skillful use of this process.

I try to make my waiting room and office, especially my office, as unlike a physician's office as possible. There are no instruments anywhere. There are no half closed doors, no screens which suggest some keen-eared secretary may be lurking behind them. There is no smell of disinfectants; no magazines on the table; no drab depressing colors. My office, I dare to think, looks like a gentleman's study. It reminds, or I trust that it reminds, many patients of "Father's library at home." There are only three chairs, comfortable ones. Of these, two stand near my desk. Not one on either side of it, for I do not sit behind a desk and stare across it at my patients. Both the patient and myself sit on the same side of my long table. Nothing separates us. From where I sit I can, in moments of difficulty, reach forward and give the knee of my patient an encouraging pat. But I am too far off to do anything more. . . .
On the walls of my office are hung the engravings from my father's old library. They give me exactly the atmosphere that I am seeking. Moreover, in a cabinet or on a small table there are one or two really

beautiful things. The importance of having something in your office that is really worth looking at cannot be underestimated. A Japanese Kwannon in her dull gilt, "looking down above the sound of prayer"; one good bit of Chinese porcelain; some woodcarving from Tirol, all reds and blues; these and things like them rest tired eyes and turn tired thoughts from the noise of the street outside and the hoots of the hurrying motor cars. Finally, there is not too much light.[22]

Something of his attitude toward students as well as his method of interviewing is revealed when he describes the psychological atmosphere he tried to create: "I take pains, always, to pay them especial marks of respect, to be very courteous, punctiliously polite. For I am trying to give them back something that they thought they had lost, their own self-respect for the things in their lives that they have held sacred while others have cursed them as impure, their respect for their loving and their loved."[23]

The dentist who allays his patient's fear by having an electric button on the chair which can be pressed by the patient to stop the drill when pain becomes too severe is providing both a material and a psychological setting.

A successful clinical psychologist always manages to have the top of his desk cleared. He also makes it a point to meet his patient at the door of his office and, after a firm handclasp, invite him to enter. Another excellent but less tactful counselor would be dismayed if he knew how often students said, "I haven't wanted to bother Dr. J. because he's so busy." Actually no busier than the other clinician, he gives the impression of distraction by piles of papers and books on his desk and a habit of absent-mindedly leafing through them while talking to the student.

A setting has been consciously created by a school social worker whose pupils are of Polish, Italian, Ukrainian, Russian, and Syrian parentage. Her office has a Polish shawl hung over the file cabinet. A framed picture of an Italian Bambino is on the

[22] John Rathbone Oliver, *Four Square*, The Macmillan Company, 1929, p. 162.
[23] *Ibid.*, p. 173.

desk. Eggs decorated by the artistry of one of the Ukrainians in the district are in a woven basket. A Russian brass icon and a Syrian wine flask complete the simple collection. They are enough, however, to indicate to the parent summoned to discuss his child's misdeeds that the woman he is dealing with is interested in him and his culture.

The keynotes of effective setting are the sense that the interviewer's time is dedicated exclusively to the interviewee, that his leisure adequately encompasses the purposes of the interview, and that privacy and freedom from interruptions are essential to its success. It is recognized that even these minimum desiderata cannot always be achieved. Any missing element, however, is a definite handicap and may detract from the skill of the interviewer. The use of setting is a process in itself and also a factor in another process, that of the *establishment of rapport*.

Skill in the Establishment of Rapport

In professional terminology, the French word *rapport* is used to denote a relationship characterized by harmony and accord. Darley defines rapport as the prevailing climate achieved and maintained throughout the interview.[24] He lists the elements of rapport for counselors as seven commandments applicable to any office interview.

1. The interviewer should be friendly and interested.
2. The interview room should be comfortable and have the appearance of privacy.
3. The interviewer should appear unhurried, even though many people are waiting to see him.
4. The interviewer should accept whatever hesitant and halting attitudes and ideas the client puts forth and should express neither moral or ethical judgment, nor approval or disapproval of these attitudes and ideas.

[24] Darley, *op. cit.*, p. 13.

5. The interviewer should accept the client as a conversational equal during the interview.
6. The interviewer must always make clear to the client the limitations of his agency so that the client will not expect too much.
7. The interviewer must always make clear that the responsibility for planning and final action rests with the client.

In such a climate, Darley comments, attitudes, problems, and the client's objective self-evaluation may emerge. If such an atmosphere is lacking, the interview may be formal and remote from the problems of the interviewee.

Successful accomplishment of rapport depends upon the worker's temperament, or an attitude of mind calculated to develop friendly cooperation. One particular attitude of essential importance is the interviewer's acceptance of his client, counselee, or patient. In her discussion of the interviewing process in social casework, Gordon Hamilton has presented a clear explanation of the meaning of "acceptance" which should be a most helpful guide to anyone who is interviewing. Referring directly to acceptance, Miss Hamilton emphasizes:

This means acceptance of the other person as he is—in whatever situation, no matter how unpleasant or uncongenial to the interviewer, with whatever behavior, aggressiveness, hostility, dependency, or lack of frankness he may manifest. This attitude can come only from a respect for people and a genuine desire to help anyone who is in need or trouble. It is translated through courtesy, patience, willingness to listen, and not being critical or disapproving of whatever the client may complain of, request or reveal about himself. The first requisite in any interview is to make the person feel welcome and comfortable, and for this the interviewer himself must be relaxed and friendly.[25]

Symonds considers the ability to establish rapport with others

[25] Gordon Hamilton, *Theory and Practice of Social Casework*, 2nd ed., rev., Columbia University Press, 1951, p. 52.

one of the marks of adjustment.[26] Ability to do this involves, among other qualities, readiness to accept a person for what he is rather than for his status, and tolerance of others whose beliefs, standards, and tastes are not one's own. To achieve these qualities it is necessary to be a helpful participant in joint undertakings, a person whose satisfactory adjustment is recognized by the ease with which others accept him. Another attribute affecting rapport is the capacity for admitting the independence of other individuals as well as understanding the basic and universal need for dependence and for being loved.

Intellectual recognition of the need to accept others is not always easy to accomplish emotionally; nor is the mere recognition of the existence of prejudice sufficient to remove that prejudice. The following admission of a public health nurse demonstrates this:

As a child, I lived in a small Wisconsin village where there were no Negroes. When I was about five years of age, construction workers were laying some pavement close by. One of them was a Negro, the first I had ever seen. To keep a younger sister and myself from going into the street, we were told by an uncle that the colored man would carry us off if he saw us.

I had no further contact with Negroes until I was in nurses' training where no particular problem was presented, since only those in the highest economic status could afford to come to a private hospital. However, when I met colored people on the streets I felt myself still withdrawing. Later, as a member of the Army Nurse Corps overseas I learned to accept the Negro soldier and care for him without prejudice.

When I returned to this country I was riding on the streetcar one day when a colored woman sat down next to me. I felt myself withdrawing and questioned my behavior. When I realized the illogical attitude of being squeamish about sitting next to this colored woman when I had taken care of colored men overseas,

[26] Percival M. Symonds, *The Dynamics of Human Adjustment,* Appleton-Century-Crofts, Inc., 1946, p. 34.

my attitude seemed to change immediately. Since that time I have been better able to accept Negroes; now I can understand readily why it might be hard for someone else to accept as an equal a member of one of our minority groups.

It is not hard to predict that this worker's prejudices and in tolerances will be detrimental to her efficiency, in spite of her appreciation of the existence and genesis of prejudices.

Children are often frank in expressing their feelings and opinions about the state of rapport. They tend to show this more quickly and openly in interviews than adults. Excerpts of a recorded interview with a seven-year-old child who was seen at a Canadian Child Guidance Clinic illustrate several crucial factors in developing rapport, including the importance of understanding the purpose of an interview. Play interviewing was the primary medium which helped to establish the purposeful communication between this child and the social worker.[27]

PURPOSE OF INTERVIEW

Janet, the seven-year-old child, was referred to the Child Guidance Clinic because she will not work at school and dawdles both in school and coming home from school. She is talkative and daydreams a great deal. The mother was interviewed first and it was arranged with her that she would explain to Janet why she was to be seen at the Clinic.

EXCERPTS FROM FIRST PLAY INTERVIEW

After introductions in the waiting room we entered the playroom, Worker said this was Janet's playroom when she visited us and that we could do pretty much what we wanted to while we were here. Worker asked Janet if her mother had explained what it was she was coming to us for. Janet replied that her mother had said it was because she was not getting on well at school. Worker agreed and said it seemed that she wasn't as happy at school as she could be, and that the mother had come to us because she wanted to help Janet be happy.

[27] From Arthur C. Abrahamson (ed.), *Social Work Practice in Canada,* Best Co. Ltd., 1955, pp. 13–15.

The child nodded but said nothing for a second but then looked up and said: *"How can it help?"*

Worker explained that as she and Janet got to know each other, Janet could talk to Worker about anything she wanted. She could tell about things she liked and things she did not like. Worker explained further that she worked with many girls and boys who had problems like Janet's and hoped that we could help her. Janet replied that *she didn't think she wanted to talk.*

Worker said she didn't want to either this time or at later times, but that as we played together and got to know each other better, maybe Janet would feel like talking. Janet nodded in agreement and asked if she could play with anything she liked. She was assured that she could.

The record goes on to describe rather fully how the child explored the possibilities of the playroom, while being very careful not to get too involved in close discussion with the social worker. When the child found a broken toy she pointed out that she would like to have played with it if it were not broken.

Worker suggested that maybe she could have the toy repaired between now and when Janet returned. Janet replied: "How do you know I will come back?" Worker said that she didn't, but hoped that Janet would want to as we had liked having her come and wanted to help her; if she didn't feel as though she wanted to come she didn't need to feel she had to. Janet said nothing and went on playing.

In a few minutes the child produced a package of candies and offered them to the Worker. When the Worker took one, Janet took two more out of the package and handed them to the Worker saying: "You can eat two now, and then keep this to remember me by." Worker thanked Janet and said that she certainly would keep the candy, but that Worker would not need a candy to remember Janet because she could remember her anyway and would save a special time for her in case she can come and wants to.

Janet put a little mark on the candy and said: "Don't forget to save it; I'll ask you if you did."

The child became very interested in drawing and made one which she asked the social worker to keep. A few minutes before her interview time was up, the worker said that there would be time for only one more picture. The child responded:

"Only one more picture and then time for our talk. You know what you were going to talk to me about." Worker replied that she had not been sure whether Janet had wanted to talk today about the things that were bothering her. Janet asked what we were going to talk about. Worker commented that she was here because she was not getting on well at school. Janet reacted with: "You can sure say that again."

After talking briefly about the school situation Janet decided she had better hurry to finish the picture. When the question came about wanting another appointment the child agreed to return in two weeks. As she was leaving she announced to her mother that she was returning to see the social worker in two weeks and referred to the social worker by name.

A review of the points highlighted in the communication between the interviewer and the child shows how the necessary features delineated by Darley are carried out. It also shows a child's frank expressions of uncertainty in the "getting acquainted" period together with progressive movement out of this which enables both the child and the social worker to advance in the problem-solving task.

Where rapport is absent and cannot be effected, the interviewer is likely to be beating his head unavailingly against a wall of resistance.

Skill in Meeting Resistance

Every interviewer encounters resistance not only in his clients but frequently in himself.

Often resistance is expressed in the form of hostility toward the worker or even on the part of the worker toward the client. Where it is directed against the worker, the interviewer tries to remember that the behavior may be based on the interviewee's inability to handle the situation which made professional help necessary. Hostility in such an instance is the outward expression of futile rebellion; the worker merely affords a temporary target for pent-up feelings. Where the worker recognizes this behavior as symptomatic of emotional stress he is able to keep himself relatively free from personal reactions. Resistance is seldom directed against the worker as a person. When it is, it may be a justifiable resentment against a misuse of authority or a dislike for some personal characteristic.

Resistance is minimal or absent when the worker and the client have the same objectives in the interview. A follow-up study[28] of thirty-two families who had received case work help from social agencies in the Twin Cities disclosed that the client's opinion as to whether the agency's services were helpful depended primarily upon two factors: (1) the client and the case worker's seeing the problem eye to eye and (2) the client's liking the worker. The client's liking for the worker does not depend on the worker's status, authority, or prestige, but on whether the client feels that he is regarded as an individual and liked as such. Clients are quick to feel an attitude of dislike or superiority and to resent it.

Garrett comments on some of the ways by which the client expresses feelings of resistance he may be trying to conceal.[29] Negative feelings are often manifested by breaking appointments or coming late to them, dismissing the worker, refusing the services of the agency, or trapping the worker into giving suggestions which can later be proved wrong and used against him.

It is at the point of recognizing resistance as symptomatic of some other element that the interviewer shows the discipline of professional behavior. As Garrett has written, the counselor cannot allow himself the luxury of yielding to his natural irritation and discouragement over unexpected or irrational behavior, nor can he insist on his own plan of action.[30] His wisest course is to

[28] Anne Fenlason (with Mary Huff), "The Follow-Up; The Client's Own Story of Social Case Treatment," *Journal of Social Forces*, March, 1938, pp. 372-380.
[29] Garrett, *op. cit.*, pp. 19-20.
[30] Garrett, *Counseling Methods for Personnel Workers*, Family Welfare Association of America, 1945, p. 17.

take the counselee's behavior and rationalizations for granted. By so doing, he can help the counselee to search for the real causes of this behavior so that they can work together on the solution of the underlying difficulty.

When resistance grows out of the interviewee's inner tensions, the interviewer needs to understand its meaning before he can cope with it. Even then he does not deal with resistance as such —his interview is around the resistance rather than at it. A juvenile court judge's hearing with Eleanor N. indicates how resistance is heightened by focusing upon it.

Eleanor, aged fourteen, had been on probation for truancy. An informal hearing before the chief probation officer was followed a few months later by a hearing before the juvenile court judge— but Eleanor continued to be truant and was again brought into court.

A student who was present at this second formal hearing records her observations on it.

> Eleanor was a pretty girl with long, blond hair arranged neatly and attractively. Lipstick was her only make-up. She was dressed in blue jeans, rolled to mid-calf, a heavy woolen plaid jacket, and flat-heeled sandals. She kept her head and eyes down for the most part but occasionally looked at the judge with an expression which appeared to be half frightened and half defiant. The judge asked her why she hadn't gone to school. She didn't answer. He reminded her that only a few days before, she had talked to him after she had spent a few hours in the city jail. Eleanor made no response. Then the judge explained that he thought he had discovered why she wouldn't talk. He had noticed the other day that her teeth were in bad condition. He suggested that she didn't talk because she didn't want anyone to see her teeth. Eleanor remained mute.
>
> "Come now," said the judge, "is that the reason you don't talk to anyone but your family? At least you can nod you head, yes or no." Still looking down, Eleanor feebly nodded her head, yes.
>
> The judge explained that since she could not be depended upon

to attend school and since she needed dental attention, the only thing he could do was to send her to the County School for Girls where she would have to attend school and where her teeth could be taken care of. Eleanor began to cry silently and wiped her eyes although she tried to control herself. The judge dismissed her and she walked out, crying more audibly.

The judge had failed to realize that Eleanor was a troubled, unhappy girl. The social workers knew that she was already having extensive dental work done, and felt that her behavior was a protest against a poor home which had given her neither love nor protection.

Garrett speaks of frequent instances in which the interviewer both senses and sees resistance in a client who obviously wants help but can't ask for it, who asks for advice but won't use it, who agrees to plans but fails to carry them out, who says one thing and does another.[31]

Such reactions generally indicate inner conflicts with resulting ambivalences which have to do with the individual and his way of meeting his life's situations.

Skill in Recognizing Ambivalent Feelings

The worker's ability to recognize *ambivalence*, which he constantly encounters, and to know its significance, adds to his helpfulness in terms of his client's needs. It has already been said that meeting resistance is a process and that meeting it successfully involves skill. In the same sense, the recognition of ambivalence is a process when such recognition aids in the accomplishment of a purpose.

Ambivalence is the existence of dual and opposing forces in the human personality. These opposing tendencies are recognized by all of us in such polarities as loving and hating; the need for being taken care of and the need for independence; desire for

[31] *Ibid.*, p. 18.

work and inertia; desire for friends and avoidance of the contacts which foster friendships.

The behavioral aspect of ambivalence most often seen by professional workers is indecision. Often the inability of an individual to make his own decisions is the result of a weak or damaged ego which needs temporary support. Sometimes it is a concrete situational thing beyond the client's ability to move without help. You recall Mrs. Kazalski's indecision to return to Baltimore; in her case the block seemed to be a solid wall of material elements which dissolved when the interviewer helped her to think her problem through.

Ambivalence always rests on the conflict of some specific basic need with another need equally strong.

In professional practice, when dependence needs are in the foreground, the interviewer cannot always carry out the concept that the client should help himself. At times clients are at a stage of needing temporary active relief from the outside. But the aim in all such efforts is to help the client move in his own behalf. Skill often lies in the timing and the ability of a worker who knows how to give supportive help without further damage to the already weak ego of his client. The points mentioned here are evident in the Swedish social worker's interview in Chapter One.

The student who fails in his grades does so for many complex reasons which are often unrelated to his intelligence. The counselor realizes this, even while he gives specific, direct help in pulling him through a course in which he has become mired. The adviser is careful, if he is wise, to assume only enough of his advisee's problem to enable him to handle his more fundamental difficulties alone. The mental hygienist in working with college students who have minor emotional problems is alert to the resistance which comes from the student's ambivalent attitude—a desire for help and a resentment toward authority. Interviewing processes around this are described in an article on interviewing in a mental hygiene clinic of a student health service.

Because the patient is in a state of mind in which he is hyper-sensitive, the role of the interviewer is an important factor in treatment. Anxious and needing help, yet reluctant to have his condition investigated, the patient is tense, uneasy, and watchful. His ambivalent attitude makes him rush up his defenses at the slightest provocation and, through long practice, he is an expert at defense. Unless he is entirely absorbed in his own condition, he watches every move, gesture, and expression, fearful of being hurt, often covering this apprehension under an appearance of easy braggadocio or sophistication. Even where the self-absorption seems complete, the interviewer may later discover that the patient has been alert to certain acts which he had endowed with special significance for himself. . . .

The mental hygienist does not comment on the defense, nor appear to accept or discard it, and, at the same time, indicates that he understands and sympathizes with the problem the patient is ashamed of and trying to hide.[32]

We have indicated that a reaction to authority may be a cause of resistance. It probably was one factor in Eleanor's behavior before the judge.

Skill and Authority

Authority has its place and, properly used, affords security to the individual. This is true in all situations where conformity to regulations is necessary, as in juvenile and adult probation work, many aspects of public health nursing, and some phases of medical and psychiatric treatment involving physical or mental health. Misused authority heightens resistance. Properly employed, it becomes a support. Its use as a process is purposive and requires skill.

Garrett distinguishes between a warranted authority and unwarranted authoritativeness.[33] The warranted use of authority is that of the expert; it comes from his specialized knowledge and skill, as in the case of physicians, lawyers, scientists. Social case

[32] Robert Hinckley, M.D., and Anne F. Fenlason, "Mental Hygiene Interviewing: A Therapeutic Approach," *American Journal of Orthopsychiatry*, April, 1942, pp. 313-314.

[33] Garrett, *Counseling Methods*, pp. 94-95.

workers and skilled counselors, Miss Garrett says, are also acquiring this kind of authority because of their specialized professional knowledge of the behavior of human beings. She adds, however, that this authority comes from careful, systematic study; without such formal background both the worker's knowledge of behavior and the authority based on this knowledge are necessarily limited.

Another kind of authority, discussed by Miss Garrett, is that in which one individual has power over another.[34] Parents have such authority over the small child. When it has been used to restrain wisely and to guide, the growing child learns to use rather than to resist authority.

The child of today thinks of the policeman who helps control traffic at crossings as his friend, and, unless his later adult behavior results in another aspect of police power, he thinks of the policeman as a protector of society.

The attitude of the client toward the interviewer may contain vestiges of his childish attitudes toward his parents, his teachers, and others who have exercised authority over him at earlier periods of his life. This is especially the case if the one needing help or counsel has no choice about accepting it and nothing to say about the manner in which it is given. The interviewer must constantly keep in mind that he is involved in another human being's problems by virtue of his profession; he is there in relation to the other's need for professional services. If he fully realizes this he is likely to use constructively the authority vested in him.[35]

In regard to the constructive use of authority, the remarks of Miss Lucy Wright deserve notice. She observes that the forces of expertness and authority have their greatest value when employed on a give-and-take basis. When the give-and-take has proved impossible and conflict is inevitable, it is still possible to have a clear understanding on both sides of the issues involved.

[34] *Ibid.,* p. 95.
[35] Garrett, *Interviewing, Its Principles and Methods,* pp. 19-20.

In all but a limited range of cases, on lines to be clearly and definitely defined, one works directly with the advisee himself. "The greatest skill of all lies, perhaps, in knowing when to postpone the use of even the force of authority and how to apply that force well when used."[36]

So far our discussion has emphasized selected processes which describe movement within the interview. The techniques which cause the interview to progress also require a high degree of skill. The two most effective and commonly used techniques are *questions* and *silence*.

Skill in the Use of Questions

Questions are more than mere inquiries; they are technical procedures in constant use in a great variety of forms. A question used to elicit only a *yes* or *no* response is ordinarily an indication of lack of skill and is a poor technique. However, when the situation demands a clear-cut, unqualified answer, such a question may be used skillfully in evoking the desired response. The salesman trying to eliminate negative responses and to call forth a series of *yes* responses in order to build up a positive attitude toward his sales talk is using the question as a technique.

With the entry into this country of displaced people since the end of World War II, interviewers may well review the warning of Miss Richmond. Although she was writing of social case work with Italian families after the First World War, her words are still good counsel in most instances. "Letting fly the question direct means receiving in return evasions, prompted by a repugnance for what seems to be intruding brusqueness."[37]

There are many different forms of questions besides the direct question: the rhetorical question, the question asked as a restatement for clarification, questions for affirmation or denial, ques-

[36] Lucy Wright, "The Worker's Attitude as an Element in Social Case Work," *Interviews, Interviewers, and Interviewing*, Family Welfare Association of America, 1931, p. 7.

[37] Mary E. Richmond, *Social Diagnosis*, Russell Sage Foundation, 1934, p. 74.

tions calling for specific information, questions in cross-examination, the leading question, the psychiatric *why*, and many others.

The rhetorical question is really a statement made in question form, which demands no answer. The question of restatement using slightly different words is generally effective in stimulating realization of the feeling, meaning, or importance of what the client has said. When Johnny vehemently tells the visiting teacher, "It isn't the school I hate, it's Miss Jacks. She's down on me," the teacher may ask, "You think Miss Jacks is down on you?" with a rising inflection, to which Johnny may respond with the chapter and verse of his reasons for disliking Miss Jacks.

The question asked for affirmation or denial might have preceded the above, with the teacher's saying to Johnny, "Do you think you're getting anything out of school?" or even more directly, "Do you like school?"

Many interviewing situations demand direct information. After rapport has been established, and after the purpose of the questions has been explained, these can be asked directly.

Questions in the form of cross-examination have no place in the field of human relations; clients, patients, or counselees should not have to defend themselves against the interviewer. When this is the case, it indicates a misuse of authority and a lack of skill.

The use of leading questions is a questionable technique for professional workers. It implies cleverness on the part of the interviewer rather than a desire to ascertain facts and understand the feelings of the other participant in the interview.

The *why* question is an attempt to help through a deeper understanding of motivation. When Johnny says, "It isn't school I hate, it's Miss Jacks. She's down on me," the interviewer who asks "Why do you hate Miss Jacks?" may arrive at the meaning of John's emotion and some explanation of its origin. The question may also lead John to understand that his own behavior may have an irrational basis.

What is a question that evokes an explanation or description. "What are you going to do about it?" is often an effective way of helping the client face his problems and marshal his resources to meet them. At times, however, this fails; if so it may not enable the client to evaluate his own weakness or weigh various possibilities or show reasons why definite help is needed. For this reason, a number of interviewers have found it more effective and helpful to ask their clients about *what plans they had previously considered* as possible ways of meeting their difficulties.

Skill and Silence

Training supervisors in psychiatry, psychological counseling, nursing, and social work report that one of the earliest and most common hurdles which arise in practicum is in the student's learning how to understand and manage silence in interviews. This is not surprising. Such difficulty is due partly to the prevalent system of values in our culture which tends to put a higher premium on noise than it does on solitude. Barbara discusses this point in considerable detail, corroborating the opinion of others.[38] Not a small amount of the difficulty is due to the mismanagement of tensions and the array of prejudices in the interviewer.

Skilled handling of silence in the interview depends upon the interviewer's acuity about what is being conveyed through silence. Often silences connote a thoughtful, meditative sorting out of what has been said and felt. In doing this, the interviewee draws on his own inner resources to help him figure out meanings behind and solutions to his problems. When such a condition exists, it is paramount that the interviewer exercise "the will to refrain." As the interviewer gains experience, and to the extent that he can discipline the expression of his own fears and prejudices, he will become adept at recognizing the true meaning conveyed in such a response and responding wisely to it.

Silence may also be an indication of anxiety or emotional blocking. Not infrequently is it a passive expression of anger or hostility in both interviewee and interviewer. A client in a mental health clinic offered a lucid explanation of how she felt her mother controlled and punished her by "stony silence." The power which the mother thus exerted was forceful and was a

[38] Barbara, *op. cit.*, p. 32, 166–181.

condition which this client had not been able to penetrate because it blocked her in every maneuver that she used in trying to deal with it and with her mother. This same client had been seen earlier by an inept interviewer who tended to be silent in many parts of his interviews. Because of this and because the interviewer was not skillful in his use of silence, the client did not return for further interviews. In fact, she reacted with intense anger because she was now encountering another adult who was "stony and silent" at a time when she was under stress. The interviewer at the mental health clinic then asked what this client would have said if she could have told the former interviewer how she felt about his response. The client's immediate reply was that she would have told him "to get off his high throne and pay attention to what was going on." The clinic interviewer then pointed out that the client might get uncomfortable if there were unavoidable silences in the interviews at the clinic as well, and that it would be very helpful if she would call attention to this discomfort, when it happened, and talk about it.

Skill in handling silence, particularly when it is due to a complicated set of circumstances, can only be developed through supervisory guidance. For this and other valid reasons, competent, careful, and close supervision is provided for those receiving practicum or field work experience in many of the helping professions.

Knowing when not to inject oneself into the interview is often as important as asking questions deftly.

Often, a seemingly unself-conscious response is actually the interviewer's expression of self-consciousness and his feeling of compulsion to break an embarrassing silence.

Darley reminds us that the secure interviewer is never afraid of *silences*.[39] He never feels impelled to rush in to fill a vacuum with words. Indeed, for him there is no vacuum; for he is actively trying to understand why the client is unable or unwilling to continue, the nature of his inability to talk, and what his own activity should be. In some instances he realizes that the subject under discussion has been exhausted and that, if the client doesn't

[39] Darley, *op. cit.*, pp. 12–13.

initiate a change, a question or comment will start the conversation in a new direction. He recognizes that silence may mean an emotional blocking. If he is wise, he will not force the conversation further along the lines that evoked the emotion but may, by his silence, give the client a chance to recover his poise or direct his own conversational course into a new channel.

The interviewer who feels he must fill every void of silence should know that his eagerness to talk is usually caused by concern about his own comfort rather than concern for his client.

INTERVIEWS ILLUSTRATING PROCESSES AND TECHNIQUES

All that we have been saying about the skillful use of processes and procedures in the interview should become clearer in the study of the two following dialogue interviews between workers and adolescents in difficulty.[40] Both interviews were conducted by teachers. Each teacher wished to be helpful; each knew there must be reasons behind her advisee's behavior; each planned before hand the processes and some of the procedures she would use. The wide differences in results obtained are due to diversities in understanding motivations for adolescent behavior, and in applying that knowledge through the use of the processes and techniques of interviewing.

The first interview is with Carleton.

The Purpose of the Interview

Carleton was a boy of seventeen in his senior year in a small consolidated high school. He had been elected the most popular boy in school a few days before the incident in this interview. His own father was dead. It was the custom of his stepfather, a teacher in the high school, to stay on to finish his work before driving six miles to their home, and Carleton accordingly waited for him every evening. Miss Martin, the teacher holding this interview, had had frequent difficulty with Carleton's insubordinate behavior in the study room which had finally resulted in his suspension from school. This meant that Carleton could not graduate unless he were reinstated.

[40] The author is indebted to the students who presented the following dialogues in class assignments.

The evening after Carleton's suspension the dramatic arts teacher, Miss Karl, came to Miss Martin much perturbed to report that her purse had disappeared during the rehearsal of the class play. When she had come to get it, she had found Carleton in the room. He seemed disturbed at sight of her and had retreated hastily after explaining that he had come for a book. She dashed into the principal's office demanding immediate action and accusing Carleton of the theft. The principal promised to take the matter up at the school board meeting that evening.

Miss Martin, fearing hasty action on the part of the board because of the principal's impulsiveness, asked if she might be allowed to handle the case until Carleton's guilt was proved or disproved. Consent was reluctantly given.

Miss Martin then wrote a note to Carleton saying that he had been accused of theft but that she could not bring herself to believe him guilty. If he were guilty, he was to stay away from class one more day so that the students would think he was still under suspension. If he were not guilty he was to come immediately after school and talk over ways and means of freeing himself from suspicion. When he did not appear in class nor after school, Miss Martin decided that he couldn't have received the note and sent a student to hunt him up and ask him to her room for conference.

As she waited for Carleton Miss Martin considered various possibilities: (1) he did not get the note; (2) he did get the note, but was staying away because he did not want to talk with her so soon after his suspension; (3) he really was guilty and was taking the means of confession she had offered him.

With these possibilities in mind she selected the first as the best way of avoiding tension at the beginning.

The two preceding paragraphs indicate the psychological setting for the interview.

Miss Martin was standing at the window nervously wondering what was going to happen when Carleton and the boy who had been sent for him came to the door. Carleton's head was hanging and he slouched sullenly against the wall near the door.

Miss Martin immediately concluded that her last assumption had been correct—he was guilty. However, she still chose to act as if the first assumption were the correct one, and the interview began on this supposition.

Miss Martin's observations and assumption are clearly stated; the effect of her hypothesis is evident.

The Dialogue of the Interview

MISS MARTIN: Thank you Robert, for finding Carleton for me. I
thought perhaps he had not received a note I wrote asking for
a conference.

The technique of dissembling is always questionable.

Robert left at once while Carleton mumbled, "I got your note this
morning."

The interview began with Carleton on the defensive—an attitude which would have to be modified before a satisfactory result could be achieved.

MISS MARTIN: Then you mean that you took Miss Karl's purse?
CARLETON: Yes, now go ahead and scold me. I know I deserve it.

Miss Martin was using the authority vested in her position
rather than trying to put Carleton at ease. She may have thought
that putting her assumption into words would be the easiest way
of bringing out a difficult admission. If so, Carleton's response
would seem to have justified her procedure. It did not, however,
do much to overcome Carleton's resistance and hostility.

MISS MARTIN: What's the use of scolding? Let's sit down and
thrash this thing out.

Carleton looked surprised but took the chair next to Miss Martin.
He still looked sullen and rather apprehensive.

Miss Martin's non-judgmental attitude was good. Her invitation
to sit down and thrash the matter out only partly allayed Carleton's fears. He was in no position to refuse the invitation. The interview continued:

MISS MARTIN: There must have been some urgent reason why
a boy like you should take to stealing, Carleton. Won't you
tell me about it?
CARLETON: Yeah, tell you and then you blat it around to all
the teachers. Then I'd be expelled and that would kill my
mother.

Miss Martin may have recognized Carleton's resistance at this
point. Instead of asking why he stole she showed him that she

knew there must have been a reason and asked him to tell about it. Because rapport between them was lacking she might have expected the rebuff. Carleton's reply indicated that he completely distrusted her but wanted assurance that his mother's confidence in him would be protected.

> MISS MARTIN: Did I blat about the trouble we just had? It seems to me you did the blatting, now didn't you?
>
> CARLETON: Yes, but I thought I'd beat you to it. I could make it sound funny and make the kids laugh at you. But I couldn't make them laugh off my stealing Miss Karl's purse. They're strong for me, but not that strong.

Note the teacher's use of Carleton's language. It may have reduced some of his tension but he was still resistant and hostile. He was aware of his leadership in the school and wanted to maintain it. Miss Martin recognized his pride as a possible asset. She now had two strong points to work from—Carleton's love for his mother and his pride in himself. Carleton's open hostility toward the teacher seemed to stem from earlier poor relationships. Miss Martin was put on the defensive by her lack of insight into the symptomatic nature of his behavior and her own insecurity caused by not understanding adolescents.

> MISS MARTIN: Have you ever known me to break a promise?
>
> CARLETON: No.
>
> MISS MARTIN: If I promise that I shall not tell a living soul anything you say unless you give me permission, do you believe I'll keep that promise?

Miss Martin was making a direct appeal for Carleton's trust and confidence. She might, however, be about to make a promise which shouldn't have been made and a commitment which she might not be able to keep. Her bid for Carleton's approval seemed to have been made more for her own reassurance than for Carleton's.

> CARLETON (*studying the teacher for a second*): Yes, I guess so. Yes, I'm sure.
>
> MISS MARTIN: Then is it a go?
>
> CARLETON: I guess so.

They shook hands on the bargain and this act was interpreted by Miss Martin as evidence of Carleton's complete confidence in her. Another interpretation might have been that he was making the best of a bad situation in which he had little or no choice. Miss Martin was now committed.

CARLETON: I don't know where to begin. But—well—you see—
MISS MARTIN: Go on, Carleton, I have shock absorbers.
CARLETON: Well, then—I'm the one that's done all the petty stealing here in the last four years. Nobody ever suspected me because I look so honest; anyway I was always active in the student council meetings, giving lots of suggestions on how to find the thief. That sure was fun!

Even with her shock absorbers Miss Martin must have been unprepared for this revelation but showed poise in controlling her astonishment. Miss Martin possibly recognized here that Carleton's thieving was symptomatic of some deeper maladjustment. He had spoken boastfully of the fun he got out of it and the sense of superiority he derived from fooling everybody. Miss Martin didn't think these were his only reasons, however, and went on:

MISS MARTIN: I can imagine it! But was that your only reason for taking the money?
CARLETON: Gee, no! I had to have the money and I didn't know how to get it.

Miss Martin records that her assumption at this point was that Carleton's stepfather was too niggardly with spending money. She asked herself why Carleton didn't work to earn the money but refrained from putting the question. These conclusions indicated superficial and premature diagnosis of Carleton's behavior, which was certainly symptomatic of something seriously wrong in Carleton's life.

MISS MARTIN: You mean you didn't have any spending money?
CARLETON: Oh, Dad gives me a dollar a week and besides I work in a garage Saturdays and earn a couple of dollars—but— well, the truth is I've been gambling over at the Zenith Pool

Hall, and I owe over a hundred dollars. Whenever Old Irish
threatens to tell, I swipe money to satisfy him, because I just
can't let my mother know. When I get out working I'll pay all
the people back because I've kept a record of every penny I
stole.

At this point Miss Martin decided that Carleton had insight
into the right and wrong of stealing but not of gambling, and that
he was gambling while waiting for his father to take him home
in the evening because he had not been able to find a wholesome
recreation for that time. She questioned Carleton on this point
and he confirmed her assumption, possibly to protect his defenses
against any further assault.

This statement of Carleton's marked the climax of the interview. Miss Martin now believed that she understood enough of
the situation to help Carleton and proceeded to take over.

She persuaded Carleton to confess to Miss Karl that he had
stolen the purse and to make plans for paying her back. Miss
Martin records that this was a difficult scene because Miss Karl
wept and insisted on kissing "the dear boy" for being so frank
about his error. Miss Martin hurried that interview as much as
possible and then ushered Carleton into the principal's office for
a similar confession. The principal, threatening everything from
a whipping to reform school, proved no asset in working out the
problem. Escaping from the storm, Miss Martin and Carleton
once more returned to her office to make plans for the future.

Miss Martin decided that whatever was to be done would have
to be accomplished mainly by her efforts. The principal must be
mollified or he might become an active danger in the boy's rehabilitation. Miss Karl, in Miss Martin's opinion, was a danger of
a different sort and would need careful evading.

With this reasoning she evolved a seven-point program. The
plans made were:

1. Carleton was to tell his father about his difficulties on the way
   home that evening and ask him to help with the debt at the

pool hall. His father was to decide whether to tell his mother.

2. He was not to go near the pool hall for the rest of the school year.

3. He was to pay back his thieveries according to a budget they worked out and to make a weekly report to Miss Martin.

4. He and Miss Martin were to organize a Hikers' Club among the students; to hike at least once a week for the rest of the school year. He was to go on every hike and earn extra points by hiking other evenings whenever he could.

5. Miss Martin was to give him a piano lesson every Tuesday and he was to use his spare time practicing on the piano in the auditorium. (He had said he wanted to learn to play.)

6. He was to refrain from stealing anything.

7. "Whenever temptation had him in its toils," he was to try to find Miss Martin or to get his boon companion, Robert, to play some strenuous game out-of-doors as far away from the pool hall as possible.

The interview ended on an exalted note. As Carleton left he said, "I can feel comfortable about going home to mother; she'd die if she knew what a bad boy I've been. But from now on, it's going to be different."

Miss Martin records that, knowing what stuff such resolutions were made of, she answered, "That's a fine feeling, Carleton, and I hope you will keep your mother in the foreground of your thinking. You'll need to think of her many times in the next few months because it isn't an easy job we have set for ourselves."

Processes and techniques[41] were employed in the interview with Carleton but without much awareness on the part of the teacher as to what their part in the interview was:

Miss Martin attempts to *create a setting* by writing a note, by

---

[41] The term descriptive of a process, in the analysis of the interview, is underlined. The technique indicates the way the process is achieved and is generally flagged by the word *by* or *of*. Where the technique is not introduced by a preposition it is contained in a phrase explaining how the process was implemented.

telling him of the accusation and her faith in him, and by asking him to confirm or refute the accusation.

When this failed she had him brought to her office "for a conference."

Miss Martin seeks to *avoid tension* by assuming that he did not get the note.

Observation of Carleton's hangdog expression when he appears compels her to revise her hypothesis and assume that he stole the purse.

She tries again to *avoid tension* and to *establish rapport* by using a technique of making a statement that Carleton could accept or reject.

She tries unsuccessfully to *meet Carleton's resistance* by putting her assumption that Carleton was the culprit into words.

Her *acceptance of the situation* and of Carleton is indicated by her question "What's the use of scolding?" followed by an invitation to discussion. Her process of acceptance is also shown by her voicing aloud the thought that there must be some explanation of his behavior, following up by an invitation to explain, in the form of a question. Such an invitation is likely to be refused unless the advisee's need to share his troubles is great and he has confidence in the interviewer. The technique alone is not enough.

Miss Martin's technique of using the interviewee's colloquial language was a way of trying to *reduce tension and resistance* and *establish better rapport*.

Miss Martin's personal appeal is a technique that is seldom successful. Where the relationship between a worker and a client is good such an appeal is generally unnecessary and where necessary is, as a rule, unfair.

Miss Martin's technique of shaking hands to bind a bargain is of the same nature as using colloquial language. The process apparently underlying it was *meeting resistance* and the closely allied *establishment of rapport*.

Miss Martin's technique of "Go on Carleton, etc.," was the reverse of a silence technique. She was attempting to *help Carleton in making a difficult admission*. It seems clear, however, that her own discomfort impelled her to speech.

Miss Martin's *acceptance of Carleton's behavior* was not as deep as the dialogue indicates in the light of subsequent happenings. Her simple comment of "I can imagine it!" is non-judgmental. It is followed by the technique of asking a question for further information and clarification.

Her question about spending money is *voicing an assumption* in a form designed to *bring further elucidation*.

Miss Martin's exhortations at the end of the interview probably fell on deaf ears as exhortations always do unless they are coincident with a motivation for change—in which case they are unnecessary.

Reserving further comment on Miss Martin's interview with Carleton for comparison with the following interview, we shall proceed to the conversation between another teacher and another rebellious adolescent. This is the interview of Jane and her adviser.

The Purpose of the Interview

Jane, eighteen years old, is a student in a small sectarian college. She has made herself conspicuous by breaking dormitory regulations and by poor attendance in classes. A series of escapades culminated in an automobile accident which seemed to point toward sex irregularity. She had been up before the discipline committee, but had been so defiant that the committee had referred her case to the Dean of Women for study and treatment. Jane had so completely identified the Dean with her duties as disciplinarian that the Dean could make no progress with her. She, therefore, asked Jane's teacher-adviser to try to get at the girl's problem and handle it as best she could. If Jane did not begin to show improvement soon, the discipline committee would have to suspend her.

Miss Dare had been Jane's adviser for two years and her classroom teacher at the same time. In spite of this connection, she had not been able to make close contact with the girl, and therefore felt extremely diffident in approaching her. She determined on the following policy: (1) not to be shocked at anything Jane said or did; (2) to avoid every appearance of being censorious; (3) to keep off the emotional plane as much as possible; (4) to be absolutely frank; and (5) to let Jane take the lead as often as possible.

These policies are good rules of conduct for any interview. The teacher set the stage by having on her desk a book of Jane's favorite poetry which she planned to use as an opening wedge if necessary.

She was marking papers at her desk when Jane breezed in, fifteen minutes late for the appointment. She was untidy, her hair, which needed washing and brushing, hung in oily strings around her face, her pretty gray dress was spotted generously, a large hole gaped in the knee of her stocking, and her orange scarf had long ago lost crispness and beauty. She always appeared in this guise when she thought she was going to be scolded, or when she wanted to be scolded. At other times she showed exquisite taste in her clothes and almost fanatical cleanliness.

This untidiness is an example of purposeful but unconscious behavior, the probable motivation being a childish desire for attention and a need to be reprimanded as a proof of the teacher's concern.

The Dialogue of the Interview

JANE: Well, how's the old maid today? *(Loudly)*
MISS DARE *(kindly)*:   Oh, hello, Jane. Won't you please sit down until I finish grading this paper?

The adviser is able to be objective, recognizing that aggression and hostility, although directed toward her, are not directed at her as a person but against the authority she represents.

JANE *(yawning, tramping around the room, dropping a book, opening the window, and shutting it again; noticing the teacher gathering up her papers)*:   Say, Miss Dare, next week I won't be in your class any more. You won't have to bother with naughty me any more.

MISS DARE: Why so, Jane?

JANE: I'm going to commit suicide. I know where I can get some poison and I'm going to take it, see if I don't.

MISS DARE: Well, I suppose if you have firmly decided that, nothing I can say will do any good. What flowers shall I send?

JANE (*long pause in which she studies Miss Dare in surprise; finally, still in a very loud tone and swaying on her toes*):   Gee, yesterday I said that to Prof. X. and he lectured me for two hours on how cowardly it is to commit suicide. And the other day I hit Prof. Z. so hard on the back it jarred his false teeth, and then he lectured me on not being a lady. Aren't you going to bawl me out for not being a lady, or hand me some sob stuff about suicide?

The adviser is able to carry out her intention not to be shocked by anything Jane does or says. Her bantering manner is effective in this instance. The teacher apparently understands adolescent behavior.

MISS DARE: No, Jane, I don't intend to lecture you on anything. A girl of your age and intelligence knows how to act properly, I'm sure (*walks leisurely to chair near where girl is standing and seats herself*), but I am interested to know why you choose to be the Athenian instead of the Spartan.

This is a reference to an anecdote read in class that morning which seemed to have struck Jane's sense of humor. The Athenian had declared his country knew good manners, but did not use them, while the Spartans both knew and used them.

There is skill in Miss Dare's matter-of-fact manner and her use of an illustration that made Jane see her behavior as a deliberate, undesirable pattern.

JANE (*laughing and flouncing into chair beside Miss Dare*):   I'll bet Dean Y. would like to know that too. I sure do keep her guessing.

This marks the end of Jane's resistance to the teacher and from now on the interview can proceed with greater flexibility and directness.

> Miss Dare: Of course Dean Y. is as human as the rest of us and wants her work to go smoothly and successfully. Did you make that dress you have on?

Leading Jane away from her grievance to a topic she would discuss freely is done purposely.

> Jane: Yes, do you like it?
> Miss Dare: It is very becoming. But suppose while you were making it I had sneaked in and broken the belt on the machine or loosened the tension, how would you have liked it?
> Jane: I probably never would have finished the dress, and I would have got even with you, believe me.

Again a figure of speech is more effective than remonstrance would have been. Having met Jane's original resistance, the adviser is careful to avoid building it up again.

> Miss Dare: Dean Y. doesn't relish your upsetting the machinery of her work any more than you would relish my tampering with your sewing machine. But of course you would consider her pretty small if she tried to get even; all she could do is try to stop you. Did you ever think of it from that angle?
> Jane: No, it isn't Dean Y. I dislike, I just can't abide rules and regulations. They were made to break and I can't help if I step on her in the process. She'd really be quite decent if she weren't dean. Gee, Miss Dare, didn't you ever break rules?

The teacher appeals directly to Jane and Jane responds by telling of her rebellion against authority.

> Miss Dare: Yes, of course. (*She relates an incident, much to Jane's amusement.*) However, I didn't make a habit of breaking rules. You do it so often I should think you'd lose the kick entirely if you do it just for fun.

There is no artificial distance between Jane and her adviser for she relates herself to Jane. She also makes a distinction between her behavior and Jane's in a manner which Jane can accept.

JANE: Did you ever go out with men when you were in college?
MISS DARE: Naturally I had dates. What made you ask? Oh, yes, I remember, you called me an old maid when you came in.

Here the adviser brings an earlier remark of Jane's back into the conversation. Her response has now made Jane feel free to approach the crux of her difficulties.

JANE: Forget it! I was trying to get a rise out of you. I like to shock people. But I didn't mean just dates with men. I meant did you pet and go to road houses and, oh—you know.

A short discussion follows in which it becomes evident that Jane has false notions of sex. Miss Dare gives her a book on the subject intended for students. She asks Jane to read it and come back in a week for further discussions. Jane eagerly agrees to the plan. There may be some question at this point as to the effectiveness of referring a young girl to books instead of having a direct discussion.

MISS DARE: What I really asked you to come for was to work out with you your reasons for acting as you do on the campus. When you first came here you gave us all the impression of a wide-awake, well-poised girl who knew exactly what she wanted. Instead of living up to that impression you have been acting like a spoiled nine-year-old on her first trip to a circus.
JANE (*in subdued voice*):   Do you think maybe I'm feeble minded?
MISS DARE (*knowing Jane's I.Q. to be above average, laughing easily and countering with*):   Do you?

The teacher now is able to use her role as adviser.

JANE: Well, something's the matter with me. I'm so restless when I'm in the house I have to make a lot of noise to keep from screaming. I hate everybody and everything, myself included; I don't believe in God nor fear the devil. Life just isn't worth a darn.

She is so tense Miss Dare lets a few seconds pass before saying anything.

Silence is an effective procedure both in lessening tension and in stimulating realization.

> MISS DARE (*in a quiet, meditative tone*): It does hurt to doubt all the things you used to think were so, doesn't it?

A comment in the form of a tentative question is also an effective procedure.

> JANE (*rigid with effort to control tears*): Did you ever doubt God?
> MISS DARE: Yes, often.

Note the adviser's freedom to exchange experiences with Jane and how she limits them to those which Jane asks about directly.

> JANE: How did you ever get over it?
> MISS DARE: I'm not altogether over it yet. It takes time and study and thought and experience of life. I console myself with the thought that doubt is a sign of growth even if the growing pains are bad.

Here an admission of her limitations without despairing over them is undoubtedly helpful to Jane.

> JANE: Then you don't think I'm wicked and damned?
> MISS DARE: Heavens no, Jane! Because I'm fond of you, I'm worried about your conduct, as I told you before. You don't strike me as being especially happy in spite of your independence and I'd like to help you work out a scheme to make you happier. But that can't be done until we both face the reasons underlying your conduct. You know that from your psychology.

The adviser makes use of her relationship with Jane in a professional way. Jane is now ready to use her adviser.

> At that Jane bursts out crying. Her defenses are down and she pours out a tale of difficulties with a stern mother, inability to become reconciled to the death of her father, disappointment in a love affair at school, long hours of prayer with an emotional adult who had a claim on Jane and used it to "purge her soul," fears, doubts, and a craving for understanding and love from an

older person. During the tearful story, Miss Dare sits quietly by, asking a helpful question now and then, but refraining from any emotional display of sympathy. When the storm has passed, Miss Dare pats Jane on the arm.

MISS DARE: I'm glad you told me, Jane. You can rest assured your confidence will be respected. We certainly have a big program ahead of us, but I feel sure of success because we understand each other now, don't you think so?

The adviser's quiet willingness to share but not assume Jane's problems is the assurance Jane needs. The rest marks the conclusion of a successful interview.

JANE: I can't tell you what a relief it has been to tell you all this. I've wanted to talk with you but hated to take your time. Anyway I thought you would think I was crazy.

MISS DARE: Well, don't bottle yourself up again. Remember what happened to that old radiator the other day.

They both laugh at the recollection of how the cap blew off the radiator the week before and broke up the class.

An allusion has been used skillfully for comparison—this time to drive home a point with humor instead of a hammer.

JANE: That sure was an explosion! Well, I guess I'd better be getting back to the dorm. I'll read the book through and come back next week at this time. I'll bet we'll have some fun with it. Thank you a lot. Bye, now!

Miss Dare smilingly waves her hand at Jane and the interview is at an end.

Processes and techniques are employed by Jane's teacher with discernment and sureness.

Miss Dare's *setting* was contrived, but arranged with skill.

She not only observed Jane's behavior but her *observation* gave her a clue to Jane's emotional state. She also used previous observations to confirm her interpretation of Jane's personal appearance.

She *met Jane's resistance* by recognizing it as such and ignoring it. Her attitude was friendly and not defensive because she recognized that Jane's resistance was against authority and not against herself.

She restrained herself from *using her authority* in a dictatorial manner.

Her question of "Why so, Jane?" was a casual response to Jane's statement that she wouldn't be bothering her by continuing in her class.

She accepted Jane's dramatic avowal of her intention to commit suicide calmly and showed that she didn't take it too seriously by humorously asking what flowers to send. If she had not known Jane as well as she did, this response would have been doubtful. It is a fallacy to think that a threat of suicide is never carried out.

Miss Dare's technique of using the reference to the Athenians and the Spartans stimulated in Jane a realization of her behavior. By this allusion she was able to convey her *acceptance* of Jane without condoning her behavior. Through the techniques of humor and the use of references which had direct application to Jane, she was able also *to meet successfully Jane's resistance.*

She used a figure of speech again as a procedure in further *stimulating in Jane a realization of her behavior* when she compared Jane's actions in school with tampering with a sewing machine. Her recognition of Jane's sewing ability is an implied compliment—her comment on the dress is a direct and tactful one. Compliments should be used sparingly, and only when they are deserved and sincere.

Miss Dare's skill was again apparent when she responded naturally but briefly to Jane's question as to whether she herself never rebelled against authority by breaking rules. Here the process might be considered *cementing rapport* and the technique one of sharing experiences. The teacher did not let this divert her from the purpose of the interview, however. She *brought Jane back* to it and capitalized on her opportunity by explaining the difference while admitting the likeness of their behavior.

When Jane asked whether the teacher had dates, Miss Dare responded honestly, inquired why Jane asked the question, and *brought the interview back* to the point which she had earlier ignored by reminding Jane that she had called her an old maid. She did this without resentment or defensiveness. By this time the rapport between them had made her comment possible.

Sharing experiences is a technique to be used with caution. The interviewer can never be sure his experience is parallel to the interviewee's, but he can be reasonably sure that the interviewee is more interested in his own experiences than in anyone else's. Differences in experience are more likely to alienate than to strengthen a sound professional relationship. Miss Dare seems to have avoided this pitfall in her interviewing path.

Miss Dare gave Jane a book on sex as a way of *offering a concrete suggestion* to a specific problem. Her action might be questioned. She did not know the details of Jane's involvement well enough to be sure her prescription would hit the mark and she had no way of knowing Jane's reaction to sex information. Her only safeguard was her invitation to a further discussion, which she had no assurance that Jane would accept.

Miss Dare *brought Jane back to the purpose of the conference* by frankly stating the reason for calling her in. This she had deferred until she thought Jane was in a frame of mind for such discussion. She tempered her criticism by stressing Jane's positive attributes before commenting adversely on her negative behavior.

She discounted Jane's question about feeble-mindedness in the same way she discounted Jane's suicide—with humor. She put the question up to Jane instead of answering it for her.

Jane's explanation brought obvious tension, which Miss Dare felt and noted but met with silence and followed by a tentative question which showed her *understanding of Jane's emotional problems* centered around religion.

Again Jane asked for *reassurance* in terms of the teacher's feelings, and Miss Dare responded again simply and honestly.

To Jane's question as to how the teacher got over her doubts, Miss Dare admitted some misgivings but followed the admission by injecting the notion that change means growth and that growth is painful. When simple techniques had reassured Jane that her problem was understood and was not a unique one, her tension subsided.

Miss Dare was often silent but occasionally conveyed sympathy by an apt question or a reassuring pat on the arm, as Jane *gained emotional release* in relating the salient points of her history.

The interview ended with the teacher's again using a fitting allusion to a humorous incident as a way of *giving direct counsel.*

The commonest elements in these two interviews are as follows: Both of them concern young, troubled adolescents whose difficulties have precipitated a crisis; both interviewers have a real desire to help; both the young people have an initial resistance either to the interviewer or to the interviewing situation. Both interviewers are cast in multiple roles in their school settings.

The desire of Carleton's teacher to understand and help was greater than her skill. The defects in the interview grew out of ignorance and a violation of some of the concepts of behavior. In the interview with Carleton, the setting was not conducive to rapport because Miss Martin's recent contact with Carleton had been severely disciplinary. Carleton's attitude toward authority prior to the stealing episode seems to have been a compound of resentment and defiance. There is no indication that the teacher understood the basis of his attitudes or of his behavior.

There is a question as to whether rapport was really achieved. Carleton was in a spot where he had to take such aid as Miss Martin offered. His acceptance of her bid to tell him all about it may have been due to the authority she represented. Through-out, she acted intuitively and impulsively. When she marched Carleton into the principal's office and made him apologize to Miss Karl she was flagrantly violating her promise to respect his confidence.

Before the end of the interview she had become emotionally involved. She herself had become the star of the performance and had taken the spotlight: it was her program and, because it was imposed and not fitted to Carleton's emotional or material needs, it would have little chance of being carried out. One suspects that its acceptance by Carleton was a momentary submission to the authority Miss Martin represented. Even if Carleton had accepted it there is little probability that such an ambitious program, planned in an exalted moment, could be maintained. We can only conjecture the feelings of frustration and failure the program's collapse would bring to the teacher and the unfortunate consequences such a failure would have for Carleton.

This interview points to a misuse of interviewing procedures, owing to a fundamental lack of understanding behavior. The teacher's sincere desire to help is responsible for the good points of the interview. It was unfortunate for her and for Carleton that her kindly impulses were not enough.

Jane's teacher knew Jane as an individual and skillfully applied her knowledge of psychology to the case. The aims first stated—to lessen or avoid emotional reactions, to be absolutely frank, and to let the interview be Jane's as far as possible—were all centered around Jane's welfare. She was able to carry out her plans because she was evidently experienced in good interviewing practices. By adherence to them she succeeded in decreasing Jane's tension. She met Jane's resistance by appealing to her sense of fairness and to her emotions by using examples keyed to the girl herself. Her humorous references were ones in which she and Jane could share a laugh.

One has the feeling that Miss Dare and Jane are at the beginning of a relationship in which Jane will ask, need, and receive competent help.

GENERAL SUGGESTIONS FOR THE SKILLFUL USE OF INTERVIEWING PROCESSES AND PROCEDURES

No rules of interviewing can be given as absolutes. However, Darley has made some general suggestions for counselors which should be helpful to the inexperienced interviewer.[42]

Since the interview is a situation in which the client learns something about himself, his attitudes, and the world into which he is going, Darley advises the interviewer to draw on his own educational experiences as a guide to effective techniques. He arrives at the following conclusions:

1. We do not learn if we are emotionally blocked or if our minds are distracted by personal problems that take our attention away from the classroom.
2. We do not learn if the vocabulary or ideas of teachers are over our heads.
3. We do not learn if too many ideas or facts are thrown at us at one time.
4. We do not learn if we are given no opportunity to participate in the learning experience. (This is a most important point.)
5. We do not learn if the halting expressions of our deep feelings and attitudes are received with scorn, a casual bit of reassurance, obvious embarrassment, or other attitudes which hinder expression.

Dr. Darley translates these conclusions into the following positive techniques:

1. Do not lecture or talk down to the client.
2. Use simple words and confine the information you give the client to a few ideas.

[42] Darley, *op. cit.*, pp. 12, 13.

3. Make sure that you know what the client really wants to talk about before giving any information or answering any questions.

4. Make sure that you sense or feel his attitudes because, if hostile, these will either block the discussion or keep out the main problems.

The following rules of procedure formulated for interviewing in mental hygiene are applicable to any type of personal counseling.[43] There are only a few rules of procedure since the difficulty of formulating them is great and most of the existing rules are in terms of what *not* to do.

1. Any show of intellectual brilliance or superiority on the part of the interviewer should be avoided. It is true that the person coming for help expects the counselor to be wiser than himself, but he does not want a display of wisdom thrust upon him.

2. Any show of haste is to be avoided if the patient's small store of self-importance is to be preserved. An easy, unhurried manner is one of the best ways of showing your interest in him.

3. Reference to the interviewer and his private affairs is to be avoided. It is obvious that the person seeking help is interested in himself, and in the worker only in so far as the worker can help him. The policy of avoiding self-reference has not been tested. There are many incidents where it has been used unwisely; there are also cases in which it has proved a valuable device. (The interview of Jane with her adviser is an illustration of wise use of personal experiences.)

4. The use of an illustration from another case history should ordinarily be avoided. It often fails to clarify the issues because, though it may apply on one point, its dissimilarities serve only to confuse. It may fail because it is not an exact parallel. It may fail because it implies that the counselor has already formed an opinion. Perhaps the strongest reason for not using an illustrative case example is that it is a violation of confidence. The inter-

[43] Hinckley and Fenlason, *op. cit.*, pp. 314, 315.

viewer who resorts to this technique is likely to see his patient lose interest in the recital or problems of other people even when the cases are parallel to his own. He sees dissimilarities rather than likenesses or he is too absorbed in his own difficulties to be interested in those of others.

5. It is unwise to make a statement that the patient is understood or to offer any explanation of why he is in his present condition. This applies to all forms of personnel work and often explains failures and limitations where a premature diagnosis may mean a faulty one. Aside from the fact that one is more than likely to be wrong in his conclusions even when the matter seems perfectly obvious, such a statement will cause the patient to recoil. His troubles have been made to seem too easy, and he feels he has been made to look a bit ridiculous. He knows very well that he has not told the whole story. He sees that the interviewer has been jumping at conclusions—that he has already classified his case. His problem is important to him. He knows it is too complicated for a quick explanation, and therefore the easy explanation must be wrong. He is right, of course. Such an explanation has only succeeded in undermining what little confidence he had in the interviewer and, by lowering his self-esteem, has forced him into closing the small opening the mental hygienist has made in his defenses.

6. It is usually necessary to supply the patient's need for immediate assistance with some bit of information or definite statement that will make him feel that the mental hygienist, too, is not blundering along in a thick fog. These statements, however, can usually be specific and confined to matters of fact. Compatible with this principle is the rule of avoiding any facile explanation of the patient's condition or any statement that he is completely understood.

7. The explanation of a mechanism can be made safely when it is obvious and sure, or when the explanation is not too far from ordinary rational thinking, as when the problems themselves are

on a conscious level. The method of putting facts in juxtaposition, so that the patient is able to draw the obvious conclusion, is the preferable and usual one, and avoids the need of explanation. It has been found in some instances that an explanation of mechanisms completely divorced from any application is a successful method. Giving the patient the abstract mechanism, leaving him to apply it personally when greater insight into his condition will permit, is more likely to succeed than any explanation in personal terms.

8. The technique of suggestion has fallen into disrepute. It must be recognized, however, that any prolonged contact of one individual with another involves suggestion. It would seem wise to study and control the use of suggestion as an implement rather than to deny its evidence or use. Whenever so-called transference is established, the mental hygienist's attitude, statements, questions, and even his very inactivity are all overvalued by the patient and carry with them the power to influence his emotional behavior.

The greatest objection to suggestion is that it is a superficial method of correcting evils or solving problems and is likely to impose on the patient an interpretation, an explanation, or a mode of action which has no validity for him and is only adopted because of his relation to the mental hygienist. An attempt is made to guard against this result, particularly in early interviews, by limiting suggestion to leading the patient to reëxamine his experiences from another point of view. There should be conscious avoidance of suggestion where there is danger of its being accepted as advice. Used in the analysis of the problem and the personality, suggestion is less dangerous than in a reëducation process. It goes wrong oftenest where it is used in a specific instance and is carried over by the patient to the general situation. It has been found most effective when the suggestion takes the form of a question implying a doubt on the part of the therapist as to the soundness of the patient's statement or attitude in regard to the matter in hand, thereby implying that there is another way of looking at the situation. Since the process of therapy consists in an endeavor to help the patient to another way of looking at things, suggestion of this kind seems valid. Optimistic suggestions are not employed for the obvious reason that the intelligent patient would be unlikely to accept them. The safeguard in the use of suggestions lies in the fact that an individual accepts only those which meet his material and psychological needs.

SUMMARY

The interview is a professional method based upon a simple but definite structure within a time-bound continuum; it accomplishes its purpose by the employment of processes and techniques; its dynamic is the interaction between the interviewer and the interviewee. Since human beings are its mediums, understanding motivation of behavior is essential.

A knowledge of structure is the framework of the interview. It keeps the interview from wandering aimlessly. Process is the movement toward accomplishing the purpose of the interview. It involves more than the use of the process itself if the purposes of the interview are to be achieved; it involves skill or expertness in its performance. Techniques or technical procedures are the devices by which the flow or movement in the interview is directed. The competent use of processes and techniques depends on understanding what is involved in the interaction between two such diverse individuals as the interviewer and the interviewee. Such understanding brings with it a sensitivity to the reaction of the other person, an idea of the meaning of the response, and an ability on the part of the interviewer to make his response apt to the purpose of the interview. Above all, process and technique must be consciously employed with an understanding of the individual—his environment, his personality, his behavior, and his problem—together with a knowledge of what the agency and the worker can do in the situation.

Good interviewing comes from the *skill* with which the interviewer uses in the client's behalf his knowledge, understanding, agency, the time prescribed, and the interaction between persons. There are no rules for skill in interviewing. There are some general suggestions as to what others have found successful and unsuccessful. The unsuccessful interviews have been primarily the result of not understanding behavior and personality or failing to utilize that knowledge in the practice of interviewing.

SUGGESTED ASSIGNMENTS

1. Describe an instance when you were given a definite period of time in which to accomplish some objective. How did you feel about this time limit? To what extent did it enable you to meet the objective?
2. Describe an interview in which you were the interviewee and where you felt the person with whom you were talking was not listening carefully to what you were saying. How did you react? What do you think might have caused the interviewer to respond this way?
3. Observe and record your observations and assumptions in some event or episode that involves social or health problems.
4. Give two examples of your own in which you either knowingly or unconsciously have applied processes and techniques. Comment on the success or failure of your attempts.
5. Have you ever been conscious of an illogical resistance to authority? On what do you think this was based?
6. Interview someone for some purpose. Record the dialogue. Analyze the elements of its success or failure.

RECOMMENDED SUPPLEMENTARY READING

Barbara, Dominick A., *The Art of Listening*, Charles C. Thomas, Publisher, 1958.

Bingham, Walter, and Moore, Bruce V., *How to Interview*, Harper & Brothers, 1931.

Bordin, Edward S., "Counseling Points of View—Non-Directive and Others," in E. G. Williamson (ed.), *Trends in Student Personnel Work*, University of Minnesota Press, 1949, pp. 120–129.

Darley, John, *The Interview in Counseling*, Retraining and Reemployment Administration, U.S. Department of Labor, 1946.

Garrett, Annette, *Counseling Methods for Personnel Workers*, Family Service Association of America, 1945.

Garrett, Annette, *Interviewing, Its Principles and Methods*, Family Service Association of America, 1942.

Gilbert, Ruth, *Public Health Nurse and Her Patient*, The Commonwealth Fund, 1940, chaps. 1, 3 (parts 1, 2, 3); chap. 6 (parts 1, 2).

Hamilton, Gordon, *Theory and Practice of Social Casework*, Columbia University Press, 1951, pp. 51–83.

Kahn, Robert L., and Cannell, Charles F., *The Dynamics of Interviewing*, John Wiley & Sons, 1957, pp. 22–65; 233–253.

Law, Stanley G. *Therapy Through Interview*, McGraw-Hill Book Company, 1948.

Lee, Porter, "Interviewing." In Mary Antoinette Cannon, and Philip Klein, *Social Case Work*, Columbia University Press, 1933, pp. 558–579.

Mann, James, "Human Relations," *Public Health Nursing*, December, 1948, p. 583.

Pease, Sybil, "Interview in Public Health Nursing," *Public Health Nursing*, March, April, May, 1933.

Reynolds, Bertha, "Dynamic Possibilities of the Limited Interview," *News Letter*, American Association of Psychiatric Social Workers, 10th Anniversary Number, 1938.

Rogers, Carl R., and Wallen, John L., *Counseling with Returned Service Men*, McGraw-Hill Book Company, 1946.

Swanson, Marie, "The Interview in School Nursing," *Public Health Nursing*, May, 1949, pp. 282–289.

Williamson, E. G., *How to Counsel Students*, McGraw-Hill Book Company, 1939.

Wrenn, C. Gilbert, "Client-Centered Counseling," *Educational and Psychological Measurement*, Winter, 1946, pp. 439–444.

Young, Pauline, *Interviewing in Social Work*, McGraw-Hill Book Company, 1935.

Chapter Five

ESSENTIAL ATTITUDES IN INTERVIEWING

> The skill to do more
> With the will to refrain.
>
> —Ruth Mason Rice

COMPONENTS OF SKILL IN INTERVIEWING

Attitudes as a Factor in Skill

A number of points made in the preceding chapters referred to the influence of attitudes on interviewing. This was emphatically highlighted in the last chapter's discussion about listening and the array of prejudices that interfere while an interviewer listens. Among the many who have dealt with the role and influence of attitudes on the interviewing process, Rogers is perhaps the most explicit about their direct influence on the interviewing method and techniques used. He points out:

. . . the counselor who is effective in client-centered therapy holds a coherent and developing set of attitudes deeply imbedded in his personal organization, a system of attitudes which is implemented by techniques and methods consistent with it. In our experience, the counselor who tries to use a "method" is doomed to be unsuccessful unless this method is genuinely in line with his own attitudes. On the other hand, the counselor whose attitudes are of the type which facilitate therapy may be only partially successful, because his attitudes are inadequately implemented by appropriate methods and techniques.[1]

[1] Carl R. Rogers, *Client-Centered Therapy,* Houghton Mifflin Company, 1951, pp. 19–20.

The term "attitude" as it is used in interviewing refers to the interviewer's reflected position of his feelings or moods.

As interviewers experience the learning which deepens their interviewing skills, they are forced to deal directly with a range of complications arising from the network of their own biases and prejudices. This is a painful process for many learners. For some persons it is impossible to break and work through the attitudinal barriers which block them from learning and mastering skills in interviewing. On the other hand, those who have overcome these obstacles in a creditable fashion have mastered the essentials of interviewing. The use of processes and techniques carries with it conscious or unconscious attitudes which affect the interviewer's behavior. Attitudes, inextricably bound up in all activities, are a salient component of the interviewer's skill.

Any skillful interview is tempered and forged by a good working relationship between the interviewer and the interviewee. Between worker and client, the relationship influences every point and can make the interview a real participation or mere intrusion into the affairs of another by taking advantage of his needs. Which course it follows depends upon the *attitudes* of the interviewer toward himself; toward his client, patient, or advisee; toward his agency, under whose auspices he has legitimately entered the private life of another; and toward the communities in which each party to the interview is living.

An attitude remains when the incidents of its origin may have been forgotten. It is a dynamic factor in the interview, always subject to change in order to fit each new situation or event. It has been rightly described as the worker's consciousness of his professional status.

Attitude and the Ability to Individualize

Attitude, according to Lucy Wright, is the dominant spirit of the individual and the core of the interviewer's skill.[2] The inter-

[2] Lucy Wright, "The Worker's Attitude as an Element in Social Case Work," *Interviews, Interviewers, and Interviewing*, Family Service Association of America, 1931, pp. 3–7.

viewer's attitude has potentialities for either good or bad. An insincere attitude, one which is donned or doffed like a coat, is always bad. Any attitude flexible enough to meet each given situation as if for the first time, "like the current with which the magnet meets the needle," is good.

Attitude is conceived by Miss Wright as the application of spirit to human affairs, an innate quality in every individual, capable of cultivation, development, and change. Attitude represents to her at the same time beliefs, principles, and plans of action; it stands for states of mind and ensuing behavior. Through her writing she makes the reader see it as she conceives it—"a glowing, dynamic word."

Miss Wright uses Mr. Bly, the window washer in Galsworthy's *Windows*, as an example of an attitude which leads to a search for significant states of mind rather than to the mere application of rules. In *Windows*, Mr. Bly's daughter, an unmarried mother, has been on trial for suffocating her baby. She hadn't wanted to kill the child, she explains, she only wanted to save it from living. Mr. Bly's comments, in reviewing the events of the trial, are illuminating:

BLY: Why, I've known people who could see nothing but themselves and their own families unless they were drunk. At my daughter's trial, I see right into the lawyers, judge and all. There she was, hub of the whole thing, and all they could see of 'er was 'ow she affected 'em personally. One tryin' to get 'er guilty, the other tryin' to get 'er off, and the judge summin' 'er up cold blooded.

MR. MARCH: But that's what they're paid for, Mr. Bly.

BLY: Ay, though which of them was thinkin' 'ere's a little dancin' creature? What's she feelin'? What's her complaint? Impersonal-like. I like to see a man do a bit of speculating with his mind off himself for once.

We are also indebted to Miss Wright for two illustrations of consummate skill in the interview, both of which demonstrate a decidedly different set of attitudes of an interviewer concerned with significant states of mind. The interviews were conducted by Francis Bardwell, at a time when he was the inspector of almshouses for the state of Massachusetts. They were given to Miss Wright in response to her request (during a telephone conversation) as examples of the potency of a flexible imagination in interviewing. Mr. Bardwell's first interview was with Aunt Anne:

> What you refer to as flexible imagination I had always been pleased to call the "angle of approach"—one of the most important things in personal contact with dependent people.
>
> Here is an episode about Aunt Anne, who wanted to be "took care of." I had been sent for because Aunt Anne had refused to do any longer the little tasks required of her at the almshouse, and had retired to her room, putting on her only best dress—a black alpaca made in the seventies. There came the expected knock, and she bowed with serenity as the caller came in. From a formal and dignified attitude she deflected not one iota. In state, best dress as an armor for aged dignity, she received her caller. "My, but you're dressed up, Aunt Anne." "Yes, from now on I'm always going to be." "No more help?" the caller queried. "No." The monosyllable was snapped out. "Is this fair?" "Yes, and ain't it time for rest and for best alpacas? If I'm to rest here, it must be from now on." This was delivered severely and in measured tones. She wouldn't weaken, although she began to wonder at the courage she had somehow acquired; she would see it through. "You're too young to quit, Aunt Anne. Just a few years longer— a little help here in the hard places—and then the best dress and folded hands." "Go on!" she taunted. "The best dress and folded hands and a handful of people saying 'Her smile is natural.' Oh, I've heard it, many funerals where I've helped. Perhaps you don't know it—you haven't looked me up in the book; if you had you would have known I should have quit years ago. I know I don't look my age. Stout folks seldom do after seventy, but I'm eighty-four. Isn't it time I quit? If I'm ever to sit and rock and rest, isn't it from now on? Fourteen years I'm living on borrowed time, so I'm through." She paused, looked out of the window, saw the near-lying meadow and beyond, the low Cape hills. A tear welled to her eye and slowly rolled down her withered cheek. The spirit of revolt was gone; she was in retreat; she was a woman again, and wept. With an effort she controlled her emotions, and quite calmly said, "I want to be took care of, only that." The caller said, "Tell me all about it, Aunt Anne," and laid a kindly hand upon her shoulder.

Then followed the complete unfolding of the story of her life: how through her childhood she had tended her mother's children, then her own children, then her children's children, finally doing tasks in the almshouse because her loyal children had died, and her disloyal ones neglected her. As you can imagine, she was given the chance she craved, even finally to the ambition of her lifetime, being waited on in her bed by a nurse in a cap.

A portion of a second interview of Mr. Bardwell's demonstrates similar skill with Bardwell's gift for individualizing the man with whom he was dealing. Mr. Bardwell called this story "Raising Dates."

Timothy had demanded an audience. Timothy evidently had a grievance, the nature of which, however, I could not fathom. So when I stepped into the smoking-room for my audience I found Mr. Murphy alone, occupying an armchair, and evidently in an anticipatory mood. I resolved to confine myself to the strict language of diplomacy, so at the door I stood and bowed saying: "Mr. Timothy Murphy, I presume?" "Your presume is right," was the answer. "Oh," I replied, "I'm pleased to renew an acquaintance," and shook hands. "You may not be so pleased when I'm through with you." "I understand, Mr. Murphy, you have a bone to pick with me, and I'm hoping it's only a chicken bone." " 'Tis not! 'Tis the hind leg of an elephant." "Oh, I'm relieved (you will notice my use of the language of diplomacy), for it might have been the wishbone of a mastodon." "Never mind all that, 'tis a big bone. If I knew my geography as well as you do, I'd be back at you with a dragon's backbone, but that's neither here or there." "Well?" I questioned, resolving to let him state his own case in his own way. The old man shuffled his feet, twitched his hands on the arms of his chair, cleared his throat and began: "Do I look like a man who raises dates? I ask you that, man to man, do I?" "No," I answered deliberately, "you do not look like a man who raises dates. If anyone had asked me what was your specialty, I should have suggested something tropical, but not dates, even if dates are raised in hot climates," and so on.

The point of this story hinged on an unfortunate misunderstanding of the expression *raison d'être*, which had been used in Mr. Murphy's hearing without explaining that it meant the reason for being.

Mr. Bardwell's own comment on these interviews shows that his skill was based in part on his recognition of the needs of the individual as a person.

"You will see the entirely different angle of approach in these two cases. I could not have used the language of diplomacy with Aunt Anne; it would have been an insult. Timothy expected it: a dignified hearing, with its humorous side patent to both of us, and only touched on in by-play—and my man was Irish. Aunt Anne was Yankee to the uttermost generation."

The other components of the interviewer's skill were his knowledge of the physiology and psychology of old people, his experience in handling them, and that ability to relate himself to other people in terms of their needs which we call *empathy*.

Empathy as a Factor in Skill

Empathy is the capacity of an individual to identify himself with another in terms of the way the other would feel and act. It is the essence of understanding the *why* of another's attitudes and behavior.

A rudimentary example of empathy is found in an apocryphal tale of Jason, a lost donkey. The whole village joined Jason's distressed owner in his futile search for the animal but it was a feeble-minded boy who triumphantly led the donkey into the village square. "Where was he?" "How did you find him?" cried the villagers as they crowded around. "Oh, it was simple," was the laconic response. "I just thought of where I'd go if I was Jason, so I went to the glen and brought him home."

Identification in terms of empathy is displayed by Miss Housman in "Home Visit." This is a glimpse of a student's reflections after a field-work visit to an old age assistance client. It reveals something of the same kind of empathy and ability to individualize as Mr. Bardwell's. A social case worker will recognize that the underlined part of the account is the recorded result of the interview. The rest gives the worker's impressions, attitudes, and a little of her philosophy.

<u>October, 1944, Visited Martha Matthews to reinvestigate her eligibility
      for Old Age Assistance</u> . . .
<u>Mrs. Matthews lives in a very pleasant neighborhood</u> . . .
Autumn is setting fire to your shabby house, Martha.
Scarlet and gold flame touches the gray unpainted shadows of your
      house,
And burns in brisk October air. Wind blows the red and golden sparks
Over the withered grass. . . .   .
<u>One market trip per week per family</u> . . . But you can walk
Over the blown leaves along October's flaming road,
To buy a Last Supper at your neighborhood grocery. . . . <u>Shall I say
No allowance is required for transportation?</u>
Will you walk proudly in October fire,
Into that last cold winter, Death?
When John got hurt, he sat and rocked and swore at the Democrats.
He said he'd worked his fingers to the bone to buy this house.
He said he'd come mighty close to stealing,
To pay taxes year after year.
He said by God a taxpayer was entitled to something
Without all this fuss. John talked real tough.
But you didn't talk tough, Martha.
You took pride in your two thin hands and strangled it, for him . . .
See, your dead pride is here in the old typewritten record:
<u>A ton of coal for John and Martha Matthews.</u> . . .
<u>A grocery order for three dollars</u> . . .
When John died, you sold your home,
But the people let you rent one room of it.
You sold your household goods:
But they let you keep that chair he rocked in. . . .
Sat and rocked and swore and said he'd be everlastingly damned
If he'd crawl on his stomach for anybody. . . .
You sold your home for nineteen hundred dollars and ninety-five cents

                    .   .   .   .

You paid the mortgage, funeral bills and the doctor bills. . . .
<u>Mrs. Matthews has cash in excess of five hundred dollars.</u> . . .
You paid the grocer and the druggist. . . .
You lived for a long time on the rest, Martha:
And when it was gone, you applied for Old Age Assistance.
Now you sit quietly in John's chair, and sometimes speak to God;
But you don't bother Him about the Democrats,
Or even about the Republicans. . . .

You figure He knows His business.
Your landlady cheated you on the price of your house.
She cheats you still. Mrs. Matthews' rent is excessive.
How shall I budget the price your spirit pays
For a room in your own house?
You pay cash for your food, and Mr. Amanti, the grocer,
Gives you each week a little more than you paid for.
Mrs. Matthews states that she manages very well on her grant . . .
Perhaps not so well, Martha, if it were not for Mr. Amanti.
Mrs. Matthews has no living relatives. . . .
But you did have a son, Martha.
You were in labor three days, and your son died
In the long violence of being born. His head was hurt;
He would never have had any sense. It was better he died . . .
Your son had soft and thick brown hair—
His mouth was small and soft and sweet—
He lay warm in your hands that brief while,
And the living minutes have sufficed the years of your life.
Mrs. Matthews is showing increasing signs of senility. . . .
Now you are old, you sit alone; and in that thin and soft and insubstan-
    tial voice, talk with your son. . . .
She has no resources. . . .
But what of the assessed value of your spirit, Martha?
It is hard to appraise.
There is no statutory limit
On the value of a human soul.[3]

Empathy depends primarily on the worker's ability to individualize. It is that attitude of awareness of the significance of
the feelings which underlie another's words. It is listening with
the heart as well as with the mind. It is not to be confused with
false sentiment, because it is built upon an understanding of
human beings as well as a knowledge of the individual's circumstances. Sympathy must be controlled and directed in professional use.

A destructive form of identification, the direct opposite of
empathy, is *projection*. Projection is the kind of identification in
which the interviewer imagines how he would act in circumstances similar to those of the interviewee's. The interviewer

---

[3] Mary W. Housman, "Home Visit," *The Survey Midmonthly*, February,
1945, p. 43.

maintains his own identity and feelings but projects them into the interviewee's position. The result is an emotional involvement where the worker sees himself rather than his client and becomes blind to the reasons for the client's feelings and conduct.

The worker's own past experiences play their part in both empathy and projection. There is no denying that everyone sees more clearly in others what he has experienced himself. Reactions differ by virtue of past experiences. It is failure to recognize this fact which makes an interviewer project his own attitudes rather than respect those of his client.

Objectivity as a Necessary Attribute of Skill

Dr. John Brown,[4] a famous Scotch physician and surgeon, distinguishes between maudlin sympathy and a sympathy that helps. Herewith he is also describing *objectivity*.

The incident he recounts revolves around an operation for breast cancer in his student days before anesthetics were used.

The following day, at noon, the students came in, hurrying up the great stair. At the first landing place, on a small well-worn blackboard, was a bit of paper fastened by wafers, and many remains of old wafers beside it. On the paper were the words: "An operation today . . . J. B., clerk."

Up ran the youths, eager to secure good places; in they crowded, full of interest and talk.

"What's the case? Which side is it?"

Don't think them heartless; they are neither better nor worse than you or I; they get over their professional horrors, and into their proper work; in them pity, as an *emotion*, ending in itself or at best in tears and a long-drawn breath, lessens, while pity, as a *motive*, is quickened and gains power and purpose. It is well for poor human nature that this is so.[4]

Dr. Brown's prescription of restraint of pity results in objectivity. The ability to be objective involves both control of attitudes and self-discipline in emotional responses so that the worker will be left free to use his knowledge and skill.

[4] Dr. John Brown will be recalled as the author of *Rob and His Friends*, from which this excerpt was taken, and *Marjorie Fleming*.

Students and beginning workers are sometimes overconscious of a professional attitude and perplexed at the seeming incompatibility of the sincere feeling of friendliness needed for a good working relationship and the objectivity which is essential.

Confusion arises first from mistaking friendliness for the deeper sentiment of friendship. Friendship is a form of love. The unwilling dependence of a client on his professional helper precludes the reciprocal response demanded of friendship. This does not preclude a friendly attitude, however. Florence Hollis has expressed a doubt that a social case worker can be really helpful to one he dislikes, since his interest in, and liking for, a person must come out of the client's need for the professional worker and the worker's competence to give help.[5] It can never be a response of the two personalities to each other in a free, responsive relationship. Whenever friendliness gets out of hand and involves a deeper attachment, it is because the worker lacks an understanding of the unconscious response and so becomes entangled in a professional relationship he is not equipped to handle. This relationship is called *transfer,* a term descriptive of a dynamic process in psychoanalysis and other therapeutic practice. Transference is a universal phenomenon which occurs in significant measure in every human relationship. Psychoanalysts recognized and named it.

Dr. Kubie explains that transference in psychoanalysis refers to the fact that in adult years our relationships to others are compounded of both unconscious and conscious elements; the unconscious elements consist largely of attitudes, needs, feelings, and purposes transferred or carried over unconsciously from the attitudes, needs, feelings, and purposes toward others developed in infancy and early childhood.[6]

Its use in professional practice calls for specific, formal prep-

[5] Florence Hollis, *Social Case Work in Practice,* Family Service Association of America, 1939, pp. 6, 7.

[6] Lawrence S. Kubie, M.D., *Practical and Theoretical Aspects of Psychoanalysis,* International Universities Press, Inc., 1950, p. 57.

aration. For the interviewer without such professional education an attitude of friendliness compounded of warmth and acceptance is sound and safe. Such an attitude is neither cold nor impersonal.

Confusion also arises from thinking of objectivity and impersonality as synonymous. An interviewer may be friendly and still be objective. He can be sensitive to the feelings of his client without becoming emotionally involved. The skilled professional interviewer is always himself. It is not necessary for him to keep his mind on his professional attitude if he is competent and has the personal qualities which make his relationships with others a natural medium.

Webster says objectivity is the tendency to view events, phenomena, ideas as external and apart from self-consciousness. The simplicity of this definition gives little indication of the importance of the term to an interviewer. Objectivity in interviewing means that personal emotions are not allowed to enter into the situation.

Sometimes objectivity is lost through identification with the client, or the projection of the interviewer's feelings into those of the client. Objectivity for the interviewer is a professional relationship showing a grasp of the situation and an understanding of the person involved which results in a realistic and practical point of view, unbiased by prejudice and temperament. It is the capacity to regard a situation or event without personal emotional involvement; it is self-discipline which enables one to withhold and restrain one's own emotional reactions while viewing the predicament of another.

Sensitivity to Another's Feelings as a Factor in Skill

Lack of objectivity generally means concentration of an interviewer on his own feelings and a resultant insensibility to the feelings of the interviewee. There is no incompatibility between objectivity and a sensitivity to the feelings of others. Seeming insensibility and the resultant lack of skill in interviewing may stem from inexperience. Miss D., one of the leaders today in her field, looks back with horror at a student interview of her training days.

Mrs. Black, a former schoolteacher, had been reported by the Public Hospital to the Family Welfare Association because she had neglected to arrange for a needed operation following her last confinement. The family had had a brief contact with the agency at a time when Mr. Black had been unemployed owing to illness. The student worker was given the task of encouraging Mrs. Black to make arrangements for a clinic appointment. An incidental purpose of the visit was to secure additional pertinent information concerning Mrs. Black and her family which would enable the agency to be of better service.

Following swiftly on Miss D.'s visit, Mrs. Black telephoned the supervisor of the agency and, protesting incoherently against the imposition of the visit, demanded assurance that her privacy would not again be invaded. The supervisor in discussing the situation with Miss D. was unable to understand from her report what could have upset Mrs. Black. She therefore asked her to reconstruct the interview as nearly verbatim as possible.

From the reconstructed dialogue the reasons for Mrs. Black's indignation were made clear to both supervisor and student. They should be equally apparent to the reader.

This is the report:

> Student R. D. visited Mrs. Black. She was writing letters but paused to greet worker and offer her a chair. Louise, the young daughter, interrupted to show mother her report card. Mrs. Black took the card and read the grades aloud saying, "No A's but I don't see any flunks either."
>
> "Why are you having difficulty with arithmetic, Louise?" worker asked.
>
> "I never could get it, I don't understand it."
>
> "Do you help her, Mrs. Black?"

"I have been helping her but they don't allow her to take any books home now. I think they want the children to rest."

"Are you sitting where you can see the board? Does it hurt your eyes to read what is written on it?"

"I sit in the front seat. I got glasses yesterday but they make me dizzy so I don't like to put them on."

"You will have to become accustomed to your glasses. Try them for about a week, then if you still feel dizzy and nauseated take them back to your school nurse. She will tell you what to do. I'm glad you have glasses. Now when are you going to see about your own condition, Mrs. Black? I believe Miss Clare gave you the clinic dates, can I make an appointment for you?"

"That won't be necessary. I'll go when I get ready. I haven't time right now," Mrs. Black said.

"You should make the time. Waiting will not improve your condition. You have waited a long time now, haven't you? Did the injury occur at Louise's birth?"

"Yes."

"Where was she born?"

"At Lake Winston."

"Was Edwin born there also?"

"No, he was born at Parker's Prairie."

"Where were you born, Mrs. Black?"

"Why do you want to know?" she asked worker.

"We have to have a certain amount of routine information on our records, and that is one of the things we want to know."

"What else do you want to know, can you tell me?" Mrs. Black asked.

Worker passed her a small piece of paper on which she had made notes of missing social information which she thought might be needed. Mrs. Black looked it over, handed it back and said, "Sorry, but I can't answer those questions."

"Why?"

"Because I don't want anything about my parents on your records. Anything I have done I'm responsible for but I don't want their names disgraced. I'm sorry I told you about the children. I don't want them to grow up knowing that they were a family welfare case and have that disgrace hang over their heads all of their lives."

"It isn't a disgrace to be known to a social service agency,

Mrs. Black. The agency wants to help you. In order to do the most for you, they have to know something about your history, and these things are just a part of the history. The information obtained from all clients is treated as confidential. When you attend a clinic you give the doctor or hospital worker this information; you give part of it to the school and don't consider that a disgrace, do you?"

"But that is not charity," Mrs. Black answered.

"Family welfare is not charity either; you are receiving no financial aid at present. Service from a family welfare agency does not mean that you are down and out. Money is only one of the many problems that come up in a family. Think this over, Mrs. Black, and see if you can't understand that we are trying to help you; we don't want information just because we are curious. You can help us a great deal by working with us."

Mrs. Black rather reluctantly gave the nationality of her parents and their religion, and said very proudly, "They were Americans."

She knew little about Mr. Black's parents.

Worker thanked her for the information, urged her to think over what she had said about the agency, and suggested that she call at the office and let them know how the family were getting along.

Mrs. Black did call back but only to ask that she not be bothered by any more calls from the agency. When the student had reproduced the dialogue as nearly as possible she discovered why the interview had been unsuccessful. She was able to see that she had been authoritative and presumptuous in the questions she had asked and insensitive to Mrs. Black's reactions. It was noted in extenuation that she was a new worker who had been briefed by her supervisor to accomplish definite objectives and given only a vague idea of why she was to get certain information and no idea of its use.

Fortunately for the worker, Mrs. Black reacted against the authoritative request for personal information. From the protest, the worker learned the important lesson that it was not the agency's policies or demands which gave her the right to ask questions of a client; it was the client's needs. These could be better met if the agency knew certain pertinent facts.

Sympathy, empathy, objectivity, and sensitivity are all fundamental attributes of the good interviewer, but without the knowledge of behavior which enables him to employ them with professional skill, they would merely be desirable personal qualities for anyone. Harnessed to such knowledge, they enable the worker to use himself wisely and professionally.

Often our own blind spots, or areas in our lives in which we are not comfortable, give rise to strong feelings which may interfere with our objectivity at any point. It is not the fact that he feels strongly which should concern the interviewer; what he is able to do about his feelings is his concern.

The worker can get some idea of his ability to be objective by questioning his own attitudes. A teacher of case work sometimes asks her students to list their own special dislikes. The answers are varied and individual. It is a superficial listing, of course, but worth careful exploration by each student; for study may lead to a discovery of intolerances and even to some inkling of their genesis.

It is fortunate for the client that there are workers who prefer work with children, others who would rather work with adolescents or delinquents, and still others who are interested in specific family problems, or in the aged. It is unfortunate that our present stage of development in helping in human problems seldom gives the client the privilege of selecting his own worker.

Feelings of Insecurity and Lack of Skill

An attitude that has a special impact on the interview is the interviewer's feeling of his own inadequacy in a given situation. Garrett remarks that the worker may worry about his ability to use the interview to put the client at ease, to draw him out, to uncover and meet his resistances, to know the significance of what he is saying, and to select the significant facts in what he reveals by his remarks and behavior.[7] Without being able to

---

[7] Annette Garrett, *Interviewing, Its Principles and Methods*, Family Service Association of America, 1942, p. 9.

articulate his worries he is concerned over his ability to use interviewing processes and procedures. Lack of experience increases his anxiety.

Darley comments on the interviewer's feeling of insecurity in slightly different terms.[8] He recognizes that the new worker is likely to be a bit frightened by the curtain's going up on a play in which he has not rehearsed his part. Because of this he may tend to omit his most important lines, or to ad-lib too much. Neither reaction is conducive to a good interview. The person to be interviewed may also be ill at ease in the presence of a stranger. "He may feel that the interview is just one more step in the run-around he has been getting; he may be particularly anxious for some kind of help"; he may cover his uncertainty by an appearance of arrogance or anger; or he may be resistant to the whole idea of the interview as an intrusion into his personal affairs.

The apprehension of the inexperienced worker is vividly expressed by students who were asked to record their thoughts as well as the give-and-take of the interview. The two interviews reproduced here were initial experiences of students who since have become proficient in social case work and interviewing.

Mr. H.'s Interview with Mrs. A.

It's no secret—I wasn't at all happy about this assignment. After all, this interview was to be my first of this type, and how in the world could I ever manage to remember the sequence of things discussed, and the particular meanings they held for me? And how embarrassing it must be to have a first interview brought to the critical attention of a class.

I studied all of the available information quite carefully and after talking the case over with my supervisor, I started out for my client's home, armed with note paper and an outline of the points to be cleared, enclosed in a large official-looking envelope.

I knew that I would find in this home a 55-year-old man, totally incapacitated with cancer: his 45-year-old wife suffering

[8] John Darley, *The Interview in Counseling,* Retraining and Reemployment Administration, U.S. Dept. of Labor, 1946, p. 12.

from phlebitis; and four children (one boy, 16 years of age; three girls—13, 9, and 7 respectively).

WORKER: Good afternoon, ma'am. Are you Mrs. A? (Certainly not—this woman is too healthy-looking.)

MRS. A.: Y-e-e-s?

WORKER: (Oh, yes it was about two months ago that she was ill. Of course, she must be feeling much better now.) I am Mr. Hart of the County Welfare Board. I have come to talk to you about your application for assistance. (What an ungodly time to visit—in the middle of a washday.)

MRS. A: Oh yes—I've been expecting you (*as worker steps into the kitchen*). I know these dirty dishes look bad, but I've been busy with the washing this afternoon, and couldn't take care of them. (*She hurries around putting things away.*)

WORKER: That's quite all right, Mrs. A. (Taking stock of room, with its table, five chairs, day bed, sewing machine, and small stand with drawers. I noticed particularly the large picture of the Last Supper on the wall and the Holy Bible on the table.) You have a nice home. (Gosh, I'd like to have a place like this. Apartment hunting is getting me down.)

MRS. A.: Yes, we like it. We have six rooms and bath downstairs, and five rooms and bath upstairs. I'd like to put in a furnace downstairs. That would help the family upstairs as well as us. And maybe I could raise the rent a little on the people living upstairs.

WORKER: Oh, yes, you do rent the upstairs, don't you? (The records show $20.00 a month—what a steal!!!)

MRS. A.: Yes—but we are only getting $20.00 a month, just enough to pay the installments on the house each month.

WORKER: (*Sits down and pulls from large brown envelope note paper and notes with which to check on vital information.*) (Her husband must be asleep, of course. I'll ask about him in a minute, if she doesn't volunteer the information. Now—how to start?) I am here, Mrs. A., to help you in every way possible. But before I can do that, I need some more information.

MRS. A.: Yes?

WORKER: Have there been any changes in your family or your financial situation since you applied for assistance, Mrs. A.? (Hope she understands what I mean.)

MRS. A.:   No, I guess there haven't been any—except when he left.

WORKER: When who left?

MRS. A.:   Mr. A. He died on the seventh of January—or was it the second? I guess it was the second.

WORKER: I'm sorry. (Rather casual about it, isn't she? But she has expected him to go soon for some time, according to the case record.)

MRS. A.:   Yes, we took poor A. to the Veterans' Hospital on December 24th, and he died on January 2nd. It was 2:30 in the afternoon, I think. No, maybe it was 7:30 in the evening. I don't know when, exactly. But any way, he's gone. He was awful bad with cancer, you know.

WORKER: Is your sister still with you? (She's not too sharp at remembering dates and times.)

MRS. A.:   No, she went back home after I got up on my feet for a while. Her husband was pretty mad because she stayed to help me for so long—about six weeks, I guess.

WORKER: Have there been any other changes?

MRS. A.:   Oh, yes—Luke came home from the Army last Saturday, and he's staying here now. He has a good job in Indiana, but he may get one here.

WORKER: Where is your son Charles now?

MRS. A.:   Oh, Charles is in Chicago, and he wrote that he will be out of the Navy in about ten days. I think he is going to a trade school when he gets back. Charles sent me some money about a month ago, and I bought a piano with it, so that Lucille can learn to play. It cost me $250. That seems like a lot of money, but I guess you can't get them cheaper anywhere nowadays. I have started Shirley taking lessons on the accordion for $2.00 a week, and Lucille is taking lessons on the piano for $1.25 a week.

WORKER: (Hm—an extravagant woman, apparently. Applied for aid and then bought a piano and started children on music lessons. Probably like that with all finances.) Will you tell me a bit about your own life and that of your husband, Mrs. A.? I mean, about your own childhood and education and the things you have been interested in, and where you have lived, and things of that sort. (Gosh, time is flying and I have so much yet to find out. This is going to be a longer job than I expected.)

We discussed at some length the history of the family and the roles played by its various members. During the last part of the interview we got down to the financial problems. I found that a Veterans' Administration representative had taken her application for benefits, and had almost promised $50.00 per month; that Mrs. A. is now receiving an allotment of $37.00 per month from her son Charles; that her sixteen-year-old boy, living at home, is at present earning $150.00 per month; that she had not as yet checked on Social Security Survivors' benefit; that she knew of no life insurance policy carried by her husband, but that someone had said that she *might* be eligible for $2000.00 life insurance benefits; that she and her husband each received health and accident benefits for about 14 weeks; and that her total debts amount to around $42.00. It appeared from these possibilities that this family might be ineligible for aid.

The close of the interview went something like this:

MRS. A. (*hunting through several boxes of old letters, clippings, etc.*): I know I can find that insurance policy for you, Mr. Hart.

WORKER: Don't bother about the insurance papers now, Mrs. A. I have taken enough of your time, and I must be getting back to the office now. I'll plan to call on you again on Monday afternoon—that is, if that's all right with you. In the meantime, you may have the opportunity to call the Veterans' Administration representative, Mr. Everett, regarding your pension chances, and check regarding the possibility of a life insurance payment. You might check with the Social Security Old Age and Survivors' Insurance Section. I can talk over your various findings with you on Monday. I can be of more aid to you then when we know more about everything. (She certainly doesn't have much sense about keeping fingers on contracts, insurance policies, bills, etc.)

MRS. A.: You have been so understanding. It's nice to have someone interested in you.

WORKER: That's my job, Mrs. A. I am here to try to understand your problems, and help you as much as possible with them. (Good thing she doesn't know that I'm new at this work. Wonder whether she really means that?)

MRS. A.: You have many strange cases to handle, I guess, haven't you?

WORKER: My work is interesting. Good-by, Mrs. A. I'll try to stop in again on Monday. (Gosh, I'm awkward at this. I'm still lacking quite a bit of necessary information. This is only my first visit. I surely hope to do better next time.)

MRS. A.: Good-by. Thank you.

MR. BOE'S INTERVIEW WITH THE DOES

OBJECTIVE OF INTERVIEW

To get acquainted with my clients. A social call only. No business transactions contemplated.

SITUATION (FROM CASE RECORD)

The Doe family of three persons live in one large room on the second floor of an old mansion at a busy traffic point just outside of the city's downtown district.

Mr. Doe is 36 years of age and has been almost continuously confined to bed for 1½ years with a serious heart ailment. He can be up on his feet only a few minutes at a time. When he goes to the hospital for treatment twice a month it is necessary to get a couple of men to carry him downstairs to the taxi. Obviously the family should live on the ground floor but such a place is not now available.

Mrs. Doe is 34 years of age and is able to work although she has a case of arrested t.b. She was about to attend business school last autumn but was prevented by the serious illness of her husband at that time.

The boy, Junior, age 4½, is healthy and normal but there are no other children in his locality for him to play with.

INTERVIEW JANUARY, 10:45 A.M.

When I come to the large old mansion I see why this family need to find living quarters on the ground floor, preferably somewhere else than here. There are steps from the sidewalk to the walk leading to the house, many high steps to the porch and a long wide stairway to the second floor. The hallways are very clean but as I peer at the dark doorways I wish I had a flashlight. I find the right door, knock and listen. Dishes are rattling. I imagine a gloomy room where a wan woman is washing dishes and an emaciated man lies in bed. I knock a little louder and then the door opens quietly and a pleasant rosy-cheeked woman stands before me. (It is Mrs. Doe.)

ME: My name is Mr. Boe. I am the new ADC worker. (After-thought—I hope she knows what ADC means.)

SHE: Come in. (She is very pleasant. Perhaps she is resigned to the necessity of these visits.)

The room is large and cheerfully bright from the three windows, which look out on a park. I walk around a table on which there are a typewriter, papers, and dishes. A man is in bed in the farther corner by the windows.

SHE: The place is terribly dirty and upset. (Usual feminine re-mark. It is disorderly all right but I realize this one room is kitchen, bedroom and parlor.)

ME: It's perfectly all right. How do you do, Mr. Doe. (Hearty tone.)

HE: Take a chair. (He looks much healthier and plumper than I expected. She's pleasingly plump also. Both are reasonably tall and nice looking. I sit down on a davenport facing the bed and Mrs. Doe stands in front of me and to one side looking at both of us.)

ME (to Mr. Doe): How are you feeling these days?

HE: Oh I feel fine. I have no pains or nothing to bother me. But I don't have any strength. I try to walk around the room but I'm too weak to stay up. I haven't any energy and I seem to improve so slowly. (He speaks so cheerfully it's almost de-ceiving. He's trying to be patient.)

ME (slowly and carefully): I understand it takes a long time to build up in a case of that kind. It must take a lot of patience to stay in bed so long. (I guess I didn't say the wrong thing.)

SHE: He's been in bed for a year and a half. (Just a statement—no sadness, censure or anything particular.)

HE: Oh the days pass very quickly for me. (I hadn't asked him if his days went slowly. He answered as if he had been asked that question a lot.)

SHE: Yes, he says the days go real quick for him. He says he hardly gets time to do all the things he wants to. (To do what things? He can hardly sit up in bed. Why this stressing of how quickly the days go by?)

ME: Well, that's good that time doesn't go slow. (It is, isn't it?)

HE: Take off your coat, why don't you? (I'd forgotten about that so I do it. He is very well mannered.)

ME: What do you do to spend the time? (Obviously he reads.)
HE: I write a lot of letters and read quite a bit. (Then he must have relatives and friends who are interested in him. Why not?)

I realize Mrs. Doe is being left out of the conversation. She keeps on standing and seems interested. They both strike me very favorably.

ME: What kind of reading do you like—magazines—books—or what? (Probably *Crazy Comics*.)
HE: I like news magazines and articles. I don't read fiction much but I like a historical novel now and then. I got a subscription to the *Reader's Digest* for Christmas and one to *Time* magazine but that hasn't started coming yet. (Somewhat baffled I note that he speaks especially well and his tastes are good—I like to read the same things.)
ME: That's just what I like to read too. (Buddies.)
HE: I like to read historical novels. They tell how people used to live. I don't think I'd like to have lived then—we have more comforts now than the best-off people had in the old times.
ME: Yes, I saw some of the old castles in England where the nobles used to live. They were very cold and drafty. Glass was hard to get so the windows were made very small. It must have been very disagreeable in winter-time. (Why did I drag all this in? Traveled, did I? Now maybe they think I'm one of those wealthy volunteer workers.)
HE: Yes, we are lucky to be so comfortable these days. (I am still irritated at my personal remarks and possible misunderstanding.)
ME (*drowning myself*):   I'm not wealthy—the government took care of my visit to England. I was very interested in the castles, churches and historical things and how the people live now-a-days. (Isn't this awful—how awkward I'm putting this. Now I've dragged in my Army service.)
HE: Oh, you were in the Army, I suppose? My brother was in the Army in Europe and he said things were pretty bad there.
ME: Yes, the countries are badly beat up and the people haven't much to eat or wear.
HE: We are lucky to be so well off over here.
SHE: It's wonderful that we have these welfare organizations. They do such wonderful work. I don't know what we'd do with-

out them. (She radiates gratitude about it all. How cheerfully they take their long stretch of misfortune. They can't be this happy all the time.)

ME: Well, these days it's possible for all of us to have some misfortune and we should get help if we need it. (Am I getting too "socially minded" in this case?)

The door opens and Junior comes in with a junior-model snow shovel. He looks healthy but stays by the door when he sees me.

ME: Here comes the young fellow, I see. (Definitely young— 4½ years old.)

MR. DOE: Come over, Junior. (He doesn't.)

ME: Been shoveling snow, Junior? (He twists about at the door. My hearty remark performs no miracle. Have to wait a while.)

ME (to Mrs. Doe): Is everything going all right? How is the new budget working out? (I was supposed to ask that. General increases were recently allowed for personal incidentals and clothing.)

SHE: Oh just fine. You know we got a lot more this month. (A lot?)

HE: It was a big increase—$11.00. (He speaks enthusiastically and seems surprised at the amount. I am somewhat surprised myself since I hadn't figured what the increase amounted to. I must do this hereafter.)

ME: The old allowance of only 50 cents a month for incidentals wasn't enough.

SHE: It would hardly buy the soap. (Feminine emphasis on cleanliness.)

ME: I have a copy of the budget here in case you would like to have it. (I was told to do this by my supervisor.)

SHE: I'd like to have it very much. (She actually seems to want it. I hand it to her.)

ME: You have a pleasant place here but I suppose you would rather be on the ground floor. But of course, just now it's almost impossible to find such a place.

SHE: We were going to get a place next door but it cost too much. It was a dark place though—it looked out on the alley.

HE: The view is so good here but of course that doesn't matter so much when I'm in bed all day. (But it would matter to his wife and boy I think.)

SHE: Junior, don't do that. (Boy was using a glass to fill the mop pail with water from the faucet. Harmless and rather fun I thought. Maybe she didn't want me to notice the mop pail and the mop. I remembered that Mr. Doe had been a janitor here so that's how they got that "professional" type of mop pail I imagine.)

MR. DOE: There aren't hardly any children around here for him to play with. (Perhaps the father feels he is handicapping the life of his boy. Or only explaining why Junior is so restless and active in the room.)

ME: I suppose he'll be going to school soon so that will give him plenty to do.

SHE: Oh, but he won't be five years old until next May. Next fall he can start kindergarten. (Almost regretfully. But it's necessary of course. His shyness may be due to his isolation.)

ME: He's a very husky, active little fellow, so that's a great help.

MR. DOE: Yes, that's something we have to be thankful for.

Junior waters a plant by making several trips with a thimble. He has to go right by me so he isn't too afraid. I think the case record emphasized his shyness too much. He begins stirring up the soil with a spoon in a plantless flower pot. Mother fortunately doesn't stop him. Apparently he has to find most of his play in this room.

MR. DOE: The doctors assure me that I'll be able to do some work later on. I'd like to study something. I know I can't do hard work again but if I could study something I could sort of prepare myself.

ME: What was your line of work before?

HE: I was a sort of mechanic. I like to work with my hands. But of course I couldn't do that any more.

ME: What do you think you'd like—what are you interested in?

HE: I really don't know. Rev. J. of our church left some tests last fall which would tell me what I should do. I haven't answered them yet and sent them in. (I knew he had a bad spell about that time. Interestingly enough I know Rev. J. I will talk to him about this case.)

ME: Maybe you'd like some sort of electrical work or something like that?

HE: Maybe I can get started with some occupational rehabilitation work later on. When I applied before, they said they had so many applications I would have to wait. (What's this "occupational rehabilitation" business. I'll have to find out about that.)

ME: Well, don't worry about it. As you get back your strength it will all work out all right. (Do these remarks do any good?) If I get any ideas or material I'll turn it over to you. (I rise, preparing to take leave.)

HE: Yes. If I could only prepare myself, but of course it's hard to know what I can do.

ME: Well, I suppose I had better move along. (*To Mrs. Doe*) I'm undoubtedly keeping you from doing your housework.

SHE: Oh no, not at all, but I suppose you are quite busy.

HE: Yes, you must have quite a lot of people to see.

ME: Oh I have quite a bit to do all right. (Especially to write up this interview.) Here's my card in case you have any questions or special problems to take up. You can call me at that number. (Omnipotent me!)

Mrs. Doe takes the card and studies it. I put on my coat.

MR. DOE (*cheerfully*): I don't think we have any problems now, have we, Mother? (!!)

SHE (*also cheerfully*): No, everything is just fine. (She means it, I guess, but it's somewhat ironical to me.)

ME: Well, I'll be in to see you again later on.

MR. DOE: Well good-by, and thanks for stopping in.

ME: Good-by, Mr. Doe. So long, Junior. (No reply from Junior.)

MRS. DOE (*at doorknob*): It was nice to meet you.

AFTER THOUGHTS: CONCLUSIONS AND IDEAS FOR NEXT STEPS

1. *Health:* There is not much evidence from the records that all three members of the family are receiving periodic physical examinations. Should the mother's arrested t.b. become active at any time it might be dangerous to the boy and fatal to the father. Very likely that matter is being taken care of by the t.b. agency but it is well not to take it for granted. There may have been so much attention to the father's heart condition that the t.b. aspect has been overlooked.

2. *Housing:* If possible the family should get on the ground floor and in a neighborhood away from this traffic intersection where

there will be playmates for the boy. He seems normal but the present condition must not continue too long.

3. *The Mother:* Although she may be able to work it does not seem desirable under present circumstances. Apparently she realizes that. In some ways she has the hardest burden. It is likely we have forgotten her needs in our concern over Mr. Doe and the boy. Further study should be given to this matter.

4. *The Father:* The question arises as to how much encouragement should be given to his desire for occupational rehabilitation and for home study. On the basis of present information it appears inadvisable to build up the hope of his doing any work for some time to come. There would seem to be no harm in encouraging his interest in home study, which might well help him to spend his time in a constructive manner. His energies are too low, however, to permit even home study to any degree, at present.

5. *Special Suggestions:* (1) See Rev. J. at the earliest opportunity. Since he has been visiting the family it may be possible for church and state to help each other.

(2) It would appear a good idea to bring along some reading material from home for Mr. Doe since he doesn't seem to be very well supplied. Apparently Mrs. Doe doesn't get around very much. The boy could use some things also. The stuff should be given tactfully as to a neighbor and not overdone.

(3) The family should be visited a couple of times a month, if necessary. The last home visit was made about two months ago.

Author's Comments

We grant that it is extremely difficult to be an actor and a critic in the same play. In spite of the difficulties, the unspoken thoughts of the two students are an interesting contrast.

Student H. resented the assignment. He was afraid the results would be embarrassing to him. He approached his case with emotions centered on himself.

Student B. doesn't record his feelings about the assignment. His observations are objective and factual, but he has an attitude of sympathy and tries to understand his clients in terms of their personalities and experiences.

Each student was concerned about the effect of the interview, but H.'s reaction was self-centered, whereas B.'s was centered on his clients and showed awareness of their sensitivity.

We do not know the backgrounds of the two students nor do we have much knowledge of their personalities. If these facts were known we would have some insight into the difference in approach of the two interviewers on their first assignments.

The Effect of Preconceived Attitudes

Bertha Reynolds ascribes the element of uncertainty always present in a first interview to preconceived attitudes in which conflicts are sensed.[9] This uncertainty can be somewhat dissipated by such devices as a smile, a friendly handshake, friendly solicitude for comfort, and casual remarks while the interviewer and the interviewee are feeling their way to a working relationship.

In spite of the importance of preliminaries Miss Reynolds believes that they should be kept at a minimum and the sooner the major question of "What are you here for?" is answered the better. There are three reasons for this: (1) Fear is lessened by telling the reason for needing professional help (the more urgent the need, the more the necessity of getting at it quickly); (2) the relationship between worker and client carries less anxiety if its limits are known; and (3) discussing the business to be done helps instead of hinders.

Many years ago, Miss Ida Hull, a social work supervisor of a district of the Boston Associated Societies known as Little Italy shared with other social workers her experience among the South Italians.[10] What she had to say about first contacts with those of

[9] Bertha Reynolds, "Dynamic Possibilities of the Limited Interview," *News Letter,* American Association of Psychiatric Social Workers, 10th Anniversary Number, p. 4, 1938.

[10] Ida L. Hull, "South Italians," *Charity Organization Bulletin,* Russell Sage Foundation, December, 1914.

alien cultures is especially important today in working with displaced people, our new immigrants.

Miss Hull advises that the worker before her first contact consider the attitude the family is likely to take toward the stranger.
"The worker is not of their country; he looks like an official; he
may be a spy; let the family beware!" It isn't always possible to
avoid suspicion, but apprehension and distrust may be reduced
through tact so that they do not dominate the interview. If the
worker gives a good reason for his intervention; if he refuses to
let the responsibility of a difficult task seem to harass him; if,
instead of seeming slow, cold, and calculating, he shows his enjoyment of the call and his confidence in himself and the family
by his words and manner, then he may expect that his enthusiasm
and evident interest will meet with some genuine warmth of
response.

On the first call the interviewer must make his courteous interest in the family immediately felt. No formula can be given which
can be used by two different individuals or in two different situations, but the great divide must be bridged and this can be done
only by the establishment of common interests.

Evincing an interest in the client's language and his life previous to emigration is an obvious way to establish this bond. Even
a few badly pronounced words in the client's tongue are helpful.
It is always possible for the worker to learn some word or phrase
from the family, who are generally glad to be of service to anyone
who wishes to know more of their language.

But such devices are not enough. Miss Hull's summary of her
advice to social workers with South Italians is sound for any interviewer with any client from an alien culture:

It cannot be too emphatically stated that an American social worker
is not adequately equipped just by being conversant with the history,
the customs, the language, the virtues and failings of South Italians;
it is even more imperative for him to be acquainted with himself. This
means not only that he must know his own heart, but that he should

know as well how to give such external expression to his motives as will make them understood. How many social workers, before starting out to visit a foreign family, have ever tried to see themselves as they will look to their hosts? How many know what characteristics Italians, from observation, ascribe to Americans? If only there were some infallible way of communicating our thoughts and hopes, how many tragic misunderstandings might be averted! It is not enough to be conscious of our rectitude; we may have sympathy in our hearts, but if a long-faced stiffness prevents any of it from ever becoming visible on the surface, of what social value is it? To learn to express ourselves so that a family from a far-off land, of another race and with other traditions, shall have any adequate conception of what we are doing and why, is a task to tax our best powers.

PREDISPOSING ELEMENTS OF A SKILLFUL INTERVIEW

Although more pronounced in an initial meeting, attitudes of both interviewer and interviewee in any interview are preconceived, preconditioned, and generally divergent. Disparities are the outgrowth of differences in backgrounds, personalities, and elements in the interviewing situation itself.

The attitudes are subjective but they may be concerned with objective, tangible factors.

A short story by Charles Rawlings, "Buzzin' Johnny Gets His Medal," shows the conditioning effect of attitudes and how they may change with experience and circumstances.

Johnny was an incorrigible "buzzer," a term for low flying, or as Johnny explains, "shinin' yore rind with an airplane." He had asked for leave of absence from the Liberator unit in Michigan in order to go to North Carolina for his wedding. The request was refused by his Colonel; so Johnny's fiancée came to the camp for the ceremony. Soon afterward the Colonel went to Washington and Johnny applied to the acting C.O. for honeymoon leave without telling him leave had already been refused by the Colonel.

Upon the Colonel's return he summoned Johnny and demanded why he had gone over the head of a superior officer. Johnny's only answer, "I don't know, sir," was no defense and he was ordered confined to quarters until the outfit sailed for Honolulu and the war in the Pacific. There he and his plane achieved spectacular success which earned him the Distinguished Flying Cross with the Oak Leaf Cluster, and he was eventually ordered home to train other flyers.

On the night of his departure the Colonel invited former buzzin' Johnny, now Major Johnson, to his quarters to join him in a highball and a talk. The Colonel began, "Well, tomorrow you are no longer confined to quarters, Johnny. Tomorrow you start home. Do you suppose that little wife of yours understands why I had to spank you? Do you suppose she'll ever forgive me?"

Johnny studied the distant mountains, his eyes twinkling. "Sir, I don' know. Sometime I reckon I'll straighten her out—"

"Tell her I'm sending you home to her a good man. I'm sending you home in good shape. You're no combat-flying-stress-screw-up. You've got the foolishness out of you and you're going to teach those kids back home a lot of tactical flying. But they're going to start buzzing, I'm afraid. What are you going to teach them about that?"

"Well, sir," said Johnny very seriously, "buzzin's good practice—if it wasn't so risky. A bomber's—" he shot the Colonel a quick dutiful look— "a pretty big plane to buzz—as you have said."

"As I have said," said the Colonel, "—as I have said."

"I reckon I'll have to steal that advice of yours, sir—'You will, in the future, please remember you are flying a B Twentyfour and not a P Twentyfour.' But I'll hate to do it. Buzzin's—buzzin's right exhilaratin'—when you're young!"[11]

Factors which made this brief interview successful were the personalities of the two men—one a young North Carolinian, aged twenty-three, the other an older man with the prestige and authority of the rank of colonel; the locale or setting in which the interview took place; the knowledge each man had of the other's personal characteristics; the knowledge of attitudes and emotions in the earlier episodes around requested leaves and the subsequent restrictions placed upon Johnny. Even with all these predisposing elements for good results, the Colonel's purpose was accomplished chiefly by his acceptance of Johnny's feelings; his

[11] A free version of the Story of Major Paul Johnson, as told by Charles Rawlings, *Saturday Evening Post*, December 18, 1943, pp. 11, 44-46, by permission of the author.

belief that Johnny could take on new responsibilities with credit; his way of making Johnny realize that he would be in the same position for making or breaking other men as the Colonel had been with Johnny. These were the attitudes expressed in words that indicated the Colonel's understanding of human relations and skill in handling them.

In a valuable monograph entitled *Common Human Needs,* Charlotte Towle summaries the essential elements in an individual's life which would predispose him to be less hostile, less anxious, and more inclined toward social goals.[12] These are (1) the individual's physical health and welfare from infancy on, and its effect upon his personality development; (2) the opportunity for the development of intellectual capacity; (3) family relationships conducive to wholesome personality development; and (4) spiritual forces.

Poverty, unemployment, illness, mental incapacity, and physical handicaps, Towle points out, have different meanings for different people, depending not only on the nature of the problem but on the person's age, previous life experience and personality development, and the timing of the problem in relation to the other events of his life.[13]

Twila Neely[14] has assembled convincing evidence that subject matter is a strong conditioning factor in the interview. Drawing her conclusions from a study of the accuracy of information in research interviews, she finds a tendency to prevaricate around specific areas.

The six clusters are: (1) personal motivations; (2) previous emotional reactions; (3) lack of information; (4) difficulties inherent in remembering facts; (5) lack of interviewing skill; (6) questions difficult to answer.

[12] Charlotte Towle, *Common Human Needs,* Federal Security Agency Public Assistance Report, No. 8, pp. 3-9.

[13] See Diethelm's discussion on this point.

[14] Twila E. Neely, *A Study of Error in the Interview,* Columbia University Press, 1937.

Under the first category, of intentional prevarication for *personal motives,* she cites a study of persons injured by motor vehicles. Such information as time lost from school and work, doctors' and hospital bills, pay lost during absences was inaccurately reported by the interviewee.

Lawyers, law enforcement officers, doctors, nurses, and social workers are all familiar with the interviewee's tendency to lie for self-protection. An earlier study of homeless men by Solenberger showed that they lied about their personal histories, work records, and earnings.

Miss Neely found that pride was an attitude which prevented the gathering of accurate information about relief received. One out of nine on relief in California concealed the fact. Pride also accounted for a tendency to exaggerate educational attainments and hesitancy to admit mental deficiency in members of one's family.

People tend to give inaccurate information when they consider an interviewer's questions too personal,[15] especially those on the amount of their savings, money borrowed or lent, investments, and sex. Psychiatrists and physicians found that sex questions were most easily answered as part of a medical examination.[16]

Miss Neely comments that question on personal habits yield more accurate information when asked indirectly. For example, instead of asking how many baths, the interviewer may say that some doctors claim too many baths are bad for health. What is the interviewee's feeling and experience on this point?

Assurance of anonymity is generally productive of response where embarrassing questions are concerned.

Sometimes fear that an employer will use the information against the interviewee inhibits or colors the response.

---

[15] It is interesting to see how readily people responded to the 1950 census takers.

[16] Miss Neely's study was made before Kinsey's famous report, in which his investigators seem to have been markedly successful in eliciting cooperation from interviewees.

A not uncommon reaction to the interviewer is one of distrust. Miss Neely's study showed that the most successful interviews were obtained by mature-looking, "reliable" persons, and that a youthful appearance or an immature manner is a handicap that has to be overcome by interviewing skill. Sometimes the reaction is a carry-over of a distortive emotional effect from a preceding situation which may have contained some one element that formed a bridge to the new situation.

Neely's examples of distortions *due to the influence of interest and emotions on memory* were drawn from United States Bureau of Crop and Livestock statistics, which showed that a farmer tended to underestimate his yield if his income depended on one crop; that worry over unemployment tended to increase the estimate of its incidence; and that there is tendency to forget, completely, shameful or painful occurrences.

Error also was found when facts were of minor importance at the time the incidents occurred. The tendency to best recall items of greatest interest is a general one.

Other sources of error were *lack of information* and the *inherent difficulty in remembering details* pertaining to developmental history, employment history, earnings and income, cost of living, and consumption. Inaccuracy in reporting budget expenditures in farm families lies in the difficulty of recalling exactly what goods were furnished by the farms and what were bought as supplement.[17]

Errors on the part of the unskilled interviewer were ascribed as follows: (1) There may be difficulty in explaining the interviewer's agency or its function. (2) Inaccuracies may be due to labeling or terminology. Miss Neely notes that Foster and Anderson, in discussing the young child and his parents, observed that one person may consider behavior vindictive while another finds it obstinate or irritable; a feeding problem may be labeled an

[17] Since Neely's study was made, farmers have had extensive experience in furnishing accurate information to the internal revenue collector.

emotional difficulty. Words have often acquired special meanings; gestures and facial expressions are differently interpreted (*Life* magazine has illustrated this fact pictorially by contrasting the different meanings of the same gesture to Frenchmen and Latin Americans). (3) Personal bias of the interviewer affects the terminology where the interviewer and interviewee have different views. (4) Other factors are lack of skill shown in answering leading questions, forgetting the answers before they have been recorded, an attitude of bashfulness on the part of the interviewer, or a sense of intrusion.

A person tends to avoid a question *difficult to answer*. Neely would avoid employing a field investigator who would be unwilling to answer his own questions. Salesmen find that diffidence results in an apologetic tone, a nervous manner of asking questions, or in failure to ask embarrassing questions even when necessary. Bias on certain questions renders an interviewer unsatisfactory in research interviewing as well as in many other types. Ambiguous questions are also a source of error.

These studies of common errors and their causes were made exclusively from research interviews. They do, however, reveal everyday pitfalls open for any professional worker.

INTERACTION OF PROCESSES, TECHNIQUES, AND ATTITUDES

Processes and techniques are inseparable from attitudes. They not only accompany them but affect them. The interviewer sensing tension in the process of observation ignores it, works around it, or heightens it because of his attitude toward its display. Where there are tears, the worker who is more concerned for his own comfort than for that of his client feels a compulsion to console. In meeting resistance the interviewer who is unable to bear hostility, or who does not understand the motivations for it, tries to assuage his fractious client instead of accepting his behavior.

In explaining an agency's function as a process, the effect of the interviewer's attitude toward it is generally apparent. The interviewer who cannot explain the purpose of his visit or the function of his agency is vague and uncomfortable, as we have seen in the interviews of Mr. Hart and Mr. Boe.

This point was tested in an educational experiment sponsored by the Veterans' Administration whereby social workers from the Pittsburgh School of Social Administration conducted courses and seminars for psychologists and social workers in training at the Winter Veterans' Administration Hospital.[18]

One discussion group dealt with the problems and techniques of preparing a patient for psychological tests. At first the psychologists felt resistant to the idea that it was their responsibility rather than the psychiatrist's to explain the purposes and expectations of testing. They also rejected the responsibility of helping the psychiatrist understand what was involved in testing. This collaboration was necessary if the patient was to accept testing as an important part of his psychiatric treatment.

Later experience proved that the psychiatrist usually cooperated when he understood the psychologist's function.

These interviewing procedures may seem simple, but two examples cited in the report of the experiment show that the psychologist's attitudes toward it are conditioning factors in skill. In the first of these two instances the psychologist reports:

> I asked the examining physician to report to the patient that testing would be done and to tell him why. The doctor did this and later asked me if I would like an introduction to the patient.

Here the acceptance of the psychologist, with an appreciation of the tests, made for confidence and trust. This rapport could

[18] John T. Dickson, Harry Levinson, Arthur T. Leader, Isabel Stamm, "Contribution to Interviewing Skills of Psychiatrists," *Journal of Social Case Work*, October, 1949, pp. 312-324.

not be taken for granted, however. The psychologist had to be sure that the physician's conception of his role agreed with his own definition.

In the second example the psychologist records his approach:

I spoke with the doctor briefly about referral and he was hesitant to discuss the case, saying he felt I might be prejudiced by his views and he would prefer to have me arrive at my conclusions independently. I agreed that prejudice was possible, and that I would not press the matter; but the referral had raised the question of the nature of the man's disability; it was important for us to have this information so that the test battery could be altered to throw his problems into relief. The psychiatrist evidenced considerable surprise at this and told about a previous contact with a psychologist who had stated emphatically that she could diagnose brain damage infallibly from a Rorschach alone. I commented that some psychologists were able to make very astute inferences from this but that this ability varied widely among individuals with experience and that we made no such claims here. We discussed further some of the limitations of tests, and the doctor seemed to appreciate our point of view.

In this case the doctor's previous experience with another psychologist gave him a wrong conception of the purpose of the tests; this would have made it difficult for him to interpret reasons for the tests to the patients.

The study also revealed an initial difference between the attitudes of the social workers and the psychologists in the interview with the patient. At first, there was a tendency for the psychologists to regard interviewing as superfluous or separate from testing; some resisted handling the feelings or problems the patient displayed in the test situation. Their resistance was based on the belief that handling such feelings or problems neither helped the patients nor affected test results. As more specific interviewing techniques were acquired they were able to integrate interviewing and testing in a manner constructive for both themselves and the patients. Here understanding the purpose of the interview and maintaining its focus involved decisions and activities on the part of both participants. Attitudes played a major part in this, as the following account shows:

> At one point in the test the patient began to speak of a number of problems, with a surprising amount of feeling—some anxiety, agitation, a kind of depressive undertone, bitterness, and a paranoid tinge. . . . Finally, he said quizzically, "I don't know if you're the one I should be telling this to." He paused only momentarily. At this point I wasn't sure either, and I blocked momentarily trying to decide how to respond and how to ascertain whether he had taken up these problems with his doctor.

An interesting question brought up repeatedly in the seminars was: Could one prepare a patient for testing by listening to his symptoms, hoping thereby to establish a rapport which would lead to cooperation in testing? After many experimental failures the answer was a decided negative. It was decided that the psychologist's responsibility as part of the clinical team was to state his purpose, indicate his professional concern and interest in the patient, and give him a chance to express his feelings directly about the tests and the psychologist himself. Some patients considered the tests were designed to measure their "craziness" or stupidity. A psychologist sensitive to the patient's feelings was able to explain the value of the tests only after he assured himself that the patient had a right to know the nature and the purpose of the tests and that he had the capacity to accept this information. The psychologists found that a frank discussion of the tests with the patient made him feel that the tests were an integral part of his treatment and reduced his anxiety by removing an aura of "mystery and magic." They credited this change in the patient's attitude to their own changed attitude in understanding the feelings of the patient and in explaining the tests to both patient and doctor.

This study, a joint one of social workers and psychologists, is important to interviewers for two reasons: (1) It marks an attempt to coordinate the work of two different disciplines through a study of the interview, and (2) it demonstrates again that there are common components in every interview, regardless of its purposes or auspices.

So far we have discussed *attitudes* as a component of the interview. There is the more important and broader aspect of *attitude* as the interviewer's *values*.

ATTITUDES AND ETHICS

Need for a Personal and Social Philosophy

Anyone has a personal philosophy who knows what his assumptions and standards are in such matters as love, sex, recreation, work, family interrelationships, money, and religion. His attitudes on these questions, expressed or unexpressed, are the ingredients which he blends into a philosophy of life.

A mature and integrated attitude must be a harmonious blend of all of its elements. For example, the man whose love interests defy his family mores or religious tenets has a philosophy which is bound to create conflicts for him rather than to sustain him.

The philosophy of the worker in human relations must embrace social as well as personal values. His social philosophy consists of the assumptions he makes as to good or bad social values and his reasons for making them—what he considers socially desirable and why. His professional philosophy is made up of his social philosophy plus what he is essentially as a human being. It is his answer to the question: What is the minimum that society should afford for everyone and what are my obligations toward securing another's rights in society? In practice, his social philosophy supplies the reasons for what he does.

The worker's professional values and obligations are found in the realm of ethics.

Ethical Considerations[19]

The obligation to be altruistic is an ethical problem of peculiar importance in any endeavor to help. Kant's maxim that one ought to treat another as an end in himself might well be used as a canon for workers in human relations. It crystallizes a basic concept in the client-worker relationships: To treat a client as an end, never as a means, is to grant him his dignity as a person, to refrain from using him as a tool in personal aggrandizement, and never to indulge in maudlin sympathy in his behalf.

In analyzing further the ethical basis of service to others we are confronted by three questions: (1) What is the worker's professional motivation? (2) Can a selfishly motivated worker serve his client effectively? and (3) Are there ethical truths in worker-client relationships which are universally binding to all persons, at all times, and in all places?

In answer to the first question, it is clear that motivation may be predominantly selfish or predominantly altruistic. Altruistic motives are undoubtedly a greater source of satisfaction than selfish motives. Altruistic motivation, however, cannot be reduced to the satisfaction derived from it. John Dewey has demonstrated that people who deliberately seek satisfaction for themselves rarely find it, and that pleasure is derived from activities directed not toward pleasure but toward people or objectives.

The answer to the second question is found in empirical ethics, which is concerned with the observable effects of a motive. If these effects increase the sum total of happiness, then the action is good, whatever the motives behind it. However, it is probable that a person whose motives are generally altruistic will engage in nonaltruistic acts less often than one whose motives are commonly selfish, because a person selfishly motivated will act

[19] The ideas contained in the section on "Ethical Considerations" are abstracted and adapted from an article by Bernard Saibel (with Anne Fenlason), "A Contribution of Ethics to Social Work," *Journal of Social Forces*, December, 1942.

benevolently only in situations which cater to his self-interest, whereas the consistently altruistic person can be generally relied upon to act benevolently in any situation. *Benevolence,* a technical term in ethics, has become *assistance, help,* or *service* in current professional practice. *Enlightened benevolence* results from determining the facts of need and finding the best-known means to meet problems represented by the facts. Enlightened benevolence enables the worker to act altruistically and effectively in the service of others.

The answer to the third question involves a discussion as to whether the professional worker's behavior should rest on the belief of *ethical absolutism* or *ethical relativity*. Ethical absolutism maintains that there are ethical truths which are universally binding—applicable to all persons, at all times, and in all places. Ethical relativity, on the other hand, maintains that ethical truth varies with different sets of circumstances, that what is true in one situation might be false in another.

The absolutist accuses the relativist of disregarding the notion of truth altogether and maintaining the position that there are as many truths as there are opinions, and that they are not necessarily in conflict. The professional worker, says the absolutist, cannot subscribe to this view unless he is willing to disclaim any responsibility for antisocial behavior.

A modification of this view is a concept of *sociological ethics:* Whatever the individual thinks is good, is good. This gives sanction for the group to enforce its ideas of what is right over those of the individual, not that these ideas are any truer for the individual. This means that various cultures cannot be compared in terms of moral progress. Some social workers, public health nurses, and counselors undoubtedly operate on this ethical concept, whereas those most interested in social action and social change find this system of ethics unrealistic. Actually, individuals do change the morality of the group through such means as education and organization. The right of the minority to express its opinions is as important a fact of democracy as the sovereignty of the will.

The point of view of the professional worker should be a naturalistic and empirical one entailing a certain degree of ethical relativity. It asserts that, although value is relative to a specific individual and can vary with different individuals, it is nevertheless independent of what the individual thinks is good for him, because the individual may be wrong. The statement "This is good for me" cannot be equated with "I think this is good for me." That is why we have the professions of medicine, law, social work, public health nursing, and counseling.

Professional workers recognize the need of a philosophy of relativity in the sense that the good is the good for a particular person. It is the basic assumption of individualization in professional interviewing.

The contribution of ethics to the practicing professional worker is the knowledge that his work is both selfish and altruistic and that its selfish aspect does not always detract from his ability to help others. An altruistic motive is not enough itself to insure helpfulness to others. Altruism plus a knowledge of ways and means, however, is the soundest foundation for constructive professional practices where client-worker relationships are involved.

Ethical Practices

When we move from a discussion of ethical theory to ethical practices, we find that there are few formulas. One universal rule for conduct in relation to others is the principle of Confucius that one should not desire for others what is undesirable for oneself, expressed in Christian doctrine by the golden rule, "Whatsoever ye would that men should do to you, do ye even so to them." No worker is competent to render professional services to others unless he can conceive of himself, under similar conditions, as the recipient of such services.

The implications of this principle are far-reaching for the

worker. It means that he will refrain from telling an anecdote about a client which he would be unwilling in similar circumstances to have told about himself. It means that he has such ingrained respect for the personality of another that he will not impose a plan upon his client which he would be unwilling to accept if he were in the client's place. He would believe such imposition a violation of the concept of the essential worth of an individual.

A worker would neither condemn destructive behavior nor condone it realizing that the tendency to condemn behavior which conflicts with one's own is due to insufficient knowledge of behavior and personality. To know is to understand. A worker must maintain his standards of behavior if he is to preserve his integrity, but he must also accept the client's right to have his own standards. Some confusion exists as to whether such acceptance entails passive inaction or whether it may involve responsibility for change. The answer is to be found in the worker's own sense of ethical responsibility, consistent with the function and policies of the agency in which he is working. Unless they are congruous, the worker's responsibility is only that of any informed citizen.

The worker's acceptance of ethical obligation is based upon his acceptance of the individual's behavior, on an understanding of behavior in general, and on the client's behavior in his special situation. An interviewer approaches unethical conduct when he asserts or pretends an understanding which he does not possess. With the acceptance of another's behavior, the interviewer has the additional obligation of controlling his own natural reactions of irritation and frustration when he sees the client behaving irrationally or contrary to expectations, or failing to carry out activities which have been planned.[20]

The professional worker needs to have convictions as to the confidential nature of his relationships with clients. Too often workers have promised or implied that confidences would be kept

[20] Cf. Garrett on "Acceptance," *op. cit.*, pp. 22-25.

and then have proceeded to violate them. Occasionally there are situations when the best interests of the client require that the information he has given be used in his behalf. Where this is done, the client should know the use to which the information is put, and his permission should be secured to so use it, except in those cases in which the individual is too young or physically or mentally unable to be responsible. In such instances the interviewer has an even greater obligation not to misuse confidences, or not to use them at all, except in his client's interests or for the protection of others. The interviewer should be frank and honest, but the attributes of frankness and honesty should be exercised with tact.

The interviewee must not be tricked by interviewing techniques into statements, positions, or admissions. Such procedures do violence to the rights of an individual to determine his own course of action. The interviewer must not have preconceived ideas of what is right or best for his client.

The interviewee's interests should transcend any other consideration unless they jeopardize the common welfare. The interviewer has a responsibility to the community and his profession. The impact of his contacts with his clients is greater than he realizes. Doctors, lawyers, ministers, public health nurses, and counselors judge social work not from the point of view of another profession but from the attitudes a given social worker has engendered by his contacts. A clumsy contact of one social worker with a member of any other calling is enough to indict the whole profession of social work. Other more representative workers may have created better impressions, but unfortunately they will be generally regarded by the critics as notable exceptions. Follow-up of complaints during community fund campaigns has shown that a single unfortunate interview, even when satisfactorily explained, may eddy into repudiation of all professional efforts. The good interviewer must remember that in the eyes of the community he represents not only his agency but his profession.

In his interviews the ethical practitioner finds he has an obligation to his co-workers as well as to his client. He often is in a position to hear criticism of the work of a colleague. Both his ethical obligation and his skill require that the complaint be taken seriously but without disloyalty either to client or coworker. This does not mean that the behavior of a co-worker must always be upheld; it means rather a withholding of judgment, discrimination in determining whether the complaint is justified, whether it should be discussed with the worker or supervisor, or whether it results from a past relationship which for the sake of the client is better now ignored. Each individual complaint must be viewed objectively and the stand taken determined by the client's best interests.

One characteristic of a profession is that it has an accepted and an articulated code of ethics. Codes of ethics are designed and established to afford protection both to the client (or patient) and to the practitioner. Each profession has its own code. Each profession has its own organizational machinery for enforcing these codes and obligating its practitioners in their adherence to them. Ethical misconduct is therefore regarded as an extremely serious matter when and if it occurs. When professional training is carefully prescribed, ethical concepts are integrated into educational preparation. The way in which this is done varies among the different professional schools.

SUMMARY

The interviewer's attitude plays a major part in the success or failure of an interview. The skillful interviewer is able: to see the person with a problem as a human being with an individual personality, to identify with him by virtue of recognizing his individuality, to be objective about him and his difficulties by not becoming emotionally involved, and to be sensitive to the interviewee's feelings and needs.

He also recognizes the basis of his own insecurities, which may be due to personality defects or merely inexperience. He recognizes that, because two individuals are involved, they bring preconceived notions to each interview which need to be compromised or at least acknowledged. There are also many elements in any individual's life which affect attitudes of the participants in the interview and, through them, the interview itself.

Working with human beings demands that the worker have an articulate and integrated personal and social philosophy. His practice involves both theoretical and practical ethical considerations.

In theory he needs to know that his motivation for his work is predominantly selfish or altruistic; an altruistic motivation is probably a much greater source of satisfaction than a selfish one. Satisfaction is a concomitant of altruism, inasmuch as any activity freely engaged in is a source of pleasure. Selfish motivation is likely to be effective in work with others only in those situations which further the worker's self-interest. *Enlightened benevolence* which determines the need for help and the most efficient ways of helping is an ethical basis for practice.

Professional practice comes under the classification of *ethical relativity* modified by a naturalistic and empirical view of new situations occasioned by human variabilities.

In practice the only universal rule of ethical conduct implies complete acceptance of the other person as a human being. It has many implications, which are recognized by the older professions in codes of ethics.

SUGGESTED ASSIGNMENTS

1. As your education has progressed, have you been conscious of changes in your attitudes toward individuals and events?
2. Are there any situations involving others where you have to guard against an emotional reaction?

3. Distinguish between impersonality and objectivity. Illustrate—from personal experience if possible.

4. Have you recently been conscious of hostile feelings towards other students? In what situations? How have you handled them? Did you try to understand the genesis of those feelings at the time?

5. Are you conscious of "blind spots" where you know that your own prejudices would be a detriment in trying to help others? Be specific.

6. Have you ever had an interview or been interviewed by another where you were conscious of such prejudice?

7. All of us are ambivalent. What recent examples can you give of ambivalence from your own experience?

8. Describe the last time when you felt there was empathy between you and an individual whom you had just met.

9. What types of problems in your chosen profession do you think you'd prefer to work with? Why? What ones would you tend to dislike? Why?

10. Have you ever tried to articulate your personal philosophy?

11. How do your personal values relate to the profession you are planning to enter?

12. What conflicts, if any, have you had between your personal values and the requirements of the profession you are working toward or in?

RECOMMENDED SUPPLEMENTARY READING

Attitudes are revealed in the interview in the behavior of the participants. Much of the published material on attitudes is discussed under interviewing principles. Therefore, instead of a separate list of references on attitudes we suggest that the reader review the selections suggested for the previous chapter with particular attention to the discussions involving attitudes. Additional references are:

Dimnet, Ernest, *What We Live By,* Simon and Schuster, 1932.

Fromm, Erich, *Man for Himself—An Inquiry into the Psychology of Ethics,* Rinehart and Company, 1947.

Hayakawa, S. T., *Language in Action,* Harcourt, Brace and Company, 1940.

La Rochefoucauld, François de, *Maxims,* Peter Pauper Press, 1938.

Liebman, Joshua, *Peace of Mind,* Simon and Schuster, 1946.

Lilienthal, David, *This I Do Believe,* Harper & Brothers, 1949.

Schweitzer, Albert, *Memoirs of Childhood and Youth,* First American Edition, The Macmillan Company, 1949, chap. 5.

Stace, W. T., *Concept of Morals,* The Macmillan Company, 1937.

PART TWO

Illustrations for Class Discussion

ILLUSTRATIONS FOR
CLASS DISCUSSION*

The examples in this section are presented for class discussion. In the previous chapters we have tried to hold to two premises: (1) that undergraduate students could profit by a discussion of concepts underlying interviewing and a knowledge of the components of the interview itself; (2) that a real knowledge of the professional use of the interview must be derived from supervised practice integrated with content of the discipline for which the student is preparing. We have limited our questions to ones that could be answered from the material in the earlier chapters. We have purposely asked a minimum number of questions and made them broad and general, in order to give the individual instructor scope to use the examples to fit the content he is presenting.

* Except where the source is otherwise designated, all of this material has been contributed by students or practicing professional workers. The only editing has been to condense and to protect clients against identification.

EXAMPLES OF CULTURE CONCEPTS

I. In Chapter Two we presented an excerpt of a talk made by Gertrude Stein to illustrate the importance of one's own culture. A fuller account is here presented for further analysis:

During World War II the late Gertrude Stein, expatriate American author, talked before a group of servicemen in Paris, chiding them for their lack of courtesy in their casual encounters with the French people. Such courtesy, she tried to explain, should be built upon an acceptance of a French culture different from, and in many ways perhaps superior to, that of the American G.I.

Miss Stein admonished, ". . . Every day somebody should say something nice about somebody else. Every nation should say something nice about another nation. Each of you should be like Boy Scouts and smile at least once a day at Frenchmen."

She went on to explain that the French were utterly exhausted. "Americans don't realize the depth of French fatigue. Their feeling in the occupation was that sometime the Americans would come and everything would be wonderful. Then the Americans came; they were all solemn, serious, hard-working boys, and the French were very disappointed.

"It is difficult to explain—you see, the last American Army sort of came over on a vacation; by comparison with your experiences it was a sort of a vacation. They had their action in concentrated doses and they then came back here and got drunk and were very gay. The French expected you to be like them and you aren't. You're serious, you do your job; you don't always get drunk, at least not all of you.

"You must smile at somebody—it's shameful—you never smile at anybody, not even at children. How many of you have smiled today at a French man or a French woman or even at a French child? Go on, raise your hands—how many of you?"

One lone hand showed.

She was curtly challenged at this point by a captain. "I rise to the defense of the American sobriety! . . ." That was as far as he got. After five minutes of trying to get a word in edgewise on the issue of sobriety, he sat down, a defeated man.

Another hand waved and was recognized by Miss Stein. "I rise to the defense of the Captain," said a coveralled G.I. The room exploded in laughter. After a while he got started again. "Miss Stein, I think you misunderstood the Captain on this question of being sober. You see, we've got the war in the Pacific to fight when we win this one."

Her response was that in the war we were in danger of losing our humanity and that everyone worried too much.

Another G.I. came into the fray, exhibiting a copy of *Woodrow Wilson and the Lost Peace*. "I'm only half educated," he said, "but I'm worried, Miss Stein. That's why I read books like this. . . . Now, I've been thinking and I'm worried."

"For heaven's sake, man," Miss Stein broke in, "don't think so much! Thinking is a solemn process. It worries you when you're thinking. You've got to stop thinking and lean over the fence and talk to your neighbor about the crops. . . . If you think too much you worry too much."

From this time, the rapport between her and her audience went from bad to worse. The majority of the audience seemed to regard her only as a scolding critic of American bad manners.

The account concludes, "When last seen, Miss Stein, in her shapeless russet coat and little brown hat mashed onto her head, was shaking hands with the soldier who worried. . . . He was still glowering but on the way to understanding another culture."[1]

[1] "Gertie and the G.I.'s," *Time*, April 16, 1945, p. 27.

QUESTIONS
1. The account produced an unpleasant reaction against Miss Stein when it was read to a class studying the interview at the University of Minnesota. Why were the students reacting as they did and to what?
2. What are your own reactions? Why?
3. What are the cultural implications of this interview?

II. "So you tell lies just like Chicken Little," my literal-minded grandmother said to her imaginative granddaughter who had just announced the arrival of the grocer's truck by saying that a red chariot had driven into the yard.

From that day "Chicken Little," hitherto my favorite story, became a hateful tale. "Run, Chicken Little, the sky is falling," instead of causing a pleasant excitement, brought me shivers of fear. I screamed when my grandmother told the story to my little sister, and was sent to bed. My grandmother was dumbfounded by my inexplicable change in literary taste. I myself scarcely realized at the time what had happened; but now the genesis of my behavior is perfectly clear.

QUESTIONS
1. What culture concept is represented by this excerpt?
2. What culture trait is involved?

III. Gertrude was adopted by Mrs. M. when she was two years old. Mrs. M. and my mother were very good friends; so were Gertrude and I. As we grew older our mothers drifted apart but we remained good friends and spent a great deal of time visiting one another, as I lived in the country and Gertrude in town. She was very pretty in high school and was popular with the boys. Her grades at first had been excellent, but she soon gave up all thoughts of study to have a good time, and began to acquire a "bad reputation"; in spite of the poor opinion my other friends had of her, we still maintained a close friendship.

She soon became the town's "wild" girl, and stories about her activities circulated with the milkman every morning. She laughed about all this, and I tried to pay no attention to the rumors for I knew the tales were the exaggerated ones which a small town loves to spread. I think she would have out-grown the boy-crazy, immature stage earlier if it had not been for her mother. Gertrude's mother believed every wild tale she heard. She would repeat the story to Gertrude with a reproachful look, adding, "Here, I adopted you out of the kindness of my heart, gave you a good home, everything you've ever wanted, and you disgrace me! You must get it from your real mother." She never gave Gertrude a chance to explain her behavior or confide in her, but chose to believe the gossip. Gradually mother and daughter grew so far apart they spoke only when necessary.

Gertrude's behavior soon lived up to its reputation, but she still appeared flippant and unconcerned. Many times she would say to me, "No matter what I do, people think I'm wild; so I may as well have a good time and give them something to talk about. When my own mother doesn't trust me. . . ." When my parents finally forbade me to go around with Gertrude she felt that I, too, had let her down. And so I had.

QUESTION

What concepts of culture are represented in this account?

IV. A middle-aged couple live in a small town in northern Minnesota where the man is a minister in one of the many little churches of the community. They have lived in this parish nearly two years, but they have not been happy.

This is a missionary church supported by larger churches in the state. The people in the community have food to eat and clothes to wear, but they do not have any of the modern conveniences which are generally taken for granted. In many of the homes, even in town, there are no indoor toilet facilities and on many farms no electricity. The people have not had much education, nor any of the cultural opportunities afforded by the larger cities. Many of them have lived their entire lives in their little town. There is no moving picture theatre, and people have very little contact with outside communities. They are, however, sincere, warm, and friendly.

The minister and his wife lived mostly in larger towns. They have never before lived without the conveniences of life. Small hardships are difficult for them to accept. They fail to understand why the church members should be so unconcerned about the comfort of their minister's family.

The minister and his wife miss the concerts and lectures of the city and the companionship of intellectual people. They do not really try to become acquainted with the townsfolk nor seek the companionship which they might find. They fail to recognize and utilize little ways which would make them more acceptable and give them an opportunity to know their parishioners. The parsonage has a large lot where the minister might raise a few vegetables. But he and his wife make no move toward having a garden; consequently they seem lazy to their neighbors.

The lack of interest in church baffles the minister greatly and it particularly concerns his wife. She becomes pessimistic and sees little good and much bad in the people of the parish.

The church members feel that the minister is not making the most of his opportunities. He is slow-moving, easy-going, and lacking the push and drive necessary to bring his parishioners out of their lethargy. He and his wife are conscious of an impasse which they seem unable to break down.

QUESTION

What culture concepts does this example serve to illustrate?

V. It is a Greek custom for parents to arrange the marriage of their children without consultation as to the children's desires.

A suitable man or woman is chosen, the prime requisite being Greek nationality. The couple may be incompatible and there is often a disparity in age. Two ceremonies are performed, the civil one, and the one in the Greek Orthodox Church. The first generation Americans usually accept this, but when they (according to custom) try it out on their children, there is often a revolt.

A young girl of Greek parentage had a marriage contracted for which was highly desirable from the parents' viewpoint, but very undesirable to the girl. She had always associated with Americans and had completely assimilated American culture. The man was from a distant state; she met him before the civil ceremony. He was ten years older than the teen-age girl, who was still in high school.

She saw no way out of this marriage other than to run away, which she did immediately after the civil ceremony. She went, as prearranged, to a large city in a neighboring state where she called at a social agency for help in securing lodging. There she readily admitted her identity (since there had been a general search for her) but refused to go home until her father met her stipulation to annul the marriage and let her choose her own husband in the future.

QUESTIONS

1. Have you encountered any similar conflict between New and Old World customs? Explain.
2. Have you encountered any personal conflicts between the ideas of your generation and those of your parents? Explain.

EXAMPLES OF BEHAVIOR
AND PERSONALITY

I. Mrs. L. came to the Travelers Aid desk in the railroad station and asked the worker if she could recommend some employment organization in the city.

She was an attractive woman of about fifty. Her iron gray hair was carefully arranged, and she wore a conservatively cut navy blue suit with a small fur scarf. However, the tremor in her voice and the nervous movement of her hands betrayed the emotional tension accompanying her simple request. When she was asked to sit down she did so with relief, and began immediately to tell of her circumstances, saying with a slight smile, "I suppose I'm really a runaway."

Mrs. L. is the wife of a druggist in a small town near D. City. She had been married 24 years and had three children, two girls, 19 and 22, and a boy, 17. She said that she had worked hard raising her family, and that now she wasn't needed any longer, and "they don't hesitate to show it." She wanted to be with her husband, but she felt her children did not want her at home any longer. Her oldest daughter wanted to usurp Mrs. L.'s position as the household manager, and the younger daughter, working as a receptionist, had begun to go to night clubs without her mother's consent.

Mrs. L. made several references to her father, who had been insane, saying that she would never become like him, and that sometimes she thought her children treated her as if she were "getting like their grandfather."

The interviewer referred her to the United States Employment Service and invited her to return and talk with her again.

Mrs. L. made several half-hearted attempts to find work, and returned each day to talk with the worker, although the talks consisted mostly of Mrs. L.'s telling of instances of her children's thoughtlessness and of her own emotional strain when her father underwent a "nervous breakdown."

On the fourth day Mrs. L. returned prepared to leave for home. Her daughter had reached her the night before by phone and told her that they missed her. During the interview preparatory to Mrs. L.'s departure she showed considerable insight into her action. She said that she supposed that her children were no more ungrateful than most children, and that it was hard for parents to accept their children's maturity. When they became irritated at her she supposed that she "took it too hard" as it seemed as if they were treating her as she had sometimes treated her father.

QUESTIONS

1. What light does Lynd throw on Mrs. L.'s situation?
2. What concepts of personality and behavior did the Travelers Aid worker need to understand in order to help Mrs. L.?

II. Mrs. Jones had been concerned about the behavior of her eight-year-old daughter, Mary, for two years. Mary had a younger sister, Jean, who was three. The two quarreled violently and could not seem to cooperate on any kind of play activity. Mary was at times openly antagonistic toward Jean, and at other times, very affectionate toward her.

In school, Mary was thought dull by her teachers. She was unable to keep up with the class in reading, and had to be tutored after school. She felt badly about this, and also about the fact that she was not accepted by the other children. They rejected her as most children reject the "dummy" of the group. Mary tried valiantly to inject herself into their favor but they would tell her to go home—they didn't want to play with her. Mary often reacted to this by becoming very unpleasant. The children would return the insults and a neighborhood battle sometimes ensued.

Another difficulty of Mary's was even more disturbing to Mrs. Jones. For the past few years, Mary had had severe nightmares. These occurred two or three times a week. Soon after going to bed she would suddenly begin screaming and sobbing loudly. She would not waken, but when one of her parents would come in and attempt to quiet her, she would become calm. In the morning, Mary could never remember what had made her so frightened and upset; or if she could remember, she refused to tell her parents.

Mrs. Jones finally called upon a social agency for help. The worker who handled the case began by trying to find the basic causes of Mary's symptoms. Questioning the parents revealed that Mary's troubles had begun soon after the birth of her younger sister, Jean, when her grandmother had abruptly transferred her attentions from Mary to Jean, who was an unusually attractive baby, and much of her mother's time had been taken up with care of the new baby.

Mrs. Jones remembered that once Mary had told her that she had dreamed that horrible things were happening to Jean—that her legs and arms were falling off, or that she was very sick.

The social worker helped Mrs. Jones to instill feelings of security and personal worth in Mary, and to spend more time alone with her. She helped bring her into group activity by organizing a Bluebird troop with Mary as one of the members. Gradually, Mary became accepted as one of the group at school, and there were no more verbal battles on the playground. Emotionally, Mary became a much happier little girl and her nightmares ceased.

QUESTIONS

1. What concepts of personality apply to this excerpt from a social case history?
2. What environmental factors are important and why?

III. Peter had been brought up in a very poor family. From the time he was seven years old, he has worked his way through school. Now he is getting his Ph.D. in bio-chemistry. His life has been a struggle with poverty. He lived on a few cents a day for food, wore cast-off clothing, and never had the social life of the average boy.

Peter's father was an invalid who lived his life in and with books. Education for him was the cure-all of all economic and social difficulties. He taught Peter to read before he went to school. By the time he was seven years old the boy had already decided to become a scientist. Whether it was his father's idea or his own, we do not know, but it is safe to say that his father had a great deal to do with this decision.

Every cent that Peter earned was used toward his schooling and the family went without many things for his sake. Little emphasis was placed on clothes, good food, or any of the things that make for gracious living. All his life at home, the need for education which came from books was the chief theme. He was encouraged to go without amusement in order to get a book.

His mother, not an intellectual herself, was completely under the influence of Peter's father and worked outside the home to help her boy get through school.

When Peter married, he chose as his wife a girl who had never known privation. Although a college graduate, she had never acquired Peter's love of books. They lived at first on a small budget and when Peter would come home with a book bought with money saved for his new shoes, his wife would scold. He would promise not to do it again, but his love of books was too strong; he would buy books with his lunch money and keep them at school so that Mary wouldn't know.

When Mary discovered what he was doing, she was shocked and a little ashamed that she had forced him to deceive her.

She talked to Peter's mother about it, and when the mother explained what the home life had been and how greatly his father had stressed the need of education through books, Mary understood.

Peter no longer has to buy books surreptitiously, for Mary took the money she had been saving for a new silver place setting and bought Peter a book he wished for but had decided was too expensive.

Peter and Mary do not have sterling silver for their table, but they do have a growing professional library.

QUESTIONS

1. What criterion of Dollard's is illustrated in this account?
2. What concepts of personality was Mary using either consciously or unconsciously?

IV. The Graveses were tenant farmers, living on a neglected farm in a weather-beaten, sagging, frame house. They had three sons and two daughters, the youngest of whom was ten years old when Stephen, the last child of the family, was born. Because he was afflicted with a spastic paralysis from birth, he had never been to school. At the age of fourteen he had, in fact, never been allowed to leave the farm on which he lived and there were stories that he was hidden away whenever anyone called. His older brothers used to torment him when he was small; they were ashamed of him and made such fun of him—he was always knocking things over, falling down, and getting words mixed up—that he had to eat in the kitchen alone until the others grew up and left home.

When Stephen was fourteen his mother, now elderly and stooped, with a weather-beaten wrinkled face and grimly determined jaw, stormed into an orthopedic clinic. Stephen followed her with his halting, spastic gait. Mrs. Graves stated emphatically to the worker who came to interview her that she had brought her son Stephen to town to satisfy the school board, who had ordered him to have an examination. She explained that he had never been to school because he couldn't learn. He was born that way, and the doctor had said at the time of his birth he would never be right. She didn't know why people couldn't mind their own business!

It seemed that the school authorities of the district where the Graveses lived had become interested in the boy through a teacher, Miss Alden, who had been hired for the one-room rural school. She had spent most of her childhood in the area, had heard of Stephen and felt that some action should be taken about the boy's schooling. Since there were only five other pupils enrolled in the school, she would be able to give Stephen individual attention. Also she had had experience with spastic children. At her insistence the president of the school board called on Mr. Graves and explained that according to the compulsory education law, the boy must either have a medical examination or be placed in school.

The county nurse was called in to secure the necessary examination which revealed that Stephen was well developed, and that he had a mild spastic paralysis with a slight speech involvement. The prescription was that he be started on relaxation and graded exercises. No psychological studies were to be made until the boy's contacts could be broadened.

Stephen had been most eager to cooperate during the examination and was almost pathetically curious about every minute detail of the proceedings. He was interested in his surroundings, delighted with the smallest attention, and beamed in response to the smiles of other people attending the clinic. So marked were his powers of observation and so keen was his curiosity that the orthopedist conducting the examination felt that the boy must have greater mental capacity than the family recognized.

The physician spent some time explaining to Mrs. Graves, who had been intent on securing a statement that the boy was neither

physically nor mentally able to be in school, that Stephen's afflic-
tion was much milder than she had always believed.

When the exercises began, Stephen was enthusiastic, and with
each explanation of the simple movements, he would say,
"Shucks, that's easy; I can learn that in no time."

Mrs. Graves remained aloof. She could see no necessity for
Stephen's going to school, but if that was the law, she supposed
it would be all right if the teacher could put up with him. He
could do the exercises, if he wanted to. She would see that he did
them and got started in the morning. But she added, "It won't
do any good, he can't learn. The doctor said when he was born
that he'd never be normal."

Stephen was thrilled with his opportunity to go to school. The
other children accepted him with little difficulty, and were skillfully led by the teacher to include him in their activities as much
as possible. At the end of two months, the children had become
so used to his defects that they were casually and normally expecting him to participate in everything they did. Stephen was
entering into the school activities so enthusiastically that much of
the time he completely lost awareness of himself. This interest
greatly decreased his spastic movements. His school abilities
varied from second grade placement in reading readiness to
sixth grade placement in geography.

QUESTIONS

1. What concepts of personality and behavior are reflected in this
   synopsis?
2. What are your own attitudes about a spastic child? Can you account
   for them?

V. "But I can't have Anne home," wailed Mrs. Peterson. The
very thought of having the crippled seventeen-year-old girl to
take care of seemed to her to be contrary to all reasonable expectations. She asserted that Mr. Peterson was suffering from arthritis

and was barely able to do the farm work so he could not be expected to help get Anne in and out of bed. Her household duties, the two other small children, and her farm work were already too much for her. She was under medical care herself, and just couldn't assume any added responsibility.

Anne had been in a hospital in a city forty miles from home for the past year under treatment for the after effects of poliomyelitis. She was now able to be up and walking with the aid of two long leg braces, crutches, and a remedial corset. During her prolonged stay in the hospital she had been quite a problem. At the time of her admission she was hostile to both the doctors and nurses, at times even striking them when displeased. Her resentment and fear of illness was acute. During her long convalescence she lost most of this fear and resentment and became deeply attached to the hospital personnel.

When her approaching discharge was discussed with her, many of her early symptoms of muscle pain, and lack of muscle power reappeared.

Her family had visited the hospital only twice during her stay, but this had been explained on the basis of their limited finances and the confining activities of farm life. An uncle had visited about once a month, bringing her candy and small gifts.

The family physician provided insight into the behavior of the girl and her family. He revealed that Mrs. Peterson was in reality Anne's stepmother. Her whole behavior was neurotic, and her illness was only feigned. He stated that Mrs. Peterson had long resented Anne's presence in the home, as she, rather than *her* children, had received most of the attention from the neighboring relatives. The stepmother had required an unreasonable amount of work of Anne before Anne's illness, possibly as a retaliation for the preference shown by the relatives.

Continued hospitalization was undesirable according to the orthopaedist. Anne was transferred to a convalescent home where physical treatment could be continued and where she could remain until some more permanent plan could be worked out. She was reluctant to leave the hospital and cried constantly the day before she left but appeared to adjust herself fairly well to the new environment after a few days. She was able to attend school in the regular classroom, and to be outside with the other children in good weather.

Shortly she began to antagonize Mary, her roommate, with taunts that Mary's grades would never be as good as her own and that Mary's parents didn't love her. Mary was given another room and an older girl was put with Anne. She responded to this by refusing to get up for several days until the ignoring of her behavior made her abandon it.

Anne then tried to monopolize her new roommate's time and was jealous if she were out of the room for long. She also became aggressive toward the other children, with whom she began to discuss her parents, drawing the picture of them as wealthy farmers living in a twelve-room house, magnificently furnished. She explained they were away on a trip, so that they couldn't visit her now. To these romancings she added stories of her lovely clothes and possessions. The story became more and more expansive and unrealistic.

The seriousness of her mental fantasies was now so apparent that psychotherapy was advised, which necessitated rehospitalization.

QUESTIONS

1. What culture concepts are operative here?
2. What personality concepts help the worker to understand Anne's behavior.

VI. My earliest experience of any significance does not lie within my own memory but is drawn from what my mother told me at various times during my life. Shortly after I was born, mother suffered a nervous breakdown which necessitated hospitalization for several months. My brother and my sisters were old enough to be sent to my grandparents' farm to be cared for by my grandparents. They didn't feel they could assume the care of a very young baby, so I was sent to the home of friends of my father's, a couple who had never had any children of their own. For several months I was the center of attention of two adults instead of having to share that attention with three other children, which I had to do when I returned home. Mother said that I was completely spoiled when I got back—even to the point where I wouldn't drink milk. I often cried and tried in many ways to get the attention at home to which I had become accustomed in the foster home. Such behavior on my part was interpreted as a result of the complete attention in the foster home and the unconscious purpose of trying to regain that attention.

The home to which I returned after this early experience was a small home on the outskirts of a small village. It was chosen and bought primarily to give my mother a chance to rest and recuperate after her breakdown. We lived there throughout my early childhood. During the time we lived there, two more boys were born, making us a family of six children, three boys and three girls. My father was the principal of the high school. I don't remember very many of the details of our life there; the first experience that made very much of an impression upon me was moving away. I was five years old when my father secured a larger school in a neighboring state.

We had been in our new home only a few weeks when I had an experience that has affected much of my life since then. We children were used to living in the country where we had been able to play anywhere outdoors with safety, so playing tag in the street didn't appear hazardous to us even though mother had warned us against it. One day when I was "it" and was chasing my brothers across the street, a car came around the corner. The driver saw the boys but in swerving away from them hit me because he couldn't see me behind them. As a result of the accident, I lost the hearing in one ear and my face was badly scarred and partially paralyzed. I can remember being constantly reminded "not to squint" and to "straighten my face" because the other children didn't squint so. The idea undoubtedly was to try to make me more like the children. The effect was to center on sensitive points for me. Two years later, when the school nurse discovered my deafness it, too, was emphasized at home, especially by my father, who often took me aside and "tested" my hearing with his watch. I suppose now that he was trying to prove to himself that my hearing wasn't impaired, since he may have found that fact hard to accept. My reaction to my parents' efforts was a feeling that I was different from and inferior to the other children.

I carried this early feeling of being "different" which seemed to develop primarily out of my accident (the principle of multiple causation suggests that I look for other contributing factors, however), over into other areas of my life such as school and neighborhood play. In grade school, for instance, I can remember being pretty constantly on the defensive about anyone's discovering my deafness. The emphasis on it at home blocked out the possibility of my realizing, as I have since learned to realize, that few people discover it unless I deliberately tell them about it. I always got very good marks in school, though, perhaps I used them as a means of getting satisfaction in my adequacy there, that I seemed to miss in other areas of my life. I was defensive about my handicap, too, among the children I played with outside of school. I can remember the frustration I often felt in games like tag or red light where it was necessary to tell from what direction shouts came—I couldn't, and still absolutely can't tell the direction of a sound. Consequently I formed the habit of spending much of the time reading that other children spent playing.

The town where our family lived and where we went to school was one of mixed population and social stratification. There were two quite definite classes—the professional and business people and the engineers and mine owners formed the first class; the laborers, who were mostly foreign-born, made up the second. There were mining "locations" making a group of people of similar nationality background. The class system carried over into the consolidated high school which served all the locations as well as the town. In the actual classrooms, of course, no class differentiation was made but in friendships and extra-curricular activities there were definite distinctions. Thus I was accepted into the "upper class" in the school and my friends were all from families of similar social and economic status.

I was quite active in dramatics and music in high school, playing a different instrument in both band and orchestra. I also belonged to a 4-H club organized outside of the school and was a participant in the activities of our church. The church reinforced my ideas of being "different." It was conditioned to a certain extent by the familiar community attitude which sets the school principal and the minister and their families apart as models. Thus I seemed to find for myself another obstacle in addition to my physical handicap in which I felt not quite accepted—that of being the "principal's kid."

When I look back now at my experiences in school and the community, they seem pretty normal and active but I don't think anyone reasoning with me then could have made me feel they were. The emotional insecurity I had learned to feel at home seemed to carry over into my life away from home so there were few situations in which I felt completely at ease and on an equality with the other people involved.

When I finished high school, I was obsessed with the one idea that I wanted to get away from home—to escape, I suppose, from the frequent conflicts I had with my mother and from the feeling of having to live up to the family's position. I read an ad in the paper one day run by the manager of a traveling magazine crew. To me it seemed like the chance I wanted. Without giving my parents very much opportunity to find out what I was joining, I got their permission and left town with the crew. If the emotional need I felt for running away hadn't been so strong in me at the time, I imagine I would have figured out that it was a pretty foolish thing to do—leaving town in the company of people whom I had just met and knew nothing about. Less than two days with the crew showed me just how foolish I was but the need for running away was still not resolved so I stubbornly stayed with the crew for three unpleasant months. I was fortunate, however, in having joined a crew with an unusually understanding couple for managers.

I think the Parkers understood my reason for joining the crew— or maybe I just thought they did. Our crew was all girls and we "worked territory" not in residential sections where we would be talking to women but in business sections where almost all of our prospective customers were men. A typical "territory" assigned to us might include a railroad roundhouse, a block with a lumberyard, several gasoline stations, or perhaps a large warehouse where there might be idle truck drivers and other men— the most important factor was that the men be working at jobs that didn't keep them very busy and might readily accept the diversion of talking to a magazine saleswoman.

Both Mr. and Mrs. Parker really helped me by emphasizing my good points and continually reminding me of my good looks and figure, pleasing voice, etc., obvious assets in a saleswoman from a crew manager's point of view. That emphasis, however, meant more to me than merely helping me sell magazines. It was one of the first times in my life that someone had gone out of his way to tell me something good about myself. Then, too, they never failed to encourage and compliment me when I had had a successful day. Through them I feel that I got a good many satisfying and constructive experiences in the crew.

The separation from home that summer was almost complete in that I was far from the physical surroundings of home and seldom got the letters that were sent me because of the extreme uncertainty of our itinerary. Yet I gradually came to realize that it was impossible to cut myself off completely from my past life and experiences and begin over again because they were too much a part of me. It was an extremely hard thing for me to admit. I thought back to that experience when, in our class discussion of the case involving a formerly well-to-do couple struggling against applying for relief, it was brought out that a problem which eventually had to be faced might as well be faced at once.

It took a year before I was able to bring myself to go back home and to work on the problem from which I had run away. But, since to "make good" psychologically one must be allowed to make good by his own efforts and in his own way, I probably profited more by waiting a year than if someone had forced me to go back sooner. I'm sure, though, that I would have welcomed going back if someone had worked the problem through with me to a point where I could have accepted such a turning back sooner.

It was during that year spent away from home that I had another experience that seems to me to have been significant. One of my jobs was to serve as nursemaid in a well-to-do family for their four-and-one-half-year-old daughter. Caroline was asleep when I made my application and appeared a normal little girl. I was very much in need of a job, having just quit the crew and being under obligation to some family friends for my maintenance. After I had moved into Caroline's home, I was told and quickly saw that she was a spastic child of normal physical development but lacking muscular coördination to the extent that she was able neither to walk or talk. Her parents about three years before that time had resorted to faith healing in an effort to "cure" her. They would not recognize her incapacity and sought no treatment nor training for her outside of monthly visits to their practitioner. If I had any experience in seeking jobs, my questions during the application interview might have led me to suspect that I was not being told all that I had a right to know before I accepted the position.

I became interested enough in the challenge I found, to stay on in spite of the obstacles. The wages were good, the child's parents pleased with my care of her, and there was another girl who served as housekeeper and cook, who quickly became my companion.

There were many limitations in working with Caroline, the greatest being my own stage of development. With no former experience in caring for a child, much less one who was crippled, I performed on a basis of trial and error. But harder to face were the other limitations of Caroline's incapacity and inability to react and develop like a normal child. It was easy to become impatient with her for she could do nothing herself—she had to be fed, dressed, exercised and watched every minute. In addition to Caroline's limitations, her parents' passive attitude toward her had to be met and accepted. I have often thought they adopted faith healing essentially as an escape from the responsibility of meeting and accepting Caroline's incapacity which they really believed was a hopeless problem anyway since medicine could promise them almost no hope of complete cure.

After a year of working after high school, I knew I wanted to go on to college and knew, too, that my family would support me in it. I chose to go to the same small denominational school to which my father, my brothers, and my sister had gone. I proceeded to make all the necessary arrangements and plans. The week before I was to leave, my mother was taken ill with a serious illness which would require periodic treatments at the State Hospital. It was also necessary that someone be at home so I, with concealed resentment, offered to give up my college plans temporarily. By the time arrangements were worked out around her illness, it proved possible for me to go college after all.

[The events of the student's life in college are omitted in the interests of brevity. They are interesting in the evidence they present of increasing maturity and greater self-understanding.]

QUESTIONS

1. What concepts of personality and behavior are there in this personal history?
2. Which of Dollard's criteria does it illustrate?
3. Comment upon the cultural aspects of these personal incidents.

EXERCISES IN ANALYSIS OF STRUCTURE, PROCESSES, AND SKILL

I. Sunday morning about 9:00 I heard a child screaming directly under my window. In the driveway between the house I live in and the one next door, two small boys in snowsuits, one about six years old and the other one little over two, were fighting. The bigger boy knocked the smaller one to the ground and then beat him over the face and chest with his closed fist while the little one screamed and wriggled and kicked futilely. The bigger boy made no sound other than panting from exertion. The younger one's screams were loud enough to be heard by anyone within the range of two or three houses on either side. Finally the little boy struggled loose and while still kneeling on the ground grasped the other boy's hand between his teeth and hung on. This brought an anguished cry of "Mother" from the older one.

At this point a neatly dressed woman in a housedress, with hair just beginning to turn gray, probably nearing forty, rushed out of the house next door and grabbed the hand of the little boy, jerked him to his feet and began to drag him into the house. She exclaimed in an impatient, scolding voice, "You bad boy, what are you doing to Jimmy?" She and the small boy disappeared into the house. Jimmy, with a triumphant expression on his face, stood absently kicking at a piece of crusted snow in the driveway and then he, too, went into the house.

QUESTION
What assumptions can you make on these facts?

II. One day last week I visited the home of a friend with whom I have worked but whose family I had not met. I had very little knowledge of her home life before this visit. The family consists of the elderly widowed mother, and the middle-aged sister of my friend, my friend, and her four-year-old daughter. My friend's husband had deserted her a few weeks after the birth of the baby, and a short time before this he had entered voluntary bankruptcy.

The young mother has recently purchased a fur coat—her taste, in dresses, runs to net and velvet—in negligees, to satins and lace. During the evening she complained that her December bills (she also stated that she had charge accounts at four department stores) totaled considerably more than her monthly salary.

While I was there she opened several drawers in her bureau— and they were in great disorder.

The little girl, who is four years old, has poor muscle tone, poor color, and talks "baby talk" to such an extent that it is difficult to understand her. She ate her evening meal with the grown-ups. Her supper consisted for the most part of two glasses of milk—scarcely any meat or potatoes—and her pudding. She refused to eat any vegetables. Before the evening meal we had been looking at some china which the family brought from Czecho-Slovakia (their former home) and the little girl insisted on playing with two pieces. Her mother explained to her that these pieces belonged to her aunt and that the aunt would feel badly if they were broken. There was considerable conversation—but the child refused to give them up until she had broken a saucer. The little girl made conversation difficult by her loud talking and jumping on and off furniture.

The apartment is small and on the third floor. When I left at eight o'clock the little girl was still up. Her mother had expressed concern because the child sleeps poorly at night and refuses to take an afternoon nap.

QUESTIONS

1. What assumptions can you make on these observations?

2. How many of the assumptions would you consider inferences warranted by evidence?
3. What inferences do you make about the observer?

III. This morning while on the street car, I noticed a man who was heavy set and about fifty years old. I do not know how fast whiskers grow, but I should judge that he had not shaved for at least twenty-four hours; however, he looked rather well-dressed in an oxford gray overcoat, hat, and suit. On his left hand, he wore a gray suede leather glove with half of the length of the fingers cut off. It looked strange to see the fingers on the left hand bare from the middle joint to the fingertips.

The thing which particularly aroused my curiosity in the man was when he took out a new red-handled paring knife and began to peel a raw potato which had been peeled before. The knife was shaped like an ordinary paring knife, but across its blade was what appeared to be a spring. When I saw him peeling the potato, my first impression was that he must be hungry; however, he let the peelings fall on the floor of the street car, and when he was through, he put the knife and potato into his vest pocket. Then he drew from his overcoat pocket a gray suede glove for his right hand which covered the entire hand; he spit upon the street car floor, and settled back into his seat with an air of satisfaction.

The observer records her inferences as follows:
The special attachment across the blade of the knife probably was to protect one from cutting himself when peeling or paring with the knife. The man was undoubtedly a house to house salesman for this special type of paring knife because the knife was new and the potato which he was peeling had been peeled before. The care which he used in peeling the potato impressed me that he was trying to develop skill in using the tool. I decided that he wore the peculiarly cut glove on his left hand because it had

been injured or disfigured. In his demonstration work, he would need his fingertips free to hold whatever he was paring. In his general conduct, he appeared very indifferent, careless, and untidy because he let the peelings drop on the floor of the car, and he also spit upon the floor which seemed to me the height of indecency.

QUESTIONS

1. How many of the worker's inferences would you think were inferences warranted by direct observation of factual evidence?
2. Which were assumptions?
3. Would you have made any different inferences or assumptions? Why?

IV. Last summer I accompanied the county nurse on her rounds. About 10:30 one morning we stopped at a farmhouse—a three-room ramshackle building sadly in need of paint. There was an old barn, and one or two other out-buildings in the yard. An old decrepit Ford coupe stood by the door.

We entered the house through the kitchen door, and were met by a woman about 23 years old, dressed in a worn-out kimono, beneath which a nightgown could be seen. She led us into the combination living-room-bedroom where a three-months-old baby lay in a crib. The baby had a slight cold, but otherwise appeared healthy, and according to the mother was a healthy child. The county nurse had come to deliver this baby's birth certificate (her means of getting in touch with new babies in the county) and inquired concerning the baby's weight, feeding habits, etc., all of which were satisfactory. I was observing as part of my training.

The mother complained of having a headache, apologizing for the unkempt condition of the house, herself, and the baby, and saying she had just got up. The remains of a very inadequate breakfast—coffee and bread—were on the kitchen table. There were four other children, of ages from about two to six scattered around the room.

The housewife used surprisingly good grammar, and appeared intelligent and cooperative. I did not see her husband, as she said he was working out in the fields.

The nurse asked her how her sister-in-law was, and she explained she had been down there the day before—taking all the children in the above-mentioned coupe, and that she seemed to be feeling better.

The nurse also asked her about milk for herself and the children, and she said they had no cow, and had to buy evaporated milk, but could not afford any more than enough to put in their coffee. They had a small vegetable garden from which they were able to get vegetables but she did no canning of any kind.

I would consider this a case for the social worker, not necessarily because of dire need or because there was an acute condition here, but because it seemed a little aid, a little sympathy, and understanding would help her. It was obvious they were barely making both ends meet—if they were doing even that. (I did not feel I was in a position to ask questions, so refrained.) The nurse said the husband was a fairly responsible person who had had no special training and had rented this small farm for a place to live, and something to work at, as jobs were scarce. She said she had derived this information from the doctor who had attended the mother when her babies were born.

The observer records her impressions as follows:

1. This young couple were trying hard to get along.

2. They had probably not been in easy circumstances since their marriage.

3. This young woman had probably never had practical instructions in home-making, or child training or child care.

4. Although she had never met the county nurse before, she was willing to cooperate with her.

5. She was on good terms with her in-laws.

6. She was probably worn-out and discouraged from the constant responsibility of five children, and having little money.

7. The mother had at least attended the local high school, and may have graduated from it. This was evident from her good grammar, and was a pretty safe inference as I knew a large percentage of the persons in that community did attend high school.

8. She was not a very good housekeeper. The headache might have been an excuse for her sleeping so late, and the house in the condition it was, but the house gave one the impression of usually being in that condition—the sheets on the crib were very soiled, the floor was very dirty, and the other children wore ragged and torn clothes.

9. She was not used to a farm. This I inferred from the frequency with which she went to town, and the fact that the friends whose names she mentioned were all townspeople.

10. She cared a great deal for her children. She was very interested in discussing the baby's care with the nurse, and asked her if she could bring all of her children to the clinic for examination.

QUESTIONS

1. How many of these inferences would you have made on the details which make up the observation?

2. There are a number of qualifying words in the account which distort the observation. Were you conscious of these emotionally toned words as you read the account?

3. Do you think there is warrant here for referral to a social case worker? Why or why not?

4. Can you make any assumptions based on the recording as to the attitudes of the observer? (They would of course be assumptions on impression rather than on evidence.)

V. There was a day nursery in the Settlement House, and it was always an eventful time of day when the children stopped to bid good-by to their friends in the office as their respective parents came for them. George was a very alert child of five. His father, who always called for him, looked in both age and dress like a fashion-minded college sophomore. He would run up the stairs, call George and then tear down the stairs to the first floor neither looking after nor slowing his pace for his offspring. George followed as fast as he could, seeming not to expect nor want aid but trying desperately to keep up with his father's long legs. Outside the Settlement House, George and his father climbed into an up-to-date Buick, a black sports model with the top down, displaying red leather seats. I could see from the office window that George was standing on the seat in order to get a better view of traffic.

From these facts the worker records the following:

The nursery children were admitted after investigation on a needy basis, and paid $.75 a week for the food costs. George's family may have owned the car and had an income equal to such expenditures, but it is not likely they would place their son in a day nursery supported by the Community Fund. The investigator would surely have been acquainted with this fact, and if George's mother were dead, other arrangements for his care could have been provided. If the father owned the car and needed one in his business, the sale of the Buick and subsequent purchase of a lower priced car would still leave a goodly sum. And having sufficient money for other care, would he want George to be in that neighborhood with many children all day, where no matter how scientific the care of the children is, they are still unable to get outdoors and romp in fresh air. The clothes may have been relics of better days, or they may have been given the young father. He may have friends who let him use the car each evening to pick up his youngster and lastly he may be a driver for a family who also keep him in this way. These are all inferences, but this much is certain: George's father was forced to ask for aid for his son, as he was unable to provide suitable care for him during the day, but in no way is this dependency carried over in his treatment of George. As a result George is independent, unafraid—knowing no insecurity.

QUESTIONS
1. What are your comments on this observation?
2. Are the worker's assumptions tenable?
3. Which would you question from the data given?
4. Do other assumptions occur to you?

EXAMPLES OF INTERVIEWING PROCESSES, SKILL, AND OTHER COMPONENTS

I. Shortly after the Visiting Nurses Association office opened one morning, the telephone rang. It was the wife of a prominent business executive.

"I have an unusual request to make," she said to the nurse. "My husband's elevator man, who has been working for him for fifteen years, has been acting strangely for the last two days. Yesterday afternoon the other men came to my husband in alarm saying, 'Jim's quite out of his head.' My husband has just called me to say that Jim has not shown up this morning. He is terribly worried. I suddenly thought of the Visiting Nurses. Of course, I do not know whether you can do anything about a case like this."

The call came about nine o'clock. Within fifteen minutes the nurse was at the address given.

"Upstairs," said a woman in the hall, when she inquired the way to Jim's apartment.

The nurse climbed the four flights of stairs. On the top landing she found a Negro pacing up and down in his pajamas. She had no doubt that this was Jim.

"What are you doing out here, Jim?" she asked casually.

"People in there," he answered, looking at her wildly, "are trying to kill me."

The situation seemed grave. It was perfectly apparent that the patient was running a high temperature.

"Now, Jim, come on in with me," she said.

"Oh no, I won't," he answered. "You'd better not either. They'll kill you sure."

The nurse walked up to him. "Jim, I've come from your boss. You know, Mr. Smith. He said I should come and see you because you are a sick man. He wants me to find the very best doctor in the city to come and make you well. Now open the door, Jim, and let me put you to bed."

Jim paused for a moment. "Mr. Smith, you say? He sure is a fine man. Guess I'd better do what he says."

The nurse took Jim in and introduced herself to the bewildered relatives, who obviously had been unable to cope with the situation. She put Jim to bed and took his temperature. It was 105°.

"Now," she said, "I'm going to send for the best doctor."

She ordered an ambulance and within an hour the patient was on his way to the hospital. The ambulance physician diagnosed the case as "double pneumonia—dangerously ill."

The nurse's comments are:

This illustrates the importance of skill in approach. Bewildered families in their desperation often do further damage to a patient too sick to know what he is doing. The nurse was not shocked at Jim's appearance in the hallway in his pajamas, nor did she reproach him for being up and about when he was so ill.

She knew that it was useless to argue or reason with a man who was delirious. She assumed that since Jim had worked for Mr. Smith for fifteen years, he probably had a regard and respect for him. When the nurse mentioned Mr. Smith's name, Jim responded, not because he thought it was the right thing to do, nor because the nurse had convinced him to go to bed, but because his respected employer, Mr. Smith, wished it.

QUESTION

Are there any other factors that you can think might have contributed to the nurse's success with this patient?

II. Mr. Jones came to a public agency which is charged with responsibility for the supervision of county agencies. The county agencies administer the Social Security aid programs, which include old age assistance. Mr. Jones is concerned with a lien that has been filed against property which he may own and wishes to have the lien removed from the records of the Register of Deeds.

Purpose of interview: To learn about Mr. Jones' problem as he sees it, and to give him advice that may help him to meet it.

The interview takes place in the office of the supervisory agency. Mr. Jones had called and said he would come in at 4:00 P.M. to see Mr. Smith.

SECRETARY: Mr. Smith, this is Mr. Jones, who would like to talk with you.

SMITH: Yes, I have your telephone message saying you would be here by 4 o'clock. You are very punctual.

JONES: I aim to be on time, part of my business training.

SMITH: Will you have a chair, please?

JONES: Thank you.

SMITH: Your telephone call stated that you wanted to talk about the lien on your property.

JONES: Yes, that's right, I was up to the capitol and they told me to see you.

SMITH: Did you get some information at the capitol that you would like me to add to?

JONES: Nope, didn't get much satisfaction from M., the attorney general. He was too busy. You know I was as much responsible for his election as any man in the state.

SMITH: I am sure Mr. M. appreciates such loyal support.

JONES: You know, I'm somewhat of a lawyer myself, in a practical way. I used to deal in real estate years ago—that's my problem, I'd like to do it again.

SMITH: You look as though you're in good health; people really never become too old to do something useful.

JONES: That's what I figure. If I could get that lien off the books, I'd be all right.

SMITH: You do have property to which the lien can attach?

JONES: No, I haven't, but in land deals you sometimes act as third person in a deal, and then the lien attaches to the property.

SMITH: I see your practical knowledge of law has been helpful to you.

JONES: Use it every day.

SMITH: Are you receiving assistance now?

JONES: Nope, not for two years.

SMITH: Did you work in the cities?

JONES: Part of the time, sometimes in the northwestern part of the state. Had some good land deals there but couldn't handle them because of the lien.

SMITH: If you didn't own land outside of the county from which you received your grant, a lien would not have been filed in any other county.

JONES: Is that so, I never thought of that. But anyway I don't like the lien.

SMITH: Did you have any property of recent years that you got through land sales?

JONES: Used to have real estate off and on. You see my family was in the banking business—lost everything but I'm not too old to try something again.

SMITH: The fact that you have gotten along the last two years without old age assistance proves that. . . . About this lien business, there are certain conditions that permit a county to release the lien with the approval of the state agency. One is for the "welfare and support" of the recipient. If you have some reasonable evidence that will show that you could get along without old age assistance if the lien were removed from the records, I think your case could be considered. Especially in view of the fact that you haven't any property now to which the lien is attached.

JONES: I see, but how do I go about it?

SMITH: You start with the County Welfare Board. You will have to prove your case to them. In other words, it will be necessary for them to satisfy their records as to the justification for release of lien.

JONES: Does it take long?

SMITH: That depends mostly upon you, how quickly you can organize and prove your proposition, so they can accept it.

JONES: Well, I'll try.

SMITH: If you have any further questions, please call me, I'll be glad to help if I can.

JONES: Thank you, good-by.

SMITH: Good-by.

The interviewer explains his assumptions as follows:

1. The man had more than ordinary work experience (knowledge of law, which was quite accurate).

2. He wanted to have some position of leadership (participation in politics).

3. He preferred to support himself if possible, a part of his pride which is rooted in his more successful days in business.

4. Physically he was able to do some work; he had been self-supporting for two years.

5. He wasn't reticent about meeting people—first place he went to was the chief legal officer for the state.

His responses were made on the basis of these observations and assumptions.

QUESTIONS

1. Do you consider this a successful interview? Why?
2. Analyze the structure of the interview.
3. What techniques did the worker use?

III. Beatrice Y. is an eighteen-year-old girl who had delivered an illegitimate child in her home two months ago. She lived with her sister and brother-in-law, their three young children, and a middle-aged aunt in an old, crowded house in the poorest section of town. The child was born with a clubfoot deformity.

The district public health nurse had given Beatrice and the baby regular bedside care for five days. During these visits she repeatedly tried to learn about the parentage of the child and the circumstances for the child's birth, thinking that she must know these things in order to help the girl. Unfortunately, her interviews always had to be conducted in the presence of Beatrice's sister, or some other member of the family.

Failing completely to gain rapport or even privacy, she tried to question Beatrice's sister but without success.

Finally Beatrice became openly antagonistic toward the nurse and told her that friends were caring for the baby and she didn't know their name and address. Realizing that she could do no more for Beatrice as a professional person with such a barrier of hostility and emotion between them, she referred the case to another public health nurse.

The second nurse decided (1) to allow for a "cooling off" period in order to give Beatrice a chance to think things out; (2) to treat her as an adult, mature person (the school record, etc., showed she was capable of this); (3) if possible, to use the approach of helping the baby grow up as healthy as possible—get a good start in life; (4) to recognize that Beatrice may have some good ideas concerning her own welfare and that of the baby; and (5) to try not to ask questions which may give Beatrice the impression that she was "prying" and wanted to know some things just to satisfy her curiosity. If she only could help Beatrice realize and recognize her problems she would be more ready to seek guidance.

The nurse found Beatrice busily hanging clothes in the back yard early one morning.

She introduced herself, "I am Miss J. from the Community Nurse Association." Beatrice didn't acknowledge the introduction, and silently kept on with her work.

NURSE: I'd like to see if the two of us, together, can work out a plan whereby your child can get good medical care for his bad foot.

The nurse thought she could tell from the girl's expression that this *was* a problem which she hadn't been able to meet satisfactorily.

BEATRICE: Well, if it won't bother you to see a lot of dirty clothes I suppose we could talk about it in the basement. The house is full upstairs (*still a trifle belligerent*).
NURSE: I don't think it would—except it may remind me of the pile *I* have to wash at home.

The nurse followed Beatrice in silence down the steps to a dark, damp basement. She didn't talk immediately, but sat down on a stool near the stairs, found a place to put her bag.

BEATRICE (*with vehemence*): My baby has to be all right! He has to get a decent start in life. This is the only thing that matters to me! If he can't grow up right there's just no—no sense to anything!

Both quietly thought this over for a time.

NURSE: That is just why we like to call on all mothers—to help them decide on ways to get their babies off to a good start.
BEATRICE: Nurse, can you—is there any way that Jimmy's—I call him Jimmy—leg can be fixed?
NURSE: Have you talked it over with your doctor?
BEATRICE: He said I'll have to take him to a specialist. But

there are none here. And I don't know how I could leave—take him somewhere else, I mean! I've been thinking and thinking! And I can't find an answer.

They both considered this for a minute.

NURSE: Have you heard about the Crippled Children's Clinics?
BEATRICE: No.
NURSE: Every year the best specialists from the University go out to different counties all over the state and set up clinics where anybody can come to see if a physical handicap can be corrected. It's free of charge.
BEATRICE: When are they having one of these clinics near here?
NURSE: I just got a notice the other day telling about such a clinic in L. (*neighboring town*). Now that's only ten miles from here. Is there any way that you can make arrangements to get there? It will be next Wednesday.
BEATRICE: Well—maybe I could get my brother to drive me over in his truck. Sometimes he gets jobs over there.
NURSE: Would you like to talk this over with your brother tonight? Then I'll call tomorrow and see how we can plan further?
BEATRICE: That'd be swell. I have lots of other things I want to ask, but, well, I'm pretty busy today—and I'd sort of like to get this clinic business straightened out first. After all, that's most important!—You *will* come back tomorrow then, nurse. I'll show you the baby!
NURSE: Yes, I'll see you tomorrow. I'm anxious to see that young son of yours. Good-by.
BEATRICE: Good-by, nurse—and thanks a lot!

QUESTIONS

1. How do you explain the differences in results between the contacts of the former nurse and the single contact reported by the second nurse in terms of processes, techniques, and attitudes?

2. Which of these is most important in this case?
3. What concepts of behavior was the second nurse using?

IV. The interview was an actual interview recorded in dialogue with the worker's inferences as part of a class assignment.

The situation of John O., age 14, was referred to the Clinic by Dr. P., because of reading difficulty. Mrs. O. then phoned Miss Miller for an appointment. I then saw Mrs. O. for the referral interview. The content of these interviews is limited as closely as possible to a statement of the problem and to such history as is essential to point it up. The case then goes to a committee for acceptance or rejection.

I approached this interview with both anticipation and apprehension; anticipation because I had been eager to handle a case from the beginning, and apprehension because I wondered if I would remember all the pertinent points to be covered.

I introduced myself to Mrs. O. in the reception room. She was a small, worn, rather stocky middle-aged woman, neatly but simply dressed. Her face bore a worried, frightened expression, and she looked as if she were about to burst into tears. Her purse was grasped tightly in both hands.

I inferred from Mrs. O.'s appearance that she was probably in very moderate financial circumstances, and that she had probably worked hard. She gave the impression of being very tense and anxious, and I thought that her tension might be involved both with her son's problem and with the new experience of coming to the Clinic.

I invited Mrs. O. into my office, and she followed me timidly.

WORKER: Wouldn't you like me to take your coat? It's so warm here.

MRS. O.: Yes, it is warm.

We chatted about the weather for a moment while I hung up her coat and we got settled, Mrs. O. contributing quietly and rather absently. When she sat down, she leaned forward in her chair, her fingers folding and unfolding the handle of her purse.

MRS. O.:   Did Miss Miller tell you about John?

I felt that Mrs. O. was quite disturbed about this problem. My small efforts to make her feel more comfortable were apparently not even perceived, and without further preliminaries she approached directly the question on her mind. She was very tense.

WORKER: Yes, she told me that John has been having trouble with his reading for a long time. She also gave me the other information you told her over the phone. There are a few more dates that we would like to know. Would you like to give them to me before we talk about John?

We spent about a minute collecting the necessary data.

WORKER: I understand you have been quite worried about John.
MRS. O.:   I've been awfully worried. (*Tears came to her eyes.*) He is such a good boy, and he feels so badly about his reading.

There was warmth and tenderness in Mrs. O.'s voice when she spoke of John, and I felt that the relationship must be quite a close one.

MRS. O.:   He's had trouble ever since he started to school. (*She hesitated.*)
WORKER: Would you like to begin with his entering kindergarten and tell me all about this trouble?
MRS. O.:   I guess that's the best way. Let's see—I get mixed up in this, so I'm not sure about all the years. I tried to remember

before I came, because I thought you'd want to know, but I'm not sure. John started to kindergarten just after he was five, so it must have been in 1942. He got along all right there, but the teacher said he was just a baby, because he couldn't do anything for himself. (*With an apologetic smile*) I guess that was my fault because he was the baby of the family for so long, and I did do everything for him. I'm like that with the baby, too.[1]

There was a pause and Mrs. O.'s eye filled with tears again.

MRS. O.:   I've wondered and wondered if John's trouble has anything to do with the baby. John has always just seemed to worship Tom and he'll do anything for him. He's never seemed the least bit jealous, but I've wondered.

Mrs. O. showed so much feeling here that I wondered if there might be some conflict within her or the home around this baby.

WORKER: Was it after Tom came that John started having trouble with his reading?
MRS. O.:   Oh, no! That's been ever since he began school.
WORKER: Then there are probably other things that have bearing on the reading.

Mrs. O. relaxed a little and we went on with the school history, which the Clinic wanted in detail. The getting of this was difficult, as Mrs. O. appeared to try hard to remember significant dates and grades but could not do so. John was retarded, but she could not recall accurately when this happened.

I felt that her inability to remember might be an indication of Mrs. O.'s own disturbance, as she spoke well and seemed intelligent.

[1] John was 11 when Tom, the next and youngest child, was born.

WORKER: We still have half a year unaccounted for, don't we?

MRS. O.: I just can't remember. I'm sure the M. School could tell you, though.

WORKER: May we call there, if it seems necessary?

MRS. O.: Oh, yes. Only—could it be done without John knowing about it? He's pretty sensitive.

I was impressed with Mrs. O.'s apparent willingness to co-operate through letting the agency make a contact like this with so little hesitation.

WORKER: I'm sure we could do it so it would not be embarrassing to him.

Mrs. O. began to twist the handle of her purse again.

MRS. O.: I just wonder if it might be John's eyes. You know, when he was in the third or fourth grade the teacher told me she thought he needed glasses, and I took him to Dr. G. He said that there was—let's see—slow transfer of vision from the eyes to the brain, and he said John should wear glasses for two years. John didn't want to wear them after that, because the children called him "storm windows" so we never went back to the doctor. (*Pause*) I was awfully upset by what the doctor said, and I thought that John might have a tumor on the brain. I knew someone who had. But Dr. G. told me it wasn't that. Dr. G. could tell you all about this, I know.

Mrs. O. impressed me as being a very anxious person, judging from her tension.

WORKER: Perhaps we shall want to call him. Did the glasses help John?

MRS. O.: Yes, I think they might have. For a year or so around that time it seems to me that he did better in school. (*Tensely*) Do you suppose he should have glasses now?

WORKER: I wouldn't know, but if you are concerned, it might be well to have his eyes examined again. You have thought a great deal about how to help John, haven't you?

MRS. O.: Oh, yes. I *worry* about him so, because I know he tries to do well. Last year, we were both upset when his teacher phoned me that John was not cooperating in school. You know, John is not a mean or mischievous boy.

I felt that Mrs. O.'s tendency to defend John might be significant, but I thought it could not be interpreted at this point.

WORKER: What did the teacher mean?

MRS. O.: Why, she said he talked and laughed a little and that he was not really bad, but his work was too poor for him to be wasting any time. I took him to Dr. W. then and he said John needed his tonsils out and that he had an obstruction in his nose. We—we couldn't do anything about it then, but Dr. W. just said that there isn't anything wrong now.

WORKER: How is John doing in school now?

MRS. O. (*tears again*): Not very well. His teacher told me last week that his reading has improved in the last six weeks, but that he needs much more improvement to pass. He gets G's in everything except spelling and reading and—I don't remember —I think it's history or grammar. I was so upset about this that I cried—and John did, too.

WORKER: Have you heard John read?

MRS. O.: Oh, yes—he reads very badly. He can't sound out words—even easy ones. Sometimes I have him read to Tom and he can hardly do it—even baby books. He says he has to picture words in his mind, and in spelling the teacher reads the words too fast. About two weeks ago he came home from catechism class crying because he couldn't read. He wouldn't tell what had happened, but he said he wished he were dead. (*Mrs. O. sobbed.*)

WORKER (*after a pause*): It's been hard for both you and John.

MRS. O.: Oh, it's terrible.

Mrs. O. moved forward on her chair, clasping her purse tightly. She spoke hesitatingly and with obvious difficulty.

MRS. O.: Miss. H., there's something about this I think you should know. That time that the teacher called me last year, and I said I was taking John to the doctor, she said, "I think his trouble is mental—not physical." You see—Mr. O.'s mother was sent to a mental hospital about two years ago. The doctors said she had hardening of the arteries, but I've wondered if that was really what caused it. She was really like that for years. She had a terrible life, because her husband left her when my husband was very small, and she brought him up alone. She could never give up my husband, and right after we were married she came to live with us. She was so selfish—and so jealous—and she said such awful things about people that no one liked her. (*Mrs. O. wept again.*)

WORKER: Was she with you long?

MRS. O.: About a year that time. Then my husband lost his job and we went to live with my folks. About three times afterward, she tried to live with us, but we couldn't get along.

WORKER: Just what was she like?

MRS. O.: Oh, she talked so terribly about people, especially my parents; and she accused everyone of talking about her and of stealing from her and my husband. The last two years before we sent her away she had to move nearly every week because she was always in trouble. My husband just *wouldn't* believe anything was wrong.

I inferred from this that, while Mrs. O. showed in her attitude a need to defend her husband as she had John earlier, there was a great deal of hostility toward him. I felt, too, that her disturbance over her mother-in-law might be due in part to some guilt feeling for the way she had treated the older woman.

WORKER: How did she affect the children?

MRS. O.: Not much because we kept them away from her. (*Mrs. O. cried again.*) They knew about it because my husband and I quarreled so much about her. (*Quickly*) We never had trouble about other things—only his mother. He blamed me for all the trouble. We had to have four doctors see her before he would believe she was insane. Since then he seems to understand that I couldn't have caused all the trouble with her before. Our quarreling was what upset John, and he cried whenever it happened. (*Mrs. O. became very tense.*) Miss H., *do* you think that John could have inherited anything from his grandmother? There's never been anything like this in either of our families before.

Mrs. O.'s anxiety was obviously very great. I had the feeling that she was asking for reassurance not only about John but also indirectly for herself. I wanted very much to explore this further with her, but because this was a referral, not a treatment, interview, I felt I should not do it.

WORKER: You know, Mrs. O., I couldn't assure anyone in the world that he or she would never become mentally disturbed, but I do think you are doing a vast amount of unnecessary worrying about this.

We talked for a while about mental illness, its incidence, its implications, and its treatment, and Mrs. O. finally relaxed completely for the first time since she had entered the office.

It had been most difficult for Mrs. O. to bring out this material, and her doing so seemed indicative of her readiness to move toward working on any part she might play in solving John's difficulties. I was aware that my reassurance was superficial, and I felt quite sure that Mrs. O. was filled with deep-seated anxieties with their accompanying guilt feelings. It seemed likely that she had many conflicts about herself and her relationships to her family, which might or might not have bearing on the problem about which she was consulting the Clinic. Her statements and her actions seemed to point in this direction. Reassurance on this particular point seemed to answer some immediate need for Mrs. O.

Mrs. O. gave the remainder of the necessary information in a calm, relaxed way. She said that her five other children seemed to be happy and well adjusted. She described John as a generous, courteous boy, who got along well with his family and had many friends. He was very close to his father, who thought Mrs. O. babied John. John had few home duties, for Mrs. O. wanted him to go to catechism class twice a week, and she thought he needed the rest of his time for recreation. He was sensitive and cried easily, especially when he was frustrated. He had a "nervous mannerism," which consisted of placing the toes of one foot on the floor and shaking the leg rapidly up and down, without knowing he was doing it. His teacher said he was a "dreamer" in school, and sometimes at home he acted as if he were in a trance, carrying out an act in slow motion, until he suddenly "snapped out of it." He was dependable, and this year was a police boy at school. He was good at basketball and hockey, both of which he played a great deal.

When this information was completed, I explained something of what a Clinic study meant, and I discussed the procedure. I mentioned that John's problem would be presented on Tuesday to the application committee to determine whether or not he could be accepted for diagnosis and treatment, and that Mrs. O.

would be notified immediately afterward as to what the Clinic would do.

At this point Mrs. O. looked at me in obvious dismay.

MRS. O.: Oh, I thought that had already been decided. Do they ever turn people down here?

WORKER: Not often. Only when the case is one where the Clinic feels their services are not the kind that would help. John's problem is one in which the Clinic happens to be particularly interested, so I think you need not worry.

MRS. O. (*relaxing again*): Oh, I do hope they'll take him.

We then discussed fees. Mrs. O. explained that the family had started a small hardware business a few months ago and that business was still slightly precarious. She did want to pay for service, however, and after some joint consideration of the income Mrs. O. decided they could pay fifty cents per interview.

I received the impression that Mrs. O. would have paid almost any amount to get help for John.

We closed the interview at this point.

MRS. O. (*as she was about to leave*): Thank you, Miss H. You'll let me know then?

WORKER: Yes, Mrs. O. I'll call you on Wednesday.

I felt very sympathetic toward Mrs. O. throughout this interview, and I was much interested in the implications of the material she had brought out, and hoped that I might be the worker assigned to work with the mother.

QUESTION

This is presented primarily as illustration of the way a worker's observations and assumptions concerning them, help the movement of the interview. It also should provide material for a discussion on mechanisms of behavior and personality problems. Unless it is used in a class where students are engaged in supervised field work and are thoroughly grounded in personality disorders, the discussions should avoid the dynamics of case treatment. A discussion of the worker's awareness of the meaning of the interviewee's behavior and responses would be more profitable for undergraduate students than a theoretical discussion of the treatment processes.

V. It was my first independent visit on my student field work for the Community Health Service, and my head was exploding with all the theory I had assimilated in my classes. Would I be able to gain the confidence of this family? Would they be able to tell I was so new at my job? Would my decisions be accepted by the family? I had much apprehension as I climbed the steps of the W. home. My supervisor had already informed me that this would be a Negro family and that the mother was worried about her little girl who she said was very weak and had a little fever. I went into a dark hall, rapped at the door, and was greeted by a smiling Negro man.

"Good afternoon, my name is Miss Peterson. I'm the nurse from the Community Health Service."

He ushered me into the house and introduced me to Mrs. W., who informed me how happy she was that I could come so soon after she had called. As I took off my wraps and set my bag down, I asked about the little girl, what her name was, how old she was, how long she had been sick, and what, if anything, had they been doing for her.

Mrs. W. was very eager to answer all my questions and kept telling me, in a soft Southern drawl, how thankful she was for my visit, all of which was very reassuring to me.

Orielle, my little five-year-old patient, was lying in bed with mounds of covers over her, yet she was shivering and whimpering.

"I'm Miss Peterson, your nurse, Orielle. You've been a sick little girl, haven't you? We're going to see what we can do to make you well. Where does it hurt the most, Orielle?"

She pointed to her throat and the glandular area near her ears, and began to cry.

"Have you been able to eat your meals and drink milk and water, Orielle?" After she replied that it hurt, I explained to her that I wanted to look at some of the places that hurt and she consented to it, opening her mouth wide while I looked at her throat, using a tongue depressor.

I tried not to appear alarmed at the glistening grayish membrane I saw in her tonsil region.

"What do you think is the matter with Orielle, Miss Peterson?" Mrs. W. asked as she attempted to keep her two younger children from climbing on the bed.

"Orielle is a sick little girl, Mrs. W. She needs rest and it looks as though she might have a communicable disease so let's try to keep the other children out of the room. She feels very warm so I'll take her temperature."

As I prepared the thermometer I talked to Mrs. W. about other symptoms Orielle might have had. I found out that the youngest boy had had a rash a week previously and was a little irritable. No other children in the neighborhood had a disease such as scarlet fever or diphtheria that she knew of.

"Orielle, I'm going to take your temperature because you feel so warm. I'm going to put this little glass stick between your legs for a few minutes and I want you to lie quietly while it is in."

Orielle cried very hard but allowed me to insert the thermometer. It read 105.8°. I told Mrs. W. that her temperature was very high and that I would like to sponge her with warm water and give an enema. I explained to Mrs. W. the things I would need and we prepared the material. While I was working, Orielle was lying quietly, almost too tired to cry.

After I completed my work, Mrs. W. thanked me and said she felt sure Orielle would be getting better.

"I don't like what I saw in Orielle's throat, Mrs. W., and her temperature is far too high. I would like to have a doctor see her to make sure. Do you have a family doctor?"

"Yes, we do. If you think he should see Orielle, I'll call him."

"I think it would be best to do so right away because he might want to give her some medicine that could be started right away and he might want her to go to the hospital."

Mrs. W. thought Orielle wasn't that sick and that she could take care of her, but if I thought Orielle should go to the hospital, she would take her there. Mrs. W. called Dr. Carle and explained to him what I said and that I was there. He asked to talk to me and I told him what I could of Orielle's symptoms. He decided that she should go directly to Public Hospital and he would like me to make the arrangements.

Mrs. W. was very reluctant to have Orielle go to the hospital. We talked about the many advantages of the hospital and the good care she would receive. "I know, Mrs. W., because I was a nurse at Public Hospital and I took care of many little children. Of course, they are lonesome at first, but in a few hours, they are happy and apparently forget that they aren't home," I explained.

This seemed to reassure Mrs. W. and she said, "Yes, I do think it would be best, because the other children are so noisy too."

"I'd like to come again and check the other children, Mrs. W. I'm glad that Orielle is going to the hospital. I'll go to her room and tell her about it."

Orielle accepted the idea of going, probably because she was too weak to do otherwise. I explained to Mrs. W. how important it was that Orielle be kept warm and we planned the amount of clothing she would wear for the journey to the hospital.

In all the following visits I brought messages about Orielle's progress in the hospital. I also found that Mrs. W. was pregnant and we discussed plans for good prenatal care.

QUESTIONS

1. What purposes do you think the visit accomplished?
2. What factors made this a successful first visit?

VI. Usually an interview between a psychiatrist and a child suffering from a psychological disturbance is held in privacy for the purposes of diagnosis and therapy. Recently, I had the opportunity to observe such an interview before a large group of medical personnel and students for the purpose of teaching.

On this occasion a famous child psychiatrist, Dr. C., was visiting a university school in the capacity of instructor in a medical extension course. One part of the program was a clinic presentation of a group of children from the university hospital during which Dr. C. participated. The clinic was held in a large amphitheatre with lighted blackboard, projection screen, x-ray show boxes and other paraphernalia of medical teaching.

Just before a fifteen-year-old child, whom we shall call Helen, was brought into the amphitheatre, a young interne described the case. Helen had a two-month history of seizures that were increasing in frequency and severity. The history indicated that both organic and psychological factors might be operating in the precipitation and continuance of the seizures. X-rays of the skull were shown in the lighted view box; other data were outlined on the board. Then the interne went to the waiting room and brought Helen in, asking her to sit in a chair in the pit of the amphitheatre facing the large audience. There was little said to Helen by the interne and that was not audible to me.

Helen slid into the chair and sat with her eyes, one of which was crossed, cast down for a tense moment while all eyes were turned upon her. After what seemed an interminable silence, the staff doctor in charge turned to Dr. C. and asked him if he would like to ask Helen some questions. Dr. C., who was sitting in the front row just in front of Helen, responded at once but quietly.

DR. C.:   First of all I would like to ask your name.
H.:   Helen Smith.
DR. C.:   Where do you live?
H.:   At Mainsville.

DR. C.:   Is that far from here?

H.:   About 200 miles.

DR. C.:   How long have you been here?

H.:   About ten days.

DR. C.:   Do you like it here?

H.:   Oh yes!

DR. C. (*laughingly*):   You do not have to say you like it just because all of the doctors are here.

Helen was mature enough to appreciate the humor in this, laughed too, and relaxed considerably.

DR. C.:   Do you want to stay here a long time?

H.:   For a while, not too long.

DR. C.:   Just long enough for the doctors to help you?

Suggestively he indicated that her stay would be terminated, that this was a temporary situation set up to help her.

DR. C.:   Do you like it at home? Are you happy there?

H.:   Yes.

DR. C.:   I understand that you have been working pretty hard at home.

Here he referred to her taking full responsibility of the farm home, the two younger children, some outdoor work, and the summer canning.

H.:   Yes, pretty hard.

Dr. C. realized that she was non-committal about her feelings when approached directly and took a new tack.

DR. C.:   What do you want to do when you grow up?

H.:   Be a secretary.

DR. C.:   You'd like that?

H.:   Yes.

DR. C.:   Helen, you are much too old to believe in fairies but I want to play a game with you. Let's pretend that a wish-fairy came to you and said that you could have anything you wanted. You must, however, limit yourself to three wishes. What would your first wish be?

H.: To be a secretary.

DR. C.: What would your second wish be?

"Don't know," Helen tensely responded.

DR. C.: Can't you think?

Helen only nodded negatively. One could almost see her withdrawing within herself as the questions became more pressing and closer to the heart of her psychological problems.

DR. C.: Where do you want to be a secretary?

Helen responded with the names of two large cities, one of which was the location of the university hospital.

DR. C.: Helen, do you know why you are here?

H.: To help me with my attacks.

DR. C.: What are they like?

H.: I get a pain right here in my chest and then I straighten out.

DR. C.: Are you afraid when you have them?

H.: Yes.

DR. C.: Why?

H.: The pain in my chest.

DR. C.: Can you show me what they are like?

H.: No.

DR. C.: Don't you know what they are like?

H.: No, I'm not awake then.

This was apparently contrary to fact as the history showed that Helen not only answered questions verbally during attacks but answered them by voluntary movements that temporarily interrupted the involuntary movements.

DR. C.: Thank you, Helen. You may go back to the ward now. I hope that your attacks improve and that you get your wish to be a secretary.

H.:   Good-by (*said smilingly and with obvious relief*).

After Helen left the room, Dr. C. rose to his feet, faced the audience, and made his interpretation of the case as far as this meager contact with the child would permit. Then he went on to point out some of the techniques of interviewing. He emphasized again the importance of addressing the child as a person and not to talk of her in the third person in her presence. The wish device was one that he frequently used with children and had found that it rarely brought forth the wishes related to the evident problem but not infrequently exposed hidden feelings. Helen was too tense in this situation to expose anything she had not already indicated.

QUESTIONS

1. Why is privacy desirable in an interview?
2. Why do you think the doctor began the interview by asking her name, etc.?
3. Why do you think he asked if she wanted to stay a long time in the hospital?
4. What was he trying to do in asking if she were happy and referring to the hard work she did at home?
5. Why did he change the focus of the interview by asking what she wanted to do when she grew up?
6. How did Dr. C. overcome the handicaps of the setting to the extent he did?

EXAMPLES OF ATTITUDES AND OTHER PREDISPOSING ELEMENTS AS FACTORS IN SKILL

I. One of my clients was badly in need of dental care. I gave her the schedule of costs. There was a dentist one block from her home to whom she wanted to go because of the problem of finding someone to stay with her two-year-old daughter. If she went to this dentist, she could have a young girl go along to the office to stay with her daughter. When the dentist sent in the estimate to the agency, he failed to itemize the work to be done, and it was necessary for me to call on him to get an itemized statement. When he had gone over the schedule of dental costs which I had brought, he frankly said he did not want to do my client's work as he could not do the work for those prices. He also protested that Mrs. R. was a hard patient to work with because she was so nervous and he did not think it worth his effort.

I was concerned because I knew it would be hard for Mrs. R. to go to another dentist and had a strong desire to urge him to do the work. I suggested that he fill out the estimates at the prices he felt he should have, but I had to restrain myself from trying to persuade him to do what I wanted him to do. While I felt hostile toward him for being unwilling to help someone who was obviously in need of dental work, I could understand why he hesitated knowing that dentists are now overworked taking care of patients who can well afford to pay. The dentist sent in the estimate; fortunately his estimate came within Mrs. R.'s budgetary limitations.

Discuss this account in terms of the attitudes involved.

II. Mrs. C. recently applied for an A.D.C. grant for her six children. Her husband is a physically incapacitated veteran of World War I. In completing the social investigation I discovered that the family was in need of financial help and also that Mrs. C. was nine months pregnant. Because of the acute situation it was necessary for me to make several home calls which involved problems other than getting the social history. After two weeks, I had recommended a retroactive grant of $103 and referred the $80 budget deficiency to the Department of Veterans' Affairs. I then made another home call to explain the budget deficiency and the referral, and to discuss plans for Mrs. C.'s hospitalization. At this time I felt my relationship with Mrs. C. was good.

About a week later on the first of the month Mrs. C. called me. She seemed quite upset that the Aid to Dependent Children check had not come that day because she was anxious to have the money in order to arrange her affairs before going to the hospital. When I told her there was no way in which I could hurry the check but that I was sure it would come within the next two days, she was angry with me. After talking with her I had a definite conflict trying to decide if I should make another home call. I realized that in her condition she would naturally be upset and would probably like to discuss with me what to do if she went to the hospital before the check arrived. However, I also felt that in calling on her she might become too dependent and also develop the idea that any time she wanted something all she would have to do was to call and I would come running. I did not go to see her. At the next home call two weeks later, I discovered Mrs. C. had received the check before she went to the hospital. It took two home calls to bring our relationship back to the level of understanding we had formerly had.

QUESTIONS
1. Discuss this example in terms of the attitudes involved.
2. What do you think was the worker's real conflict?

III. I was doing my first adoptive home placement for the agency: had made several contacts, visited the prospective foster parents several times, and was checking everything prior to writing up the case. All details checked except for one thing: I had no idea of the financial status of the foster father. In all of my interviews, although I knew it was important, I managed to forget to ask about this point. Inquisitiveness has never been one of my characteristics, yet at no other time do I recall having any hesitation in regard to questions about money. They were clients, it was my job, and that was all there was to it. Yet I still avoided asking this particular couple about wages, insurance, and savings. Somehow they didn't seem like "regular clients." I finally overcame my problem by phoning the woman, and carrying on the interview by telephone. I had no hesitation about doing this, and easily obtained a full report.

QUESTIONS
1. What mechanism of behavior does the worker's attitude illustrate?
2. Why was it easier to carry out this assignment by telephone?
3. What would you have done?
4. What are the ethical implications?

IV. For one of my cases it was necessary to get verification of school attendance of the children to facilitate the making of an A.D.C. grant. At the school, I was referred to the school social worker. When I asked if I could see the cumulative record card, she insisted that she wanted to review the record cards, see the children's teachers, and then discuss the children with me a week later. I told her that I would appreciate this additional information later as it would give me a better idea of the children's school adjustment, but asked if I could just see the attendance cards, explaining that verification of attendance was all that was needed to complete the eligibility requirements. The school social worker refused to give this information. At that point I felt frustrated knowing the grant would be delayed another week. However, since the worker seemed antagonistic, I did not think it wise to force myself on something that was her domain.

When I called a week later, the school social worker still had not seen the teachers. I was then more insistent about seeing the cards. After the interview, I went away hoping I would not again have to contact this school social worker.

QUESTIONS

1. How would you have attempted to overcome the school social worker's antagonism?
2. Hostility of teachers and other school personnel with professional workers is not unusual. Can you think of some of the reasons why this might be so? If you can, you are more likely to establish good working relations.

V. This, to the best of my recollection, is the text of an interview that took place in the office of the Lieutenant of the Police Department who handled children's cases. The names have been omitted or changed but the conversation has not been changed nor added to.

Paul, aged 13, suspected of larceny, arson, and "breaking and entering" is just entering the office of Lt. P. to be questioned on truth and content of the alleged offenses.

The office is the usual high-ceilinged, sparsely-furnished room that one finds in county court houses. The Lieutenant was seated at a large desk near the center of the room and to his left was an officer in uniform. To the right was a representative of the Fire Department. On either side of the door, as Paul entered, stood another policeman. The mother of the boy sat at the rear of the room with a friend of the family.

As Paul entered the room, he glanced quickly around and, see-ing all the strange people, seemed ill-at-ease. The Lieutenant began the interview.

"Listen, you. All I want from you is the truth." He pointed to some papers on his desk. "Unless you tell me the whole truth about this stealing business I can send you away for a long time from what we already know about you."

Paul hung his head and said nothing.

"Well, what about it? You set the fires, didn't you?"

"No," said Paul.

"No, what?" said the Lieutenant.

"No, sir," said Paul.

"O.K. Now let's get these facts straight. You started fires in the following apartment houses [reads the addresses of the apartment houses that had been set afire by the person tentatively identified as Paul]. And then when the fire got going good and the people in the apartment had run out, you went in to their apartments and stole all that you could carry away. That's about what happened, isn't it?"

Paul either would not or could not answer; he stood there in front of the desk silent and dejected.

The Lieutenant stood up and, with a certain amount of feeling evident in his voice, said, "Look here, boy. You are in a serious position and you don't seem to realize it. With all these charges against you we can send you away for ten years. You wouldn't like that, would you? I'll tell you frankly that if you can't or won't tell us what you know about all this, we won't have any choice but to send you away."

Paul gulped, and looked around until he caught his mother's eye. After a second or two, he turned his head around to face the Lieutenant and just shrugged his shoulders.

"Look, son! We haven't time to sit around all day waiting for some stubborn kid to make up his mind to tell the truth. You know you're guilty as hell and you can't get by with it. If we are going to be able to help you when your hearing comes up, we will have to know something more than has been told us by others."

This elicited from Paul the answer "I didn't do it. I don't care what they say, I just didn't do it." There was a desperate tone to his voice.

This only served to make the Lieutenant angrier, and for the next hour he and the two men who had been standing beside him took turns asking questions. They alternately pleaded, cajoled, shouted, and threatened, but through it all Paul refused to admit one single piece of information that would have a bearing on the case.

Paul did answer a few of the questions that had no obvious bearing, and they were as follows: he liked the Boy Scout Troop he was in; he loved his mother, but not his father; he did not like school, but he did like his friends, he had $.50 a week to spend and he used it to go to the movie and to buy ice cream.

For several minutes after the questioning, the Lieutenant and the other men conversed in low tones and then the Lieutenant finally spoke again. "Paul, when you were seen coming out of the apartment house you had something in your hand and when you were searched a few minutes later you had a purse in your pocket that belonged to one of the women in the apartment house where the fire originated. How do you explain that?"

Paul replied, "I found the purse by the window of the apartment house basement and I thought someone had lost it so I picked it up. You didn't give me a chance to tell you about it before you searched me."

"That's a damn lie and you know it. That kind of stuff won't get you anywhere. Is that all you've got to say?"

"Yes, sir," said Paul.

"All right. If that's your attitude, I'll turn you over to the court and let them handle this from here on."

At this point Paul's mother spoke up, "Excuse me, Lieutenant, but if you will let me talk to Paul alone I can find out what you want to know without all this shouting and threatening."

The Lieutenant answered, "You had thirteen years to talk to your boy and don't seem to have had much luck with him; so we'll take care of this ourselves, if you don't mind."

The interview ended shortly afterward with nothing more being learned from Paul. The boy was sent upstairs to the detention cells to be questioned by the Judge of Juvenile Court the next morning.

NOTE: The student who handed in this interview comments that it is not typical of most of the interviews in cases handled by the Juvenile Court.

QUESTIONS
1. Make your own analysis of the interview by paragraphs, commenting on the whole.
2. What poor use of processes and technical procedures is displayed?
3. What concepts of behavior were ignored?
4. What attitudes are evidenced?

VI. I made a follow-up visit to the home of a serviceman to learn how his wife had recovered from a recent operation. My agency had paid the hospital bill and obtained an emergency furlough and several extensions for her husband. The wife informed me her husband was now out of service and back on his old job. I proceeded to explain the services my agency offered to veterans and asked her to tell her husband of our interest and willingness to discuss such things as pension claim, insurance, G.I. educational provisions. She agreed to do so and went on to say "Oh, yes, my husband remembers you. He asked me when he got home from service if I hadn't gone back to Red Cross to ask for help." She had told him no; that she would rather manage on her own.

This statement "hadn't she gone back to Red Cross to ask for help" got me. I left the house with a sense of antagonism toward the young man. I had a feeling that he was out to use the agency for all he could get and wondered what my reactions would be when he came in for help, as I was almost sure he would do. I had been glad to be of assistance up to this time but now I wondered whether my agency was being used unfairly.

I wrote this part of the conversation into my case record and later called it to the attention of my supervisor, telling her of the antagonism which had been developed by those few words. She was surprised and said she had not made the same inference when she read the dictation. She felt he might have spoken because he was worried that his wife was managing alone so soon after an illness.

I would have to see the veteran to know whether I have eliminated my feeling about him. At the date this report is being completed he has not contacted me, so perhaps I misjudged the implication of his remark.

QUESTIONS
1. Discuss the worker's attitudes.
2. What would have been your reaction? Why?
3. Do you think the worker's attitude affected the interview?

VII. I have long been a champion of the "equality regardless of race, color, or creed" thinkers. To my knowledge the only time I have ever been put to the test was when a friend of mine married a man one-eighth Indian—a very likable fellow, well thought of by everyone. At that time we lived in a community where anyone you might meet was either Indian or in some way related to Indians. The other day in a staff consultation regarding one of the girls in my group, it was suggested that she was hoping to spend the summer with her sister. Some did not think the sister's home was suitable; others were doubtful; it was suggested I make a visit and report on conditions. This I agreed to do and was leaving the room when someone said, "Oh, by the way, that's the brother-in-law who's part Negro, you know." Immediately I found myself thinking "It won't be a suitable home." Now I am continually worried for fear that, when I make the call tomorrow, I will be influenced too much by the picture I already have in mind of what constitutes a suitable home.

QUESTIONS

1. Discuss the worker's attitudes in terms of culture and personality.
2. What would have been your reaction? Why?

VIII. I do not like to work with small children, so I was far from thrilled when I was told I was being given Dora, a small three-year-old, for study. For two months she had been in the nursery not speaking to anyone, child or grown-up. She would not play, and if brought into a group would merely stand there. I visited the nursery two or three times and could make no headway with the child. I arranged for mental tests which were useless, as rapport could not be established; so, on the advice of the psychologist, I started making arrangements for the child to be seen in a child guidance clinic. All this I have done in a mechanically correct way, without enthusiasm—in fact at times with distinctly antagonistic feelings. However, plans with the child guidance clinic hit a series of snags: Dora had mumps, I couldn't make appointments at convenient hours, I was unable to get the cooperation of the parents, and finally an automobile accident sent the mother to a hospital for several weeks. We had been counting on the mother to accompany Dora to the clinic.

With all these difficulties, the case has become more interesting to me, and I find myself quite determined to see it to some conclusion, even although I am no longer assigned to the agency as a student. As yet Dora does not respond to my friendly overtures. However, I feel I have made as much progress as any other adult. She waved to me from across the playground on my last visit although she still froze when I went over and spoke to her.

QUESTIONS

1. Discuss the attitudes involved.
2. Would your reactions have been similar to those of the worker?
3. After the worker has discontinued her contact with the agency, has she any right to continue her contact with Dora? Explain.

IX. The case history of John and Mary Adams was handed to me last week in a thick folder with even a thicker supplement. Mrs. Adams comes from a family of a poor social background. Before her marriage she had several sexual episodes resulting in an illegitimate child whom she kept with her. The Adams' marriage was stormy and unsuccessful, ending in separation and divorce. Since that time Mrs. Adams has been working continuously and successfully with Aid to Dependent Children and has become a conscientious mother. There are three children. Her problems seem to be Marian, her eldest who is thirteen and so abnormally tall that the child's personality is visibly affected; the poor quarters in which she must live because of housing shortage and limited means; and the irregularity of the alimony sent her by her husband who has remarried.

I introduced myself as Miss Haislet from the County Welfare Board. Mrs. Adams smiled graciously and asked me to come in, apologizing for hands which were grimy from cleaning her stove. She led me to a combined living room and bedroom where we sat down on the edge of a bed. I remarked that Mondays are always busy days.

(Although recent case records had shown Mrs. Adams as a

good mother, I still was surprised at her appearance, a neat, plump, and rather pretty housewife in an immaculate apron. I struggled to bridge the gap between this and the slatternly Mary Adams of the earlier records. This observation relieved me unaccountably and I felt less tense.)

"It's nice of you to come out on such a cold day," Mrs. Adams commented.

(It seemed to me that this was a good opening to explain my presence. She didn't quite understand why I was here and looked questioning, even anxious, for she frowned and twisted her hands together. I wondered if it were because she was nervous or genuinely embarrassed since she had been working with the stove.)

"Since new workers are coming into the office and several are leaving," I explained, "some of the families will have new workers, and instead of Miss Blake I'll be with you, Mrs. Adams. It's getting toward the end of the month, and I've been wondering how you're coming along with the new budget. Do you have a copy?"

"No, I've been allowed more for several things, you know, and that's fine, but I've been worried about clothes."

I pulled a copy of the budget out of my purse and handed it to her. She pursed her lips and ran a finger down each item and its explanation.

(Mrs. Adams looked interested. I felt that she was relieved with something concrete in her hands; that it would help her to express herself better.)

She hesitated when she came to "Alimony, $20.00."

"Have you heard from Mr. Adams regularly?"

"He don't send the money until the end of the month and that makes it hard to plan." (She frowned slightly and I remembered this to be one of her worries.) "But he's regular with his payment now." She looked at me straightforwardly.

(Even defiantly? I wondered. It seemed to me that I'd better not discuss that until I knew her better.)

I smiled and nodded. "And how about clothing?"

She frowned again. "Marian's getting to be such a problem. You see, she's taller than me. And women's clothes are so expensive. She has to look just like everyone else."

I commented that it must be hard to find a suitable style for her. "And Peter and Pamela?"

"I manage with them all right. But Marian—"

"How are the children coming in school, Mrs. Adams?"

"Fine. Marian felt so bad, though. She's been on the honor roll all through school and gotten all A's. But this time she got one 'unsatisfactory.' You know how girls are. She talked about it all the time for a couple days and then I went to meet her teacher at the school. And right in the hall I bumped smack into Marian!"

I laughed with her. "What did you say?"

"I told her to go right on home, that I'd be along in a while. So then the teacher said that Marian hadn't made up an incomplete paper. I asked if that weren't a small thing to dock a child for, but the teacher said that she's always so particular about everything that they expect a lot from her."

(All of this came out in a gush. It seemed to me that she had been anxious to talk to someone about Marian, who apparently was a problem to her since she had dismissed the other children with a single reply.)

Mrs. Adams paused and then continued. "But you know, I think that'll be good for her—to learn that people can't do perfect all of the time. And she studies so hard to be ahead. She says, 'I'll never be poor like you, Mom.'" Mrs. Adams looked at the floor for a moment.

(I wondered if I should say something but nothing seemed appropriate, and she went on right away.)

"But she's so young. She don't realize that things like that just happen sometimes."

(She looked directly at me with an expression on her face that might have been almost a plea for sympathy, or for confirmation.)

"You've done a good job with your children, Mrs. Adams."

(She'd expect me to know her family history so after a slight hesitation, I hoped that such a statement would satisfy the moment.)

"And I understand that they're healthy and attractive, too."

She nodded and flushed. "Yes, they are. If only Marian weren't so tall. She's so conscious of it. The other day I saw her—well, the boy next door has been in school right along and he walks home with her at night, carries her books. She can't see him for dirt, though. Puppy love—anyway, they were walking home and she was down in the street while he was up on the curb, so she wouldn't be taller. You see, she's so conscious of it. She comes home and cries sometimes. And there's nothing to do."

(Mrs. Adams apparently has taken Marian's problem on herself and is acutely worried about it although she doesn't quite know what to do about it. I wondered if she mentioned it frequently to Marian.)

"Doesn't Marian go into high school next year?" I asked.

"Yes, I've talked to her about it, thinking that it'll seem that much nearer. Then she'll be with taller kids and won't seem so strange. We're going to pick out a graduation dress soon and pay a little down on it."

(Mrs. Adams' feelings weren't all hopeless, apparently, and she had tried to employ a little psychology.)

I suggested that if Marian were noticing her personal appearance already perhaps in time and with a little encouragement she'd begin to work on her good features and make her height an asset.

"Is Marian in any school activities?"

(Perhaps Mrs. Adams would get the idea of encouraging Marian to compensate through something like this.)

"Yes, she was in the school play here at Christmas time. She has a nice singing voice and some of the teachers have hoped that she could have lessons, but I can't manage that. Sometimes down here at the Salvation Army Store there are pianos for five or ten dollars. Most of them play even if they are out of tune."

(Here I decided that it wouldn't do any good to try to get back to the other children again, since Mrs. Adams had repeatedly drawn the conversation back to Marian, who had been rather thoroughly discussed. I'd broach Peter and Pamela some other day and try to change the subject now.)

"Did you have a nice Christmas?"

"Oh, yes! My mother really made it for us—brought over the dinner and three presents apiece for the children. And the Salvation Army sent a grocery order to a store down here. Of course, none of my folks are here any more except my mother, so it was strange, but you get used to that, I guess. But as I said, my mother really made the Christmas nice for us."

(She's loyal to her mother, who is supposed to be somewhat disreputable and has harmed Mrs. Adams in one way or another several times.)

"And did you manage a Christmas tree?"

She smiled and looked down, saying that Mr. Adams had given them the tree. "A big tree. It stood right there. He came over the day before Christmas (I wondered why but decided not to ask) and asked the children where the Christmas tree was. You know how kids are—they said 'You bring one!' And he did. I'd kept all my ornaments and we had a few strings of lights."

(She sounded almost apologetic about Mr. Adams, yet had a defensive tone to her voice. Perhaps she expected me to disapprove.)

I commented that she was lucky because lights had been difficult to find this year.

She replied that her neighbor had a "surplus" so that took care of it nicely. She added (as an afterthought, apparently) that she thought I'd find this section of town "good to work in."

"It would be nice," I smiled, "but my families seem to be scattered all over town."

Suddenly she asked, "Do you have any cases down in the Mexican section of town?"

I said that I hadn't.

"I hate to see young girls like you go down there. My, when I took Marian down to the bus to camp last summer I could hardly wait to get out of that part. They say that they're all right, but you never know."

(This spurt of concern took me back somewhat, and I wondered just how "young" I did look. Ignoring it and going on with the conversation seemed safe.)

"Has Marian thought of camp for this next summer, Mrs. Adams?"

No, Marian had planned to take care of children around the neighborhood this summer. "She can save for her own clothes without it being taken off of the budget, can't she?"

I assured her that she could, up to a certain amount with certain conditions.

(I was pretty uncertain about this, thinking that it was about forty dollars and contributions to personal incidentals but decided not to commit myself until I'd checked rather than to let the client know I wasn't sure.)

"The coal's gone up a dollar, too. And the new linoleum—they told me that it would be allowed next month, too."

(Remembering the supervisor's admonition not to commit oneself when in doubt, I suggested that these things called for a budget conference down at the office where we'd talk about next month's expenses. This might be a good way to end the interview.)

"Your hours are ten-thirty to noon, aren't they?"

(She had remembered them, and this confirmed the other workers' reports of her cooperation with us.)

"How about a week from Wednesday, Mrs. Adams? Let me see, that must be the thirtieth of January."

"I have two calendars right here."

We rose and stood in front of the calendars and checked the date, so on her calendar and in my notebook.

(I wondered about the notebook but decided that this would give the forthcoming appointment a more businesslike aspect.)

"How about ten-thirty?" I suggested. "Is that convenient for you?"

"Oh yes!"

(She smiled broadly. The coal and Marian's pin money had probably been on her mind and she welcomed an opportunity to check on them. I felt that this established a working relationship with a mutual problem.)

I walked toward the door remarking that I'd be expecting to see her then. She thanked me for coming, and we both said good-by.

QUESTIONS

1. Why do you think the worker was relieved to find that Mrs. Adams presented a good appearance?
2. Do you think the worker's explanation of her visit was sufficient?
3. Comment on the worker's change of the direction of the interview from Mr. Adams' contribution to the clothing item.
4. Discuss the relationship of physical attributes and feelings of inferiority? Do you think the worker handled this phase of the interview well? If so—why? If not—why not?
5. What is the significance of Mrs. Adams' personal interest in the worker? Do you think the worker handled this well?
6. What do you think about the advisability of using a notebook in your interviews? Discuss pros and cons.
7. The worker was conscious of her status as a student. The agency policy was to have the client assume the students were regular staff workers. What do you think of the policy in its effect on the interview?
8. Do you consider this a successful interview? Give reasons for or against.

X. An executive secretary of a County Welfare Board had antagonized all of the merchants in the county by insisting that they could make no substitutions in the grocery orders of clients receiving relief. A check on their compliance disclosed that only one grocer was obeying his dictum. He thereupon wrote a letter notifying each of them that he had removed them from an approved list and they would no longer receive relief orders. The merchants were dependent upon the orders inasmuch as three-fourths of the adult population was on some form of relief.

The relief clients were naturally in sympathy with the merchants. After three weeks in which the aroused community held protest meetings and sent a delegation to the governor and the state director of welfare, the secretary was summoned to the office of the director of Public Welfare. By now, he realized that his problem was to reinstate the grocers without appearing to go back on his earlier mandate. As he neared the State Office Building his apprehension grew about receiving the criticism he knew he merited.

The director greeted him cordially, invited him into his office and said with a smile, "I see you still can hold out against a community of rule violators."

He then asked the worker to describe the situation, although the worker knew this had already been thoroughly reviewed by the merchants. When the worker had finished, the director asked, "What do you think should be done?" Not until he had finished did the director make any comments. These took the form of general approval of the worker's plan and some suggestions, tentatively made. The worker seized upon the ideas and incorporated them into his plan. They then discussed the probable reaction of the merchants to the proposals as if they were entirely the worker's.

The worker called a meeting of the merchants upon his return home which resulted in a more flexible arrangement and the conflict was resolved.

QUESTIONS

1. What do you think were the predisposing factors in making a conflict situation resolved so easily?
2. What interviewing techniques are evident?
3. The worker's comment on the interview was, "The solution to an individual's difficulty lies within the individual." Is this invariably true?

FOUR DIALOGUES FOR
CLASS ANALYSIS SHOWING
VARYING DEGREES OF SKILL

Tape recordings and dialogues of interviews are useful in helping the learner to acquire mastery of good interviewing techniques. However, such instruments involve a great deal of time, so must be chosen and used with discretion. Then, they afford an excellent means of assessing the many important factors that interviewers must take into account in order to achieve their purposes. The learner usually needs time in which to become comfortable with such a procedure, but it will help him if he can listen to and analyze verbatim interviews of others before having to submit his own for close and critical analysis. The following four dialogues are examples of interviews, each in a specific occupation.

SELLING A PAIR OF SHOES

I. A woman accompanied by her daughter, entered the Elite Shoe Store on a busy Saturday afternoon. As soon as they stepped inside the door,.a salesman came quickly forward to meet them. The woman remarked that she had noticed a shoe that she liked in the window. Smiling, the salesman asked her to be seated so that he could take her foot measurement and show her the shoe. She hesitated for a minute, but finally acceded.

As the salesman removed her shoes and took measurements he noticed that her foot was very slender, requiring a certain type of shoe, different from the one that she had picked out in the window, a one-strap, toeless, high-heeled shoe of a cheap make. He slipped the shoe on her foot.

SALESMAN: How does it feel on your foot?

CUSTOMER: It doesn't seem to fit. It gaps on the side and my toe sticks out, although the shoe seems to be plenty large.

SALESMAN: Yes, madam, I realize that is not the proper shoe for your foot. You have a long, slender foot which requires a tailored shoe. May I show you one that will fit your foot to perfection—make your foot neat and dainty?

CUSTOMER: Yes, I would like to see the shoe. I always have a lot of trouble being fitted.

In the meantime the salesman has noticed that the customer has a weak arch so he selects a tailored shoe with an arch support. He slips the shoe on her foot.

SALESMAN: Madam, will you please stand in the shoe and look in the glass?

CUSTOMER: My! I have never had such a comfortable shoe on my foot; it seems to fit real snug around the heel and yet gives me plenty of length. I never realized how a shoe of this type really felt before.

SALESMAN: That is the proper shoe for you; it will give you service, comfort, and look very attractive on your foot.

CUSTOMER: Yes, but it is patent leather and that always burns my feet.

SALESMAN: Yes, but this is a different type of leather. This is a new patent skin, which means that it is almost as soft as kid and just as comfortable, although it gives you the daintier appearance of kid. This shoe is the same shoe in the same leather as the shoe you have on.

CUSTOMER'S DAUGHTER: Mother, that looks too old for you; why don't you get one with a higher heel?

SALESMAN: Well, I wouldn't advise a higher heel on account

of arch trouble. This shoe has an arch support which takes the strain off the ball of the foot, where you have the arch trouble.

DAUGHTER: Well, what objections are there to the high heel?

SALESMAN (*then slipping on a high-heeled pump*): Just stand on this shoe and see how you like it.

CUSTOMER: Oh my! I like the looks of this shoe! But all the weight of my body seems to hit on the ball of my foot right where I have the arch trouble.

SALESMAN: Naturally! The high heel forces you to walk on the ball of your foot, while in this other shoe the arch and low heel take the strain from the front of the foot and equalize it throughout the shoe.

CUSTOMER: This shoe feels very good on my feet, but I am not quite satisfied. What do you have in color?

Salesman selects a brown shoe and slips it on the customer's foot.

CUSTOMER: I like this brown shoe very much but I generally have only one pair of shoes. Do you think this will go with different dresses?

SALESMAN: This shoe is all right if you have other shoes to wear for formal or dress occasions. Otherwise, the shoe might clash with different colors, while a black shoe can be worn for any occasion.

CUSTOMER: Let me see a lighter colored shoe.

The salesman selects a tan shoe on the order of the tailored shoe that he originally showed the customer; he realizes that he cannot fit her very well with sizes he has in the blond shoe.

CUSTOMER: I like that shoe very much on my foot. It certainly appeals to me.

DAUGHTER: That is really becoming to you, Mother. Why don't you take that shoe?

SALESMAN (*realizing that the shoe the customer has on does not properly fit her and will not give her the best satisfaction*): Madam, that shoe looks very nice on your foot but it will not be the most practical buy, since you are only buying the one pair. Also this type of shoe will be much harder to care for, as it soils more easily than another color.

CUSTOMER: I hadn't thought of that. I wonder if they would be hard to care for.

DAUGHTER: Oh yes, Mother, I had a pair of light tans and they were very hard to keep clean. Nearly everything seemed to spot them.

In the meantime the clerk has removed the shoe and has slipped on the original shoe that he recommended.

SALESMAN: Now, madam, doesn't this shoe look just as well and feel much better and give you a better fit and wouldn't it be more practical as an all-around shoe than any of these others?

CUSTOMER: Well, what is the price of this shoe?

SALESMAN: This is the combination last, a very fine fitting shoe and sells for $12.95.

CUSTOMER: Heavens! I have never paid over $6.00 for a pair of shoes in my life.

SALESMAN: Most likely that is one of the reasons that you have arch trouble and this enlarged joint. This tailored shoe will hold its shape, wear much longer, and give you more satisfaction for twice the length of time that a cheaper shoe would.

CUSTOMER: I know, but this is too much to pay for a pair of shoes. I can't afford that much.

SALESMAN: This shoe will cost you less money at the end of the year than the cheaper shoe will. This shoe will outwear two pair of cheaper makes and in the meantime you are getting comfort in a shoe that retains its shape, and will look good during the life of the shoe.

CUSTOMER: Why can't you fit me in a cheaper shoe like this?

SALESMAN: Well, this is a three-way combination last which means that it gives you the width through the ball that you require, two widths narrower at the waist of the foot which makes it fit through the arch, and three widths narrower at the heel which makes it fit closely around your narrow heel. They make up this shoe on a wood last and almost every day for three weeks the leather is drawn over the last and tacked down, which means that it will always hold its shape very well.

CUSTOMER: Don't they do the same thing with a cheaper shoe?

SALESMAN: No, madam, they use a cheaper grade of leather and rush them through the factory in a very few days. You see, for the difference in your money you are getting better quality, better workmanship, and a better fit than you are in a cheaper shoe.

CUSTOMER (*to daughter*): How do you like this shoe?

DAUGHTER: Well, how does it feel on your foot, Mother?

CUSTOMER: It seems just fine; I have never had such a wonderful fitting shoe on my foot before. I can't afford to pay that much for my shoes. I generally have to buy three or four pair a year.

SALESMAN: Well, madam, this shoe wears the average customer a year; so you can see for yourself that it is economy to buy this particular shoe. It will cost you less per month and give you more comfort in the long run.

CUSTOMER: Now that I have the shoe on my foot, none of the rest of the shoes seem to feel good.

SALESMAN: Well, let's slip on the mate, and you can see how they feel.

As the salesman says this he slips the mate on the left foot. The woman rises and walks over to the glass.

CUSTOMER: These shoes feel good on me. I really like these shoes.

SALESMAN: Wouldn't you like to leave them on and wear them?

CUSTOMER: Yes, I think I will; they feel much better than my old shoes.

SALESMAN: Yes, I am very sure that you're going to get a lot of satisfaction out of that pair of shoes.

SALESMAN: May I show you some fine hose? We have a large assortment in all the new spring colors.

CUSTOMER: I really wasn't thinking of buying hosiery, but I will look at them.

SALESMAN: Perhaps you will like a nice nylon hose for dress?

CUSTOMER: Well, what are your prices?

SALESMAN: We have different grades; they range from $1.35 to $1.95. The $1.95 hose are the full fashioned and very sheer.

CUSTOMER: Let me see the $1.35 hose.

SALESMAN: Which do you like best?

CUSTOMER: Will this $1.35 hose wear as well as the $1.95?

SALESMAN: Yes, it will; this is a service weight, a little heavier weight, and will really wear longer than the sheerer hose, although it isn't quite as dressy.

CUSTOMER: Well, I really want them for dress, so I think I will take the better grade. Do you have a 9½?

SALESMAN: Yes, madam.

CUSTOMER: Well, I think I will take a pair.

SALESMAN: May I suggest that you take two pair as it is more economical than buying just one pair. In case you get a run in one hose you still have a pair to wear. Two pair are worth as much as three pair, if you get them in the same shade.

CUSTOMER: Well, I guess I will take the two pair.

The salesman wraps them up with the shoes and hands her the package.

CUSTOMER: How much is my bill?

CLERK: $16.85 is the total.

The customer hands the clerk $20. He rings up the sale and hands her the change.

SALESMAN: Thank you very much. I am sure that you are going to be more than satisfied with your shoes.
CUSTOMER: Good-by.
SALESMAN: Good-by, and call again.

He bows, smiles, and closes the door after the women have stepped out.

The salesman has made a friend for the store and a successful sale for the company.

QUESTIONS
1. What has this interview in common with other interviews analyzed in this book?
2. Has this interview any cultural implications?
3. What interviewing processes and techniques were used to influence the sale?
4. What predisposing factors do you see?
5. Wherein does the skill used in this interview differ from the skill demonstrated in the interview with Mrs. James?

THE SPECIAL TEACHER

II. Ed was an intelligent high school student in an average sized school. He paid just enough attention to his subject to get C's in order to stay on the basketball and football teams to which he was a real asset, although he was not eagerly accepted into either of the teams, or the social activities of the school. He had worked hard to obtain places on the teams, at times even at the expense of losing a friend. He was boastful and insisted upon telling every detail of each point he had made in the last game. Criticizing other players and explaining what fools they were was a favorite pastime of his. He was crude and boisterous around the girls and would laugh loudly and long at his own jokes. He stuttered, but if any teacher or pupil happened to mention that he stuttered he would deny it. However, he always avoided speaking in a formal situation, in front of the class or at any time when he couldn't discuss his achievements. Finally, his English teacher, telling him that everyone in the school was required to take a speech test, made an appointment for him with the speech clinician.

Ed defiantly came for the interview, walked into the clinician's room without knocking, and slouched down in a chair. The clinician had previously looked up Ed's intelligence, social and athletic tests, and records. She had decided to make the interview strictly routine at first, by testing his speech the same way she had tested that of the other pupils, and to avoid letting him know that she had any special interest in him.

T.: You're Edward John, aren't you? I hope you didn't have to miss a class to come here today. When I was checking over the records yesterday, I noticed I had missed a few when we gave the general speech tests at the beginning of the year. Will you just read this little paragraph aloud for me, please?

Ed begrudgingly read the paragraph having several bad blocks and accompanying these with facial and bodily distortions.

T.: How long have you been stuttering, Ed?
Ed: A-a-ah, but, I don't s-stutter hardly at all, and I-I, a-ah, but, I don't want any help from you quacks. I-I a-ah, but know your techniques, a-a-ah, but besides I wouldn't even h-have to t-talk to get along. You've read about me a-ah but in the sports pages haven't you?
T.: Yes, you've really made a name for yourself. How did you become interested and so good in athletics?
Ed: I-I a-ah but s-suppose it comes naturally, but a-ah but it t-takes brains too. You a-ah but should come a-and see m-me a-ah but play sometime.
T.: I was at the last football game you played at home when you

made that thirty-three-yard run for the second touchdown. That was a clever play.

ED: A-ah but I c-certainly got a-ah but a write-up on that one. You know, it's too bad a-ah but you're mixed up w-with a-ah but all this k-kind of people.

T.: What kind of people do you mean, the teachers?

ED: A-ah but not them s-so much. These k-k-chiropractors, a-ah but psychiatrists, doctors, and a-ah but things who think they c-can cure stuttering. I-it's a-ah but j-just a way a-ah but of getting money. I-I g-get a-ah but along s-swell even if I-I do have a little trouble.

T.: You have gotten along well, but wouldn't you like it if you could speak more easily?

ED: A-ah but sure, b-but you can't cure m-me. I-I don't want to be sitting a-ah but around in a s-speech c-class instead of p-playing a-ah but ball.

T.: No, I wouldn't want you to either. You're far too valuable on the team. But speech is a lot the way you look at a football game.

ED: A-ah but how c-can it be? When you look at a g-game, you look at the players and the trick plays they use to a-ah but defeat the other side. With speech all you d-do is tell a-ah but people to t-talk s-slower and they won't s-stutter and it a-ah but doesn't work.

T.: That's what a lot of speech teachers try to do, but we really work very little with speech alone. We try to get to see ourselves and the tricks we use to cover up as objectively as we look at people out on the gridiron, playing a ball game.

ED: Yeah? A-ah but what good does that d-do?

T.: It helps us to evaluate ourselves and others frankly. You know, most of us have something we're ashamed of. Now, when I was in school I used to think the only thing people noticed about me was my large nose and that was what they talked about.

Ed: A-ah but your n-nose? A-ah but I-I didn't even n-notice it.

T.: It's there just the same though, and with a woman a nose is very important.

Ed: A-ah but it d-doesn't seem to matter to you like not b-being able a-ah but to t-talk s-straight does to m-me.

T.: It took me a long time to realize that that was just my way of looking. That's what we speech people try to get everyone to do regardless of what the difficulty is. You see, the way you react to your difficulty affects the reactions of others.

Ed: A-ah but I suppose I c-could give it a try.

T.: If you would like to come, we'd be glad to have you, but we don't want to force anyone to come.

Ed: A-ah but I'll t-try it a bit anyway. A-ah but I-I guess maybe I'll s-see you next week.

T.: Good-by, Ed.

QUESTIONS

1. What was the purpose of the interview?
2. Wherein did the teacher's attitude affect the achievement of the purpose?
3. By what techniques did the teacher meet Ed's hostility?
4. How does Ed show his hostility?
5. Ordinarily it is not good interviewing procedure for the interviewer to interject herself into the discussion. Was she warranted in doing so here?

MRS. P.

III. Mrs. P. is a sweet-faced, pretty young woman, 36 years old, who gives every evidence of being a good mother and home-maker, and appears to be naturally capable and well-balanced.

Mr. P., 46 years old, had a cerebral hemorrhage nearly three years ago. He is still paralyzed and almost helpless. Each day he manages, with the aid of a crutch and his wife's assistance, to get from his bed to a chair, where he sits until he goes to bed at night. He can feed himself if the food is cut for him. He is of an

independent spirit and deeply resents his incapacity. In spite of
the doctor's prognosis, he plans on getting well and again providing for his family. Recently he had been having attacks re-
sembling epilepsy, after each of which he was ill for several days.

Built on the front of their house is a small store, which brings
in an income of from thirty to forty dollars a month.

For five months, Mr. P. had asked the worker if he might go to
the County Home, each request being followed by a telephone
call stating that he had decided he did not want to go.

Finally the nurse called to inform him that there was a bed
available for him at the Home if he was certain that he wished to
go there. He said definitely that he did want to go, but only
because he knew that his going would be a relief and a help to
his wife. Mrs. P. was positively in favor of the plan, saying that he
had become so cranky that she could not stand his harping at
her any longer. IIe was getting so nervous that he made her
nervous, too; so that half the time she did not know what she was
doing. In addition to having the house and the store to attend,
Mr. P. had gotten scabies from the children. For four weeks she
had tried various remedies without success. She changed sheets
and pillowcases on the beds every day, and besides that she had
to bathe his numb foot each evening. She now saw that the store
did not pay, and felt that if Mr. P. were gone, she could dispose
of the store and secure work outside. She added that the landlord
wanted them to move out, as he intended to sell the building.
The nurse felt that she was tired out and would profit from a
much needed change.

The nurse suggested that Mrs. P.'s husband remain with them
over the coming week end, to give her a chance to get a supply
of medicine for him to take to the County Home.

When the nurse telephoned the next week to tell Mr. P. that
she would call at a certain hour to take him to the Home, he
answered the phone, saying that he had changed his mind about
going as he had learned he would not get any help there. He had

hoped someone there would help him to walk so that he could regain some of his strength. The nurse asked if he would like to have her find out for him just what attention and care would be available at the Home but he did not appear to be interested.

Shortly thereafter the nurse called at the house, and the following interview occurred:

MR. P.:   I consulted two of the best doctors in town, one of whom is a personal friend. They told me that my condition cannot be improved. So I have decided that there is no use of my going to the County Home.

NURSE: The decisions of the doctors will have to be accepted, of course, but I feel sure you would be well cared for there. Don't you think that perhaps you would enjoy being one of a group of men again, because it has been a long time since you have had any opportunity to associate with men?

MR. P.:   (*This idea appeared to impress him for a moment, and then he said quite suddenly*) Forget the whole thing.

After a short interval he asked if changing his mind had cost the county much.

NURSE: No, it hasn't and if at any future time you wish to reconsider the matter you may call again.

MR. P.:   (*looked much relieved, was silent a moment, and then said*) It would break up the home if I should go. . . . The children would miss me. . . . They would not want me to be gone when holidays come.

NURSE: Yes, I expect they would miss you. But have you thought that it would be possible for your wife to break down, and then she would not be able to care for either you or the children? Don't you think we should think of your wife's strength?

MR. P.:   If she should have to go to a hospital then the children would have to have me here. They could not run the store without my assistance. My wife needs my advice, and I always supervise her. In the time she has been here she has gotten to be as good at it as if she had been running a store for twenty years.

MRS. P. *spoke up here*:   It is good training for the children, too; that was John's reason for buying the store.

MR. P.:   Yes, I thought it would keep them off the street, besides being a good business experience for them.

NURSE: And do you feel now that it has served that purpose?

MR. P.:   Oh, yes. Virginia is only twelve years old, but she can make change as well as anyone. She will be able to go out and get a job as cashier some day.

NURSE: You realize, don't you, that the income from the store is not actually an addition to your income? If you did not have it, the Welfare Board would add the amount to your grant, so that you would have as much as you now have with the store.

MR. P.:   Well, we get our groceries at wholesale prices this way. My wife can sell it if she wants to, but she is her own boss here. If she isn't feeling well in the morning she needn't open the store at all. And she knows that she can rely on me for advice and assistance in planning and managing it.

His wife said that this was true, and added, "He is a help to me in other ways, too. Only he is so crabby."

MR. P.:   Sometimes I do take my crutch to the children, but I always notice that if I call for them immediately afterward to do something for me, they are right here to do it for me.

MRS. P.:   You should see how those children minded him before he was taken sick. He had only to shake his finger at them.

It was evident to the nurse that Mrs. P. was less sure than she had been of wanting her husband to go to the Home; so she drew the visit to a close, making an appointment for Mrs. P. to come to the office the next week. When she came, the nurse asked, "Does Mr. P. still feel that he wants to remain at home?"

Mrs. P.:   Oh, he changes his mind all the time. He doesn't know what he wants. The landlady is going to sell the house in the spring, and I don't see how I can move with him there. . . . Still I would be willing for him to stay if only he were not so cranky.

Nurse: Do you think you will be equal to carrying your many duties? I've been afraid you were getting tired.

Mrs. P.:   It isn't as bad as it was. The children's itch has begun to get better, and I have started to hire the washings done. There may be some days when I'll have to neglect things in the house, but I think I can do the work.

Nurse: It would be a shame for you to overwork until you were unable to do for either yourself, your husband, or the children.

Mrs. P.:   I'm sure that will not happen. I've gained weight suddenly, since he has been sick. And I have better color than ever before.

Nurse: That sounds good. Perhaps you are equal to doing the work. But how do you feel about your social needs? You are very closely confined and must want to get out once in a while.

Mrs. P.:   No, I don't believe I do. I have never gone out very much; even when John was well, I stayed at home most of the time. He was the one who paid the bills and took the children to the store when they needed clothing; he always bought their Christmas presents.

The way she said this was as if she were adding, "He was such a good husband that I had no need to go out then, and now I have no wish to do so."

Nurse: He must have been an unusual husband.

Mrs. P.:   It may be just as well if he doesn't go to the County Home. I know I would be worried about him, as I was while he was in the hospital. The house didn't seem like home without him, and I worried about him all the time.

NURSE: But his condition has become stationary now, so there would not be the same uncertainty.

MRS. P.: Mickey's teacher sent for me to come to school last week. She says he is lazy and impudent. I know I have spoiled him. I am just too tired to make him do things he doesn't want to do. But his father was always good at making him mind. . . .

NURSE: It looks to me as though you have thought this matter through from every angle. I wonder if you don't want him to stay as much as he wants to remain with you?

MRS. P.: Yes, I think it would be best for him to stay home.

QUESTIONS

1. Discuss the interview in terms of ambivalence.
2. Wherein did the nurse show skill?

MRS. H.

IV. The following interview was made in the home of a client. Mrs. H. is receiving a small supplementary grant for Aid to Dependent Children, and the present visit was recommended by the supervisor to see about initiating dental work (orthodontia, badly needed) for at least one of the two children included in the grant.

Mrs. H. has been married twice. The first husband, father of the daughters in the grant, was a brilliant, erratic man who made a well over average salary until he was forced to resign his position because of habitual alcoholism. Mrs. H. had worked for a time following her separation and divorce from her first husband, Mr. C., and then had married Mr. H., a man much older than herself who made a very modest living but was reliable, steady, and hard-working. They have one small daughter.

The ADC grant was given to cover clothes and incidentals for the two older girls. Their own father had died leaving no property or insurance, and their mother's second husband was deemed not legally responsible for their care. He had, however, willingly agreed to furnish food and shelter but did not feel he was able to assume the whole burden of their expenses.

Orthodontia was recommended for both girls, most especially for the younger one, and this expense had been decided as allowable in their budget. My visit was to plan with Mrs. H. about this dental program, especially to see if the family could some way pay the first flat fee, if the agency could assume the monthly payments. This was the first time I had seen Mrs. H.

The family live in a two-room apartment on the third floor of a frame apartment house. It was originally a one- or two-family house, now converted into small apartments. One bathroom served several families, but each had running water in their own kitchen. The rooms were crowded with furniture but were clean and orderly and nicely arranged. The furniture was all of good quality and in good condition.

Mrs. H. is a thin, tired looking young woman. She showed signs of nervousness—repetitious gestures and continual movements of her hands. She talks well and has a pleasing voice. She seems to be well educated and well informed and is sincere in her manner of talking. She expressed feelings of discouragement and fatigue. She does not appear to be too strong.

8-6-45

I visited Mrs. H. at her home, having arranged the time for the interview by telephone August 2.

Mrs. H. was feeding 16-month-old Bernice her lunch when I came for the interview and she continued feeding and caring for the baby during my visit.

I introduced myself and Mrs. H. responded cordially, "Oh, yes, come right in. Excuse me if I go on feeding Bernice here—she slept longer than usual today and we are late with her lunch. Aren't we, sweet thing? (*to the baby*) Now just sit down anywhere, I will sit here by Bernice so I can help her. She makes quite a mess sometimes. I know she shouldn't have the bottle any more, but she takes more milk that way and she needs all she can get."

I said "Thank you" and sat down near the dining part of the large room which serves for kitchen, dining room, and living room. Mrs. H. was fixing a banana to feed to Bernice. She continued, "It's hot up here. I guess an attic is hot all the time even when it is supposed to be insulated. This is a pretty poor place to live but it is all we can afford." She busied herself with the baby.

I commented, "It's warmer outside today so it's probably not too cool anywhere. I know it's hard to have children in a small apartment but places are hard to find now, especially where there are children. Are the older girls home now?"

"No, they aren't and I'm sorry that you couldn't see them. Today is the picnic for one of their classes and Mabel went to that. Caroline is out with some friends who took her to the lake. I have some little pictures of them though." She jumped up and got pictures of the older girls. "Those are not so hot but you can see how they look. Mabel is the blonde one—Well, they are both blonde but Mabel has the lightest colored hair."

I admired the pictures, which indicated the girls were attractive, and asked about their summer activities. Mrs. H. went on, "They sure are good kids even if I do say so. They keep busy all the time and they sure are good to help me with the work here. I try to give them enough to do that they don't have to be asking me what they can do to keep busy. I don't have trouble that way like some of the mothers do. I guess we are too poor to have any spare time."

"Sometimes time does hang heavy on their hands at that age," I suggested, "so you are lucky that you don't have that problem. Which one of the girls is it that is supposed to have the orthodontia?"

"Well, they both need it—you can't tell so much from their pictures but their teeth just don't meet right. When I first talked to the dentist he said that Caroline's were the worst but hers are getting a little better and Mabel's have been getting worse, so they both need the work done about the same now. If it didn't cost so much! But they say it ought to be done now before they get too old. And he said if they could get it started before they go to school this fall, it would help to keep them from feeling so queer about it all. Wearing the wires and so on I mean." Mrs. H. looked at me and said again, "If it just wasn't so expensive."

"That was one of the things we wanted to talk with you about. I think that we could allow at least part of it on the budget and increase your ADC grant to take care of it. Do you remember how much it would cost?"

"Yes, I sure do know that—I have thought about it until I am nearly crazy. It will be $50 down—for each of the girls—and then $10 a month. That seems like an awful lot. I don't see how we can possibly get it done unless you can get the check increased."

"Is that the price from the University Hospital or from your own dentist? Or have you asked both places?"

"That is from Dr. B., but he has some classes or teaches or something at the University and he said that he would have to do the work himself because there were not enough Senior dental students to do it, and the price would be the same."

"I think the agency would pay the same amount toward either place, but the only thing is we would have no way to pay the $50 down for you. We might be able to add this expense and budget it monthly, but we couldn't give you the money to pay down. Can you think of any way you could get it? Then we could budget for the monthly payment."

"Well, well, I'll tell you—or maybe I'd better not—I don't know—" she stopped and appeared to be thinking—she played with the banana she was feeding Bernice in an abstracted way and after a long silence which I made no effort to break, she went on resolutely, "Well, I might as well tell you, you will find out about it anyway—I do have the $100. I have been working extra for the doctor I used to work for this summer so I could save it up." Then violently, "I suppose you will take away the $9.50 a month I get now—but I can't bear to see the girls unhappy about how they look, and there wasn't any other way I could get the money." She stopped for breath and watched me closely—I thought to see what I would say and do about it. Then she went on before I had a chance to reply, "I wonder how far they think that $9.50 will go. You're married?" At my nod she asked, "Do you have any kids?"

I said I had a little boy. "Well, then you know how it is—you want things for your kids and you want them to have it easy and it costs so much to live—and there are so many things and so little money." She stopped. Then after a time, "They said I wasn't supposed to work and I haven't worked all the time—just when they needed something extra. I am a medical technician and I could make $150 a month if I did work all the time. I get to thinking sometimes that is what I should do—then I wouldn't have to ask anybody for help." She added hesitantly, "Do you think what I have worked this summer would count against me on the ADC?"

I explained, "The purpose of the ADC grant is to make it possible for the mother to stay in the home and care for the children. If you were working full time or even working regularly a certain number of days a week we would take your earnings into consideration in making your budget. Of course, in that case your expense would be greater too and that would have to be considered. We would want to know it if you were going to go back to work full time."

"I might go to work again if it weren't for Bernice. But I don't know what I could do with her. I really am needed at home, I guess. I should be here when the other girls come home, so they can bring their friends home too. Only living here the way we do it seems like there isn't much place to bring them to. We really should have more room. Most of the other kids live in real houses and mine don't even have a room of their own. Come on and see where we have to sleep. All of us in the same room like a bunch of tramps. And we have colds all the time from it. Of course this room is big and we all try to keep it neat and clean but it isn't so good for the girls to sleep in the same room with Bill and me. And he isn't their own father, even, you know." During this she had jumped up and led the way for me to see the sleeping room.

I did not immediately comment. There were in the long room a double bed, a twin size bed, and a baby's crib. Mrs. H. continued, "I have another of those twin beds and no place to put it up. If we could afford it we might be able to get another room on the next floor and fix it up for the girls. But it would cost more than we could pay. The girls shouldn't be sleeping in the same bed any more either—they are getting too big." She made a despairing little gesture and said, "I get so tired of things costing more than we can pay."

I said, "I can see it is crowded and inconvenient to have to make these sleeping arrangements. It must be hard for all of you."

Mrs. H. pushed her hair back from her face with a gesture that was becoming familiar to me from her repeated use of it and said again, "I get so discouraged. The former worker thought I couldn't quite realize the change in my circumstances but I do really. It's hard to think that at one time we had so much. Mr. C., the girls' father, used to make over a thousand dollars a month until he decided to try to drink himself to death. My God, what I wouldn't do for a thousand dollars now!" Mrs. H. was quite worked up at this point and she stopped and blushed and said embarrassedly, "Oh, excuse me—I just feel so bad when I think how much my kids could have had if he had just been different. He carried $30,000 life insurance at one time, and the first I knew that he had cashed it all in for drink was when he died without a cent. If he had even kept part of it, it would have helped me so much with things for the girls." She sighed, "They remember when we used to have a lot; it's hard for them to live like this and work so hard for everything they do get."

I said I could see how it would be hard for them, and for her too, and then, "Of course, you have said you are teaching them to help you with the house and the baby and maybe learning those things will be good for them. With a lot of money, people sometimes get too involved in other things to take that much time with their children."

Mrs. H. looked at me intently and I wondered how she was going to take this; then she smiled and said, "You sound like I try to feel about it. I keep telling myself that if the kids have the right stuff they will come out all right, and that maybe their father should have been spoiled less as a kid. But I can't help wanting a nice home for them and I want them to marry well and be happy. I would like money so they could go to college—but I suppose if they wanted that enough they would work to get it themselves."

"Of course, we all want to do all we can for our children," I said, "but a great many do work and pay most of their own way through school, and maybe they are the ones who appreciate an education the most."

Mrs. H. went on, "I would rather the kids would be happy than anything else. Maybe it is for me that I want more money. I am so tired of living this way and Bill makes so little. I wish he could earn more, I wish I could make him see that he should be earning more. And then Bernice is so little and he is so much older; we don't know how long he will be able to work. I guess it's really for me and Bernice that I worry the most. Bill does try— only I married him because I thought he would be so good as a father to the kids and now he gets so cross with them. You'd think he would be patient with Bernice—his own kid—but he isn't. He seems to think the kids are in the way, sort of." She thought a while—then smiled, "We are so crowded here I guess we do get in each other's way."

"It would be nice if the girls could have a room of their own. I mean, it would be nice for you and Mr. H. as well as for the girls."

"Oh, yes, I think Bill would be more patient with them if he had a place where he could get away from them and rest sometimes. And the girls are too old to sleep in the room with us. I worry about that too. It's beginning to be embarrassing for him as well as for the girls."

I asked, "Would you like me to talk to my supervisor about it? Perhaps since the extra room would be needed because of the older girls, some extra allowance could be made to help on the increased rent. It would be much better; I see that—and I could let you know if it might be possible to help you get it that way."

"I wish you would. Oh, that would make it so much easier and the girls would be so happy! I'd just do anything to try it that way, and on Bill's pay I don't see how we could."

AUTHOR'S NOTE: The outcome of the foregoing interview was that Mrs. H. was able to rent an extra room in the same building for the girls. The agency provided for its furnishing and the necessary dental care.

QUESTION

Review the interview paragraph by paragraph watching for (1) processes, (2) techniques, (3) attitudes, (4) the elements of the worker's skill.

SOME ETHICAL CONFLICTS
FOR DISCUSSION

I. Mrs. S. is emotionally unstable and also has a long history of physical illness. She constantly feels tired, has bad varicose veins, and was told by her doctor some time ago that she needed an immediate operation. Since then she has had no medical treatment. The case history reveals a continual conflict between Mrs. S. and the former workers about her refusal to have medical treatment.

On my first home call I felt a compulsion to persuade Mrs. S. to go to a doctor. She was increasingly elusive and vague as to when she would go to see the doctor as I became more insistent. I was in conflict with Mrs. S. in thinking that she should immediately go to a doctor, and also with myself in my inability to persuade her. It seemed to me that sympathetically listening to her troubles would get me nowhere, yet I hesitated to treat such a serious problem lightly.

We discussed the pros and cons of General Hospital and as I left, I pleasantly suggested that Mrs. S. go down to the General Hospital on the next nice day, which she agreed to do.

I left with the feeling that she would not be going, but two weeks later she called to tell me that she had been to three clinics and had made arrangements for treatment.

QUESTIONS
1. Why do you think the worker accomplished her purpose?
2. What ethical concept would she have violated if she had continued her insistence?

II. The N. family has been receiving an ADC grant for three months. Their eligibility is based on the husband's temporary physical disability. The family lived on their savings until their resources were exhausted and felt humiliated in having to apply for aid. The N.'s have four older children, three of whom have college educations; two are continuing to get their MA's; one has a good job and the other has been offered a commission in the navy because of his musical talent.

I recognized that the N.'s standard of living was considerably above that allowed by the ADC budget. From observations of house repairs, music lessons, etc., I had a feeling that the older children were contributing to the family income. I felt that in fairness to the agency I should discuss this with Mrs. N., which undoubtedly would result in a reduced budget. I was reluctant to do this because I thought it would be hard on the family to make them lower their standards. I was especially concerned about the three younger children who would have to discontinue their music lessons and who might have their social relationships with their high school friends marred. The agency won out in this conflict, although it left me with a feeling of futility in regard to the rigidity of eligibility requirements.

QUESTIONS
1. What do you think were the bases for the worker's conflicts?
2. Do you identify with the worker? Why or why not?

III. Mrs. M. is the mother of four young children. She and her husband have a long history of separations and reconciliations. Mrs. M. at one time went to Legal Aid for advice about a divorce but refused to accept their advice. When I was assigned the case, Mrs. M. had definitely decided on a divorce. I suggested she go to Legal Aid explaining that their service was good but less expensive than a private attorney. She, however, insisted on having a private lawyer because of her past experience with Legal Aid.

Mrs. M. already had a budget deficiency and had the possibility of being on ADC for many years before her. In view of her financial situation, I felt that it would be much wiser to get her divorce through Legal Aid. Even after I had tried to interpret the function of Legal Aid and offered to write a letter of referral for her, Mrs. M. still insisted on having her lawyer. Realizing that it was her right to make her own plan, I did not again attempt to sway her toward Legal Aid. She proceeded to obtain her divorce and was happy about the outcome, although I feel that the financial strain probably will be harder for her than going back to Legal Aid would have been.

QUESTION

Discuss this in terms of the worker's obligations.

IV. My work at the Y.W.C.A., which is supposed to be counseling, has so often involved rather irksome duties of an authoritative nature (such as bill-collecting and more or less tactful evictions) that I was especially pleased to have one resident come to my office voluntarily, with a problem which called for more personal help.

The client, Mrs. H., was a young married woman who had recently left her husband. She was extremely worried and upset about her marital difficulties and seemed to be under considerable tension. During the course of a rather long interview, Mrs. H., who appeared to have a good deal of insight, was able to express freely her many anxieties and conflicting feelings toward her husband. I attempted to interpret these emotions on a conscious level, of which she was quite aware, and then, since her problems needed more intensive case work than the agency was prepared to give, I suggested a referral to Family Service. When the type of help which they could offer was explained to her, Mrs. H. was very receptive to the idea, and an appointment was subsequently arranged. I was rather disappointed to discover later that she had failed to keep her appointment and had meanwhile moved out of the "Y" so that I lost contact with her.

QUESTION

This is presented as an example of what not to do. Why do you think the worker failed in her purpose?

V. The baby was to be the Pauls' first luxury. Married when just out of high school, they asserted that unless they could provide for a child, they must wait. For the first time in eight years, they now had their own little home and it now seemed possible to look forward to parenthood.

The house had long been an eyesore, so the neighbors were intensely interested when the Pauls purchased it for seven hundred dollars and began its renovation. Mr. Paul's work as a carpenter and bricklayer was irregular, and he was able to spend his spare time on the house. The three rooms were completely redone. Odds and ends of discarded furniture and a second-hand davenport were lovingly worked with. Fresh paint and flowered chintz gave the living room an attractive, comfortable lived-in appearance. The bedroom with its dainty blue and white dotted swiss draperies, dressing table, and spread was the envy of all the neighbor women. The attractive bed had been salvaged from parts of two beds found in the village dump.

Edward's arrival was awaited with great anticipation. Mr. Paul spent long hours making a baby bed, using discarded lumber and some old coaster wagon wheels. He equipped it with removable screens so that it could be used outside if necessary.

Both parents were dismayed when the baby was born with a partial harelip. It seemed incomprehensible that this should have happened to them. Could anything be done? Was the baby to go through life this way? Was there anything to this old wives' tale that a mother could so mark her baby by seeing a rabbit? These were the things they pondered until the family physician explained the probable cause, and told them surgery could be done with amazing success.

Edward and his mother came home from the hospital, but it was not the joyful homecoming they had anticipated, for both parents were wondering just how they could afford the necessary surgery on their average income of eighteen dollars a week. Both maternal and paternal grandparents were sympathetic, but were financially unable to assist.

The family physician, knowing the financial circumstances of the Pauls, suggested that they allow him to write to the State crippled children's agency to see what could be done. After much deliberation the parents consented.

A home visit was made by the public health nurse, and explanations were made of the state agency's provisions for this type of plastic care to the children whose parents were unable to secure it. The operation required the services of a skilled surgeon, so the baby would need to be sent to a hospital in a large city three hundred miles away. The surgeon preferred to have the baby as soon as possible for the repair work, as the scars became less perceptible as the baby grew.

Both parents were reluctant to make any decision because of the distance the breast-fed baby would have to be from home. They were left with their problem which they wished to think over before making their decision.

Two weeks later they requested that arrangements be made for the baby's care, having decided that nothing could be gained by waiting. The mother made her own plans to accompany the baby to the hospital as she had located a distant cousin with whom she could stay, who lived a short distance from the hospital.

Arrangements were made for the baby's hospitalization. A plan was worked out by the hospital for the mother to come there twice a day and express her milk to insure the baby a continued

348 ESSENTIALS IN INTERVIEWING

breast-milk diet, and to maintain her milk supply during this period.

QUESTIONS

1. What attitudes and philosophy of helping did the nurse reveal in this account?
2. Discuss the question of a worker's right to insist on plans for another's good.
3. What would you have done in this situation?

AN INTERVIEW OF AN EXPERIENCED SOCIAL CASE WORKER FOR DISCUSSION OF INTERVIEWING SKILLS

Analysis of the following dialogue in terms of concepts of culture, behavior, structure of the interview, skill in the use of processes and techniques, attitudes, and predisposing factors should afford a test of the assimilation of much of the material presented in this volume. The worker's personal attributes are undoubtedly a factor. In this case she is friendly, warm, young, attractive, and well trained for her profession. The Catholic agency in which she is employed is a general agency handling both family and children's problems.

INTERVIEW WITH ANN

Paragraph 1. Mrs. Andrew Taylor telephoned to make an appointment for her sister, Ann Walters, who needed help badly. An appointment was made for the following day. Mrs. Taylor, though, protested Ann might not be willing to come in but she intended to see that Ann did. I suggested perhaps it might not be a good idea to force her to come if she did not wish to do so. Mrs. Taylor answered grimly that Ann would come in or be taken into police court; her mind was made up. I asked if she would rather have me call at the house at a time when Ann might be at home. In that way whatever Ann's problem was might come to my attention in a natural way. Mrs. Taylor replied that neighbors could tell a social worker when they saw one and she didn't want the neighbors to know. I offered to keep an appointment open for Ann for the next two days in the event that Mrs. Taylor might be able to persuade Ann to come in if she knew she had some choice in the matter. Mrs. Taylor said she would talk to Ann.

Paragraph 2. Ann came in the following day to keep the appointment made by her sister. She was a blonde, blue-eyed girl, graceful in her movements, about 5′5″ tall. Her face was flushed; she appeared to be embarrassed or angry. Her features were nice, skin clear and light; make-up moderate. Her clothing was neat and attractive. Her coat was of dark blue material, a lighter blue hat tipped to one side, and red accessories.

Paragraph 3. I smiled at her as the receptionist introduced us. "I was expecting you, Ann," I began. "Your sister made the appointment for you yesterday, but she didn't know if you would care to come in today. I'm glad you came." She didn't reply so I invited her to sit down and to take off her coat. She sat on the edge of the chair and held her coat tightly around her.

Paragraph 4. "I'm not going to stay long. I didn't want to come, but my sister made me. I might just as well tell you that now because I don't intend to have you snooping in my business." Her voice was harsh, and she was near tears. I said, "I really don't want to snoop. Your sister thought you might like to talk some things over with me, but if you don't want to, you won't have to." She seemed surprised. I said as long as she was here, why didn't we get acquainted. She said yes she thought that would be pleasant. She would have to stay in my office for a short time or her sister would be "mad as blazes." If she walked right out her sister would know she hadn't told me anything. I remarked it would be a funny situation and Ann and I both laughed. I repeated it wouldn't be necessary to tell me a thing she didn't want to tell. She said I was a funny social worker. She knew they always snooped. I said maybe she had an incorrect idea about them. I said they really were very much like other people and if they seemed a little inquisitive sometimes it was probably because they wanted to help. She said she had never thought of that and she guessed she might not mind talking to me only she had made up her mind not to talk. I said of course I respected people who knew what they wanted to do and stuck to it if they were sure it was the best plan to follow, but sometimes it helped to talk about things with someone who really wanted to be a friend. Sometimes talking about problems made them seem less frightening and relieved worry. She said she didn't intend to talk about anything important. Her sister was waiting in the outer office and when enough time had passed she (Ann) would just go out and tell her sister nothing. She supposed I would tell her sister, though. I said no I wouldn't betray her to her sister in any way at all. She seemed pleased.

Paragraph 5. I noticed she was beginning to perspire around her nose and mouth so I said, "It is warm in here, isn't it? I'll open the window a little." I walked to the window and attempted to open it, but it stuck. Ann said, "Want a little help?" I said, "Yes, thanks. Maybe together we can do something about it." Ann came over to the window and helped me to push at it. It finally opened. She said, "That was easy." I said yes and it was probably because we had tried it together.

Paragraph 6. When she sat down she seemed a little less tense and she allowed her coat to fall open. She said, "Would you laugh at me if I changed my mind about something?" I said I often changed my mind about things and I didn't expect people to laugh so of course I wouldn't laugh at her. I waited but she didn't say anything further, so I asked, "What have you changed your mind about?" She said, "When I came in here I thought I would hate you and I made up my mind not to talk to you about anything, but I don't hate you and I think I might tell you." I said that was fine.

Paragraph 7. Immediately, however, she seemed to change her mind again. She said, "I don't hate you, but I certainly hate my sister." I said, "Why?" but she ignored that and said, "Sometimes I could kill her, I hate her so much!" I said her reason for feeling like that must be a very strong one. She sneered and said didn't I wish I knew what it was? I said I would be glad to know but only if she really wanted to tell me. She began to cry and she said I was different. She thought I would force her to tell and I wasn't doing that. She couldn't understand that. I said again that I would like to be her friend and to help her in any way I could. She said she didn't know what to do. I said, "Perhaps if we talk about what's bothering you, it won't bother you quite so much." She said, "Well, I'm not going to tell you just the same." I said, "All right, Ann. You don't have to." She said, "Don't you care?" I said, "I'm really very sorry you won't let me try to help."

Paragraph 8. Ann had been glancing at a scrap book containing some pictures. Each picture had a short story under it. I said this usually was of interest to children and that I kept the scrap book as a hobby. Then I asked, "Do you have a hobby?" She said she used to have one. She played a saxophone in the high school orchestra. Her voice got resentful and she seemed tense again. I said, "It must have been fun to play in the orchestra." She said yes it had been and she had played until she had to leave school. I asked, "Why did you leave school?" but she ignored the question and went on to say she had met John while in the orchestra. He was very fond of her and liked her a lot. I said I could understand why he would. She said her sister found out about John and became very angry. I said, "What did your sister find out about John?" She said, "John is the father of the baby I'm going to have." Then very fiercely she said, "I can't tell you about it!" I said, "But you have already told me the hardest part. Getting started is usually hardest. You know, it won't make me think of you any differently if you tell the rest of it now. You don't have to tell, though, unless you want to."

Paragraph 9. Ann didn't answer, so I said after a pause, "From what you have said, I imagine you live with your sister." She said yes she did. She had lived with her sister ever since her parents were killed in an auto accident when she was only three. She had no other relatives. Her sister didn't want her to live in the home and she didn't get along with the brother-in-law, but there was no other place for her to go. After she met John in the school orchestra her life had been happier because John seemed to care about her and he wanted to marry her when he was older. She didn't know how Mrs. Taylor, her sister, had found out about John, but she was going to be sent away to a "house of correction." Both her sister and brother-in-law called her a "no good little tramp." Finally they had made Ann come to see me. They said if she didn't they would take her to the police and have her sent away. I said I didn't think she needed to worry about that.

Paragraph 10. Ann began to cry again, and plead, "You won't help them send me away, will you?" I said no, and I explained that generally girls were not sent to correctional institutions because of pregnancy.

Paragraph 11. She cried, "I hate my sister so much I wanted to kill her." I responded, "Ann, you know that would not be a very smart thing to do. You would be in much worse trouble. I think it is more important to find out why you feel that way. Maybe we could change things so you wouldn't feel like that."

Paragraph 12. Ann began to voice loud accusations against her sister. Finally she said, "My sister told me if I bring home this baby she will drop it on its head and make it queer." Ann put her head on the edge of the desk and began to sob. I waited a few moments. When Ann looked up she said, "Please help me." I said I would. Then she showed me large bruises on her arms and shoulders. These she got from the sister who beat her when she found out about John and Ann's relationship with him. Then she begged me again not to send her away. I said, "Ann, I don't want to do anything except to help you. You have to understand that and to believe me. I will help you." She said, "I do believe, but I wish I never had to see my sister again."

Paragraph 13. "Perhaps," I suggested, "we can arrange for another place for you to live." She said, "Oh, I'd like that, but where could I go?" I explained that we had a Maternity Home and it could be arranged for her to go very soon.

Paragraph 14. She did not know when the baby would come but she thought in May or June. She had not seen a doctor. She became enthusiastic as I showed her some pictures of the Maternity Home and she wanted to know if she could enter today. I said I thought so, but it might be better to wait until tomorrow or at least until we had consulted her sister. She thought her sister would like the plan as she would be glad to be rid of Ann.

Paragraph 15. I explained that I would need some additional information before I could make very good plans and I hoped Ann wouldn't mind if I asked her a few questions. She replied, "No, I don't mind now and am I ever glad I changed my mind and told you."

Paragraph 16. She proceeded to give the following facts without display of emotion: She was seventeen, a senior in high school, Catholic and of French-German descent. Her parents had both been high school graduates, her sister, Mrs. Andrew Taylor, was also a high school graduate. The two sisters never got along very well. Ann could assign no reason for this. She had never been seriously ill and was in fine health now so far as she knew. She had planned to go on to college to study music. Some day she hoped to write music. She would like to marry John Martin but she supposed his parents would object as he was only 18 years old.

Paragraph 17. As Ann talked about John she seemed to become tense, so I put aside the admission blank and said, "Well, that's all I need to know now to have you properly admitted." Ann asked, "Won't it cost money?" I said that was what I wanted to talk to her sister about. Ann said she knew her sister would be glad to pay money to get rid of her. I asked Ann if she would want to talk to her sister alone or if she would want me to explain the situation. She said, "You tell her. I get so mad when I see her. I hate her a lot." I rang the buzzer for the receptionist and asked that Mrs. Andrew Taylor be shown in. Ann said, "Do you want me to stay?" I said, "I think you should so that we can work the plan out together."

Paragraph 18. When Mrs. Taylor came and was introduced I said, "Ann and I have become acquainted and have talked over some plans for her, but we do need your help to complete them." She smiled and said she would do anything she could to help. Ann grunted sneeringly. Mrs. Taylor started to make a comment but she refrained and repeated she would like to help. Workers, she thought, were easy to talk to and she was glad Ann had "seen fit" to do as she was told for a change. I interrupted immediately as Ann was angry. I said, "Ann would like to go to the Maternity Home we operate and we thought this should be done as soon as possible. Would you agree?" Mrs. Taylor answered, "I suppose I can't keep Ann from doing whatever she wants." I said I thought it would be nice if she cooperated in the plan because she had reared Ann and was more or less responsible for her. Mrs. Taylor said she hoped Ann would want to go to a home and was glad we could arrange it. I said there were costs involved and wondered what arrangements she and Mr. Taylor could make. She said without hesitation that she and her husband had agreed to bear all financial responsibility for Ann's care if a plan could be made for her. I told her what the cost would be and she agreed to it.

Paragraph 19. She then wanted to know if Ann would like some spending money while she was in the Home. I turned to Ann and said, "Will you need some, Ann, or do you have enough?" Ann said she had spent all of her present allowance. Mrs. Taylor volunteered to give her some money.

Paragraph 20. Mrs. Taylor then asked Ann when she wanted to go to the Home. Ann answered her civilly saying she would like to go right away. Mrs. Taylor said she would like to take her there. Ann asked me if she had to go with Mrs. Taylor. I said to Mrs. Taylor, "I imagine you must be quite busy and perhaps haven't too much time. I should be very glad to take Ann to the Home. You could be of much help, however, if you would pack the things Ann will need." Then I said to Ann, "Will that be all right with you?" She said yes. Mrs. Taylor said she would go immediately and get whatever Ann needed. I gave her a list of what girls usually needed. She asked if she could visit Ann. I said it was permitted, but perhaps it would be well to wait a little until Ann could get settled. I then excused myself saying I would telephone the Home to say I was bringing Ann over.

Paragraph 21. When I returned Ann had been crying and so had Mrs. Taylor. Mrs. Taylor was standing with her arms around Ann's neck. I said, "The Sister at the Home said she would be very glad to have you come tonight, Ann." Ann said, "Would you care very much if I went tomorrow instead?" I said no if she would rather go tomorrow that would be all right. Ann explained, "I want to pack and then my sister can take me." I said that would be all right. Ann wanted to know what time to go. She would like to go about one o'clock. I offered to arrange it and said that I would come to see her in a few days. She said that was fine as she thought she might have some other things to talk about. I said I would be glad to talk with her.

Paragraph 22. Then Mrs. Taylor very nervously said, "I suppose you think I'm terrible." I said I could understand her anxiety for Ann and I knew she probably was very deeply interested in seeing her happy. She said yes she was but that maybe she needed some help because she wasn't always sure she did the right things for Ann. I said, "If you would care to come in sometime, I would be glad to talk with you." She seemed pleased and said yes she would like to come next week. A definite appointment was made for the following week.

Paragraph 23. Ann said she was glad she had come in and she was sorry if she had seemed mean during the first part of the interview. I told her to forget about it, that I could easily understand how hard it probably was. Mrs. Taylor thanked me and she and Ann went out together, Mrs. Taylor saying she would take Ann to the Home the following day.

QUESTIONS

1. Paragraph 1. Comment upon Mrs. Taylor's attitudes toward Ann and toward social work. How do you think they might affect the interview in the event Ann is prevailed upon to come to the office?

2. Paragraph 1. Describe the social case worker's attitude toward this application.

3. Paragraph 2. Is the worker's observation of Ann's appearance important enough to record? Why or why not?

4. Paragraph 3. What process is involved here?

5. Paragraph 4. How does the worker's attitude enter in this as contrasted with Ann's?

6. Paragraphs 5 and 6. Comment on the worker's skill in procedures.

7. Paragraph 7. Underline the worker's part in this section of the dialogue. What was she trying to accomplish?

8. Paragraph 7. What processes and procedures are involved?

9. Paragraph 8. What part did the setting of the interview play?

10. Paragraph 8. How would you describe the interviewer's skill in this paragraph?

11. Paragraphs 9 through 14. How does the worker's attitude affect Ann?

12. Paragraphs 9 through 14. What are the processes and techniques in this part of the dialogue? Use your own terminology. Comment on the worker's skill in their use.

13. Paragraph 15. Why does the worker need additional information?

14. Paragraph 15. How do you explain Ann's willingness to give in at this point?

15. Paragraphs 16 and 17. Speculate on Ann's history in terms of the concepts in Chapters Two and Three.

16. Paragraphs 18, 19, 20. Comment on the worker's part in this section of the dialogue. How do you account for the contrast between Mrs. Taylor's attitude as shown in her telephone conversation and afterward?

17. Paragraph 21. Was this outcome a surprise to you?

18. Paragraph 21. How do you describe the processes involved?

19. Paragraphs 22, 23. What attitudes are revealed in the discussion between Mrs. Taylor and the worker?

20. Review the entire dialogue according to Porter Lee's outline of structure.

21. Summarize in your own words the processes and techniques which were used skillfully.

AN INTERVIEW WITH AN EXPERIENCED PUBLIC HEALTH NURSE FOR DISCUSSION OF BACKGROUND KNOWLEDGE, ROLE CONCEPT, AND INTERVIEWING SKILLS

DATA ACQUIRED PRIOR TO THE INTERVIEW IN THE INTERVIEWEE'S HOME

A young mother telephoned the county public health nurse and asked the nurse to call on her in her home because the three-month-old infant was spitting up food, crying, irritable, and colicky. She wanted the nurse's advice. A check with the family physician had revealed that there was nothing physically wrong with the baby, but the doctor did think that much of the difficulty was due to the mother's inability to handle and care for an infant. The baby was gaining weight and progressing according to its growth pattern. Moreover, the doctor thought that it was the mother who needed the nurse's professional assistance.

The nurse knew the community well and the year before had been on the staff as school nurse in the high school where the mother and her husband had then attended. The nurse also knew that the young mother had been forced to discontinue school during that year because of her pregnancy and subsequent marriage. The young husband and father was an active leader in the high school's athletic program. The community was relatively an agrarian one centered in a small city of approximately forty thousand inhabitants.

THE HOME VISIT AND INTERVIEW

[*Karla is the young mother. Mrs. Jenkin is Karla's mother. The nurse is recorded as "I."*]

Karla had asked that I call at about 3:45 P.M. and at that time I knocked on the door of her home. Mrs. Jenkin answered; she was an attractive woman in her early forties, nicely attired and very active in all the community sponsored social and cultural activities. (I had met her previously at a community meeting and knew her as one who was very conscious of community feelings and mores.) Mrs. Jenkin asked me to come in and said that she was sorry I had come so late because she wanted to talk with me. She hastened to explain that she had to be present at a meeting at 4:30 P.M. Without interruption she mentioned that she had ended a two month vacation from her job and had taken complete care of Karla's baby during this period. Now that she was returning to work it was necessary for Karla to care for the baby. According to Mrs. Jenkin this had brought nothing but "trouble! trouble! trouble!" She explained further that Karla knew nothing about baby care, and added emphatically her hope that I would be able "to pound something into Karla's head." While Mrs. Jenkin was talking I noticed the young mother sitting in an adjoining room and listening to the conversation.

I replied to Mrs. Jenkin's emphatically voiced expectation that I could see how a new baby could certainly disrupt a whole household.

Mrs. Jenkin then remarked that she supposed that I had known Karla from school.

I said that I had not been introduced to Karla when she attended school, whereupon Mrs. Jenkin added that she was certain I had undoubtedly "heard about her." I said nothing. At this point we went into the living room and I introduced myself to Karla since Mrs. Jenkin made no effort to introduce me. I explained that I was very glad she had telephoned and that I would be happy to help her with any problem she might have; perhaps between the two of us we could work out something.

Mrs. Jenkin interrupted at this point and said that I would have to tell Karla what to do because she "just doesn't know anything . . . and it isn't because I haven't tried to teach her!" After this remark she left the room and prepared to leave for the meeting.

There was a short period of silence and I broke this by asking Karla about what ways she had been having difficulty with her baby.

Karla went into a lengthy description of the baby's colic and the behavior accompanying the attacks. Throughout she always referred to the infant as "It." During this part of the interview the baby began to cry and Karla brought the infant into the room and put the young child on the davenport. While Karla was leaving the room to get milk for the baby I moved over to the davenport so that the baby would not roll off. (I thought this action would be a better teaching method at this point than my telling her not to leave the baby without support.) I also noticed that Karla took a bottle and filled it with milk directly from the refrigerator and brought it to feed the infant. After a few moments the young mother took the tiny daughter into the nearby bedroom and put the baby to bed with the bottle.

When Karla returned to the living room she said: "I suppose you don't think I should leave the baby with the bottle but she is old enough to handle it now." Karla went on to explain that she had heard her mother tell me about what a poor mother she thought Karla was. Karla asked me if I had brought along some books about babies for her to read.

I said that I hadn't because I thought there was something special she wanted to discuss. I mentioned the infant health care course which had been required of all girls at the high school and commented that she undoubtedly had some instructive books from that course.

Karla explained that she still had several of the recommended books and she had acquired several more from her doctor. She had decided, however, that there was "more to having a baby than what you read in a book." After I had agreed that this was so, she indicated her supposition that I had heard "all the gossip about us at school," hastening to add that she had been forced to leave school while her husband had been allowed to continue. She expressed marked annoyance at the school policy which required that a married woman discontinue high school. After she had again referred to her husband's continuance in school, I commented that perhaps she thought it unfair that a policy had discriminated against one member and not the other.

Karla pointed out that she thought the whole situation was most unfair. She spoke about all the time her husband spent in sports activities, and when talking about the many parties to which he gets invited and attends, her references had several stinging notes of sarcasm. Before pausing she mentioned her mother's adamant reaction in which the mother reiterated that had her advice been followed, "I would not be where I am today." Karla weakly suggested that perhaps this was her own fault but hastened to add her opinion that much of it was unfair.

I remarked that I could see where she would feel that much of it was unfair and I added that maybe we could make some arrangements whereby she could go to some of the senior dances and other social functions with her husband. I said that I thought she needed to gain more opportunity for some social life and it was especially important to participate in this with her husband. (At this point in the interview I felt myself strongly identified with Karla because I feel much anger at a social order which permits men so much freedom in these instances and leaving all the social stigma attached to the young woman.)

Karla's response to my supportive effort revealed something of her perceptible social role conflict in relationship to peers. In a plaintive tone of voice she said: "But don't you see that I had to get married and that no one would want me around. I guess I did wrong and I will have to live with this as long as I live. I was so lucky that there was nothing wrong with the baby when it was born."

As I was finishing the first part of my reply I realized it was a poor one because I had said: "Many people do wrong things during their lifetime and are able to overcome them and lead good lives." I hastened to inquire as to whether she really did feel as if she was being punished for having had the baby.

The discussion which followed from Karla are her amplifications in agreement with my suggestion. After vehement indication that she felt very guilty she mentioned several attempts to induce an abortion. She had talked to her doctor about this and he had laughed about it, pointing out that many women make such attempts. After these had been unsuccessful she had undergone much worry fearing that the baby might be born malformed.

Karla brought out her fear of becoming pregnant again before her husband was established on a job. For this reason she had refused to have sexual relationships with him. She pointed out how difficult this refusal was for her and the strong discomfort which it created because of her love for him.

I asked whether she and her husband had talked about this with their doctor.

They had not done so. She then described her furtive attempts at trying to get information about contraceptives from various advertisements and labels at the drugstores. Karla pointed out that it had never occurred to her that the doctor would be able to help them on this matter. After a short meditative pause she said that she would ask her husband to go with her and felt that he would be agreeable to doing so. It was after this remark that she commented that it was so easy to talk with me, explaining that I was unlike her mother who always told her to do things or did them for her.

Because it was near the time that I should leave, I wondered whether there was anything else she wanted to discuss with me today. I reminded her that if she wished we could have further interviews.

She asked if I could see her at the same time the following week, and when the appointment had been arranged Karla said: "You know I don't do a lot of things for the baby that I know should be done, such as warming the milk. This week I am going to try to do some of those things." As she was saying goodbye she referred to the time of our next appointment.

QUESTIONS AND DISCUSSION POINTS

1. What kinds of specific background knowledge does a public health nurse need in order to understand the problems which Karla raises?

2. Explain how cultural, community, and individual attitudes as well as those of the nurse intermingle in this interview.

3. How does Karla perceive the public health nurse's role?

4. What is indicated that suggests lack of clarity about professional role expectations? How does the nurse deal with this? How would you handle the situation as presented here?

5. Using the material brought out in this interview as a basis, discuss how social role perceptions and expectations change with marriage and parenthood.

6. What points are brought out that show the beginning-middle-end time continuum and how did the nurse deal with these?

7. What particular skills did the nurse employ which helped Karla establish rapport with her?

8. What are the critical incidents in this interview? What skills were used in managing them? How else might different skills have been used?

9. What pertinent observations are noted in this interview which heighten the importance of knowledge, role, and skill?

10. Show how the ten concepts of behavior discussed in Chapter Two apply to this interview.

AN INTERVIEW WITH A TEACHER FOR DISCUSSION OF BEHAVIOR, PROCESS, AND SKILL

At the end of the first nine weeks of the school year Donna entered my classroom one morning before classes started and asked to have me arrange a permit to see me during her free period. This was arranged and she came later in the day.

Neatly attired, she entered the room in a hesitant manner. Except for the worried expression on her face her appearance and bearing were not unlike that of the majority of girls in this high school. Noting her timid gait, I asked her to sit down. She looked at me and then looked at the floor and blurted out: "Miss Cressey, I am going to quit school."

I replied, "Oh? Do you have a particular reason for wanting to quit school?"

Donna complained that she could not catch onto shorthand and that she did not have the time necessary to study it. She suggested that maybe she was too stupid for high school and wondered whether she ought not to go to a vocational school instead. In a rush of words she exclaimed, "I don't know. I'm just all mixed up."

"What makes you think you are too stupid to go to high school?" I inquired.

She repeated her opinion that she did not have time to study shorthand in the way she should and this kept her getting farther behind in the course until now she felt she could never catch up with it.

I wondered why she did not have the time needed to study.

She sat silently for a few moments appearing to be thinking through exactly what it was she wanted to say. (I let her wait until she was ready and there were no observable evidences of discomfort about this short period of silence.) Donna finally looked directly at me and said: "Well, first of all, I baby-sit every night with four kids until 1:00 A.M. Their mother is a waitress and works until then. I can't study there because it's always too noisy. By the time I get the kids quieted down, the dishes washed, and the house picked up, I'm so tired that I fall asleep over my book."

When I expressed my belief that this was a work load that was too heavy for a high school student to carry, Donna burst into tears. She explained that she had to have the money because her parents were "really destitute." Because I was yet uncertain about the evident extent of her parents' implied financial poverty, I asked her if they agreed that she should work so many hours.

Upon mentioning the subject of her parents, Donna stiffened. She emphasized that they did not care how long or how hard she worked because "someone *has* to get some money for us to live on." She explained that her father's employment record was quite erratic, explaining that he was a manual laborer. When he received his pay it was customary to stop at the tavern, spend most of the money there and remain drunk for several days. Often he lost his jobs, and often would be out of work for a month or two until he could locate another job. Donna indicated that this was a repetitious pattern of the father's.

There are two other children in the home, a brother who is fourteen years of age and another brother who is eight years old. The oldest brother has had some odd jobs that have helped the family to some extent. Donna then indicated that she seemed to be the most regular means of support. Now she feels as if she has come to "the end of the rope" and reiterated that she could not continue both jobs, the school work and the one she was doing after school hours.

I wondered if her mother had ever sought any help for this family situation.

Donna pointed out that her mother would never permit herself to do such a thing. Indeed, the mother would be very angry with her if she knew what we had now been talking about. (While listening to her account I had been thinking about our public welfare office but after listening to Donna now I realized this was not the right moment in the interview to mention outside social agencies.)

I explained that I would not tell anyone that she had been talking with me nor would any of her information be used without her permission for me to do so.

Donna followed with a long recitation of grievances against her parents. She described how her father beat her mother when he was drunk. She mentioned that the mother was quite ill but would not go to a doctor because of finances. She complained further that the father was suspicious of her every move. For instance, whenever she went downtown with a girl friend, the father would drive past to see that "I was not with some of those 'good-for-nothing' high school boys." More recently the father's driver's license had been revoked for drunken driving. Since then he has forbidden her to go anywhere after dark.

She explained further that the finances of the family were of such a low state that the finance company was going to reclaim the television set, the kitchen stove, and the living room furniture. She appeared to accept this rather calmly and added that the family did have an electric plate which could be used for their cooking. She went on to admit that many times when she had been absent from school and had given illness as an excuse, this was not the real reason. Rather she had been too tired from baby-sitting or had been unable to do the required assignments. She stated that she attempted to avoid the teachers' disapproval by avoiding school. At this point she wept.

The pace of her weeping lessened after a few moments and it

was then that I asked her if she thought it would really help the situation at home if she were to quit school? (Donna was seventeen years old and the state law compels school attendance until the student is eighteen years of age or has graduated from high school.)

Her response was to say that the family would have to have more money to live on.

I wondered if her parents would be happy if she were to quit school?

Donna pointed out that her mother was eager that she finish school because the mother did not have a chance to go to high school. She repeated that her mother very much desired that she graduate. However, the father does not care. She cited several lucid examples to illustrate the father's extreme self-centeredness.

I asked Donna about what kind of work she thought she would like to do should she be able to finish school.

She had hoped to obtain an office job because she liked working with figures. Furthermore, she thought most office jobs paid fairly well. This had been the reason she had registered for shorthand and typing. Donna explained further that if she could get located in an office job she could earn enough to take care of her mother.

I wondered if Donna thought she could get an office job very easily without a high school diploma?

She thought not and suggested the alternative of getting a waitress job or employment in a store or in a mill. Donna volunteered that these jobs were becoming hard to find. A long pause ensued which she recovered by stating: "I guess, really, I don't want to quit school. I like it when I'm here, if I have my work done . . . all except for shorthand. I would not want to do office work that requires shorthand anyway because I would rather do bookkeeping or something like that."

I asked Donna whether she thought it might be wiser for her to change from shorthand to some other subject at the end of the semester?

"Oh, could I do that? I would really like to take business principles if I could. I have always liked arithmetic. I think I could get that, and then maybe I would not have to quit high school."

I said that I saw no reason which would disallow such a course plan. I also commented that if she could manage to pass her shorthand by working hard for the rest of the semester she would still have the half credit.

We talked further in somewhat more definite terms about Donna's future. She explained that it would be up to her to earn her own living and she could earn a better standard of living if she completed high school. After we had reaffirmed her educational plans, she again expressed her uncertainty about managing her school work and continuing with the same job. She finally suggested that perhaps she ought to consider getting another part-time job which paid better and one that did not require so many hours.

I offered to help her locate and discuss some possibilities, explaining that the superintendent's office had a listing of part-time vacancies.

Donna reacted to this with a sigh of relief and said, "Gee! Miss Cressey, I feel so good now that I have talked it all out with someone. I guess I really didn't want to quit school, but I felt so sort of helpless. Now I feel as though I can really stick with it."

This cue of her readiness to terminate the interview prompted me to ask her if she wanted to come in to discuss the employment situation further. She agreed to do this saying that she would arrange for an appointment after she had seen about the posted vacancies in the superintendent's office. I noticed that she had a much springier step in walking out of the room than she had when she came in.

QUESTIONS AND DISCUSSION POINTS

1. What behavioral characteristics and changes are noted during the various periods throughout this interview? How would you account for them?

2. Which of the ten concepts of behavior discussed in Chapter II apply to this interview and in what way?

3. In what ways did the teacher keep focus on the purpose of the interview? Were these skillful? Why?

4. At what points in the interview were the critical incidents or moments evident? How would you assess the teacher's management of these and on what bases do you make your evaluation?

5. In what ways is it made clear that the professional role of the teacher is different from that of the nurse or social worker? In what ways does this teacher wisely employ interviewing techniques that are like those noted in the interviews presented of nurses and social workers?

6. What are the indications for referral of this family for other help? How would you expect this to be achieved and under what circumstances?

Name Index

Subject Index

Adjustment, of the individual, 59–61, 90

Ambivalence, 165–167

American Council on Education, 59–60

Attitudes, as component of the interview, 199–259
  as interviewer's values, 236–242
  examples of, 303–320
  interaction with processes and techniques, 232–236
  of interviewee, 158–167, 229–232
  of interviewer, 199–242

Attitudes of the interviewer, 199–242
  ability to individualize, 200–204
  effect of, 225–227
  empathy, 204–207
  ethics, 236–242
  identification, 204–207, 209
  inadequacy, 213
  objectivity, 207–209
  projection, 206
  sensitivity, 209–212

Authority, use of, 167–169, 175, 188

Background, effect on personality, 7
  needed for interviewing, 8
  understanding, 12–19, 357–362
    See also Culture

Behavior, ambivalence, 165–167
  and culture concepts, 20–21, 24–25
  concepts of, 72–86
  examples of, 255–270, 363–368
  need to understand, 56–59, 139–142
  resistance, 162–167, 175–176, 180

Biography, see Life history

Case record, example, 93–96
  in understanding personality, 92–96
  objectives of, 92–93

Concepts of behavior, 7, 72–86
  examples of, 255–270

Concepts of culture, 4–37, 52
  application to interview, 37–51
  examples of, 249–254
  meaning to interviewer, 4–6
    See also Culture

Culture, 4–52
  concepts of, 4–30, 37–52, 249–254
  effect on personality, 7
  in life history, 88–89

Dollard's criteria, 87–91, 259, 260

Drive, 75

Empathy, 204–207

Ethics, 236–242
  conflicts discussed, 343–348
  practice, 239–242
  theory, 236–239

History, personal, see Life history

Identification, of interviewer with interviewee, 204–207, 209

Illustrative interviews, ambivalence, 331–335
  attitudes, 73–74, 200–203, 210–212, 214–224, 284–286, 306–311, 312–318, 335–342, 349–356
  auspices, 357–362
  background, 11–12, 15–18

370